Beyond Positivism:
Economic Methodology in the Twentieth Century

Beyond Positivism: Economic Methodology in the Twentieth Century

BRUCE J. CALDWELL
University of North Carolina at Greensboro

London
GEORGE ALLEN & UNWIN
Boston   Sydney

George Allen & Unwin (Publishers) Ltd,
40 Museum Street, London, WC1A 1LU, UK

George Allen & Unwin (Publishers) Ltd,
Park Lane, Hemel Hempstead, Herts, HP2 4TE, UK

Allen & Unwin Inc.,
9 Winchester Terrace, Winchester, Mass 01890, USA

George Allen & Unwin Australia Pty Ltd,
8 Napier Street, North Sydney, NSW 2060, Australia

First published in 1982
This edition first published 1984
New edition first published 1984

British Library Cataloguing in Publication Data

Caldwell, Bruce J.
  Beyond positivism.
1. Economics—Methodology
I. Title
330'.01'8   HB131
ISBN 0-04-330342-0

Library of Congress Cataloging in Publication Data

Caldwell¹, Bruce J.
  Beyond positivism.
Includes bibliographies and index.
1. Economics—Methodology. I. Title.
[HB131.C37 1984]   330'.01'8   83-25672
ISBN 0-04-330342-0 (pbk.)

Set in 10 on 11 point Times by Alan Sutton Publishing Ltd, Gloucester
and printed in Great Britain by Biddles Ltd, Guildford, Surrey

Contents

For my parents, Clyde and Maryann, who taught me by example that method and substance are often inseparable.

Acknowledgments

The writing of an acknowledgments page is a pleasant endeavor, for at least two reasons. First, though one's thinking on methodology is never completed, it is mercifully true that books *are* finished, and when one begins writing acknowledgments, the realization that one is nearly done with the job brings with it a feeling that borders on rapture. Second, reflecting on all of the people who have been helpful along the way also produces gratifying emotions. So I address this task with relish.

In a first book the temptation is great to mention everyone who has provided guidance and assistance in one's journey. I resist that temptation here, not with the intent of slighting the many who have been helpful, but in order to single out those whose generosity has been inspiring.

In this category, two individuals stand out: Professor Robert Barry of the College of William and Mary and Professor Vincent Tarascio of the University of North Carolina. Bob Barry was the first to show me that economics was not simply a field worth studying, but an interesting one. His encouragement during some of the more bleak periods in my graduate training gave me the will to persist. Each time that I would return to my undergraduate alma mater to discuss economics with him, I knew that on previous visits my ideas had been naive; he had the grace and patience never to point that out. His role model as a teacher and an advisor has been a difficult one to duplicate, but is an ideal to which I aspire.

Vince Tarascio was my major field professor and dissertation advisor, but far more important, he has been a constant source of sound advice throughout my academic career. I went to the trough often, and always came away satisfied. Though his duties as an academic and as the editor of the *Southern Economic Journal* make large demands on his time, he always gave unstintingly of it to me. His support of my interest in methodology, his advice on matters of substance, style, procedure, and strategy in the execution of this manuscript, and his continued interest in my professional development comprise a list of debts for which these few lines are grossly inadequate compensation.

I would also like to thank Tony Esler of William and Mary, who first introduced me to the study of intellectual history, and Ralph Pfouts of UNC, who made the first grim weeks of graduate school exciting with his lectures on economic methodology.

Two groups of individuals are mentioned next: my colleagues in the Economics Department at UNC–Greensboro, and the members of the 1981–82 Colloquium on Austrian Economics at NYU. The former could not have been faulted if they viewed with disdain their strange colleague who wandered the halls mumbling about positivism and falsifiability; instead, they offered their support. More to the point, there is a sense of community in this unique group of people that makes it a pleasure to work among them. The professors, graduate students, and interested observers who attended the Austrian Colloquium provided a year of intellectual stimulation that both broadened my understanding of matters methodological, and piqued my interest in a number of new areas for study.

The thankless task of typing and retyping the endless drafts of chapters that I kept slipping into the "To Be Typed" box was graciously performed by Vicki Sparrow and Becky Askew; their efficiency was only surpassed by their alacrity.

Research funds permitted me to devote large and uninterrupted blocks of time to this project; they were generously provided by UNC–Greensboro (Excellence Fund Faculty Summer Research Grant), the UNC–G Economics Department (John Kennedy Hours Reduction Grant), and NYU (Post-Doctoral Research Grant in Austrian Economics).

The editors of the *Journal of Economic Issues* and the *Southern Economic Journal* were kind enough to grant me permission to draw on ideas and exposition previously published.

Finally, I want to thank my friends. They helped me more than they know, just by being there. And along these lines, I would be remiss if I did not thank God for allowing the games of pool, poker, and Risk to be invented, and for letting so many people play them poorly: these activities brightened my leisure time, and made my work time more bearable.

As a youth I ate cupcakes from the bottom up, saving the icing for last. This trait carries over in my final expression of gratitude to Betsy Ranslow, who bolstered me when I lost confidence, cheered me when I was sad, laughed at me when I was preposterous (she laughs a lot), and gave up part of herself so that I could selfishly devote myself to this project. Thanks for being you.

BRUCE J. CALDWELL
New York City
April, 1982

1

Introduction

When you are criticizing the philosophy of an epoch, do not chiefly direct your attention to those intellectual positions which its exponents feel it necessary explicitly to defend. There will be some fundamental assumptions which adherents of all the variant systems within the epoch unconsciously presuppose. Such assumptions appear so obvious that people do not know what they are assuming because no other way of putting things has ever occurred to them. With these assumptions a certain limited number of types of philosophical systems are possible, and this group of systems constitutes the philosophy of the epoch.

> Alfred North Whitehead — *Science and the Modern World* (1925)

The study of methodology is an agonizing task; writing a book on the subject requires the skills of an individual who is at once presumptuous and masochistic. By the very nature of methodological work, solutions to important problems seldom seem to exist. One's thinking on a particular subject is never complete; indeed, it is more likely that one's opinion will change often through time, and sometimes change dramatically. Even more troublesome, the prolonged study of methodology forces a person to examine his or her own preconceptions, to see why certain ideas make sense, and why others seem so patently absurd. Nor is that self-examination a simple task, since preconceptions are not truly prior to experience, but invariably reflect both the material studied and the process involved in its study.

One preconception of mine that is admittedly unoriginal is that there is no single infallible method: there is no 'best way' waiting out there to be discovered, neither in the form of some Platonic ideal, nor by the careful objective study of the history of method. Rather, I am a methodological pluralist, by which I mean that, just as there exist many tasks for theories to perform, there are also many methods for the evaluation and criticism of theories. Most methodologies are prescriptive; they limit the range of acceptable theories and explanations in science. Such normative methodologies also place restrictions on what constitutes legitimate criticism; they prohibit not only certain types of theories, but certain types of methodologies as well. I would argue against both theoretical and methodological monism. Like any methodological view, methodological pluralism has problems associated with it, and, in light of my earlier comments, I would certainly like to retain the right to change my mind. But for now, methodological pluralism seems to be a reasonable, and potentially fruitful, approach to economic methodology.

One disquieting implication of methodological pluralism is that the present study and others like it are ineffective, that they are little more than a form of twentieth century scholasticism. What sense is there in studying methodology if one asserts at the outset that there is no hope of finding the best method? My particular approach must seem especially superfluous, since there is almost no discussion of the practice of economists, the focus being a discussion of the interface between the philosophy of science and the writings of economists on methodology.

The claim that the independent study of methodology divorced from the practice of economists is ineffectual is a serious one that must be considered. It is most plausible if one believes that the goal of methodological study is the discovery of an infallible method. If that is the goal, such study is truly a Sisyphean task that is best left not started. But there are more modest, and I think more attainable, goals of methodological study. In particular, I hope to make progress towards three of these.

First, methodological study aids one in understanding the essence (that word is chosen carefully, and not without trepidation) of various methodological views. Methodological discussion often involves the advocacy or critique of a particular theoretical formulation, and as such seems little more than the partisan rationalization of a preferred worldview. Methodology in such cases is perceived as simply another instrument of persuasion. But there is another aspect of methodological debate that must not be ignored. For there is imbedded in every methodological position a unique perspective on the question of how to gain knowledge, of how to most fruitfully investigate a given phenomenon. Methodology systematizes man's curiosity; each methodological view directs the scientist to seek knowledge differently. By 'getting inside' a variety of such views, one gains new ways of perceiving the subject under investigation. Perhaps most essential, one may avoid the chains of a narrow perspective. This is especially important given that one's methodological views are rarely consciously held: methodology is nowhere explicitly taught in modern curricula; rather, the modern scientist learns his methodology by plying his scientific trade.

A second goal of this study is to assess the cogency of various arguments made by economic methodologists. We can assess the cogency, though not, I think, the ultimate validity of the positions we investigate. My particular approach is to examine the writings of economic methodologists from the vantage point of twentieth century philosophy of science.

At first I supposed that more could be done. I thought that, since the philosophy of science analyzes the methods of all the sciences, and the methodology of economics is a particular instance of that larger study, the philosophy of science could be used to judge various pronouncements in the methodology of economics. But it cannot, for there is no guarantee that the propositions gleaned from the philosophy of science have either prescriptive force or descriptive accuracy when applied to economics. Moreover, most of the philosophy of science with which economists are familiar was written with the natural sciences, and particularly physics, in mind; its application in a social science like economics can and should be questioned. (There is a philosophy of social science, but few economists have expressed any interest in it.)

On the other hand, the study of philosophy of science can be useful as an aid to clear thinking on matters methodological. Philosophers of science, after all, have thought about the issues more than have most scientists. More to the point, many economic methodologists borrow phrases, terms, and concepts from the philosophy of science; yet often such expropriation has only brought further confusion, that is, economists who disagree about the meanings of those phrases, terms, and concepts. A study of economic methodology from a philosophy of science perspective may help one to clarify, unify, categorize, and explicate debates in the former field. But it will not provide ultimate grounds for arbitrating among well-developed and well-argued alternative positions. Fortunately, there is a sufficient number of poorly-developed and badly-argued cases to keep us busy. In addition, I will on occasion pause to offer suggestions of what forms potential criticisms of certain positions might take. There is no malicious intent; methodological pluralism insists that there are many roads to criticism, and these efforts are undertaken with that sentiment in mind.

A final goal of this study is to shake up some preconceptions that may presently exist in the economics profession. The chapter begins with a pertinent quote from Alfred North Whitehead – it is no easy job, but it is a vital one, to enumerate the assumptions of the epoch in which we live. I submit that one operative assumption of our time is the almost unquestioned authority of science. Its particular manifestation within our profession had its origins many years ago, when the notion first blossomed that economics could be, and should try to be, a scientific discipline. In the twentieth century the dream seemed realized with the emergence of positivism, a philosophical doctrine that appeared to offer a solid epistemological foundation for those sciences willing and capable of adhering to the rigors of the scientific method. Positivist exhortations soon dominated the methodological rhetoric of economics, even if they did not always inform the actual practice of working economists.

Positivism in its many variations has been in decline within the philosophy of science for the last twenty years or so, and that knowledge is now filtering down into the special sciences, especially since the works of the 'growth of knowledge' philosophers (Thomas Kuhn, Imre Lakatos, J. A. Agassi, and others) have gained prominence. Few economists keep up with developments in the philosophy of science, and as such it is understandable that many may still labor under the illusion that economics is, or can be, a positivist discipline. Part of the purpose of this study is to dispel that illusion by carefully documenting the demise of positivist thought within the philosophy of science.

Of course, positivism may not be dead, it may only be temporarily in eclipse. If the growth of knowledge approach which seems to be its successor leads nowhere or to speculative excess, we may witness a return to the rigorous and prescriptive models that characterize the positivist contribution. Whether or not that occurs does not concern us here; what is needed is a solid understanding of the present situation.

Thus we find that the study of economic methodology from a philosophy of science perspective has at least some chance of bearing some fruit. But it should also be emphasized that this is only part of the story. A complete study would include the practice of economists in various research traditions as a topic to be explored along with the writings of philosophers of science and of method-ologists of economics. Though the scope of this work is restricted to the last two areas, that focus should not be interpreted as indicating that I believe the first area to be of less significance.

The format is straightforward. I begin with a review of some of the major themes in twentieth century philosophy of science from the logical positivism of the Vienna Circle to the present. Next I review in a collection of critical essays some of the major methodological writings in the positivist era in economics. In four concluding chapters I address the question: What form should methodology take in the post-positivist environment?

The amount of space devoted to the philosophy of science may seem too large in a book written by an economist for the use of economists. The rationale, again, is straightforward: so many errors and misrepresentations regarding ideas taken from philosophy have been made by economic methodologists, both past and present, that a lengthy summary is absolutely necessary if clarity is to be brought to the field. No such summary yet exists in the field, though a first step is contained in the first section of Mark Blaug's admirable recent study, *The Methodology of Economics* (1980). As I will argue presently, however, Blaug's presentation is less than complete because he is a falsificationist, and as such he sees the world of the philosophy of science through the glasses of a convinced Popperian. The treatment presented here differs from others most dramatically in its emphasis on the evolution of positivist thought from the dogmatism of the Vienna Circle to its most sophisticated form, logical empiricism. Neither proponents nor adversaries of positivist thinking in economics have previously devoted sufficient attention to the mature forms of positivist thought, and that needs remedying. In addition, it is my intention to show how the analyses of men like Kuhn, Lakatos, and Feyerabend are primarily a (as yet unassessed) response to a presumably failed positivism, a point that is too often overlooked by economists enamored with the particular models of historical change that are found in the writings of these growth of knowledge theorists. Each of the four chapters in the section on positivism and economic methodology begins with a review of either a famous debate between two economists, or a position statement by a prominent positivist economist. The four major topics treated are the Robbins–Hutchison debates on the status of the fundamental postulates of economics and the proper method of economic analysis; the Hutchison–Machlup debate on the necessity of testing assumptions; Friedman's unique contribution, which I label methodological instrumentalism; and Samuelson's espousal of operationalism and descriptivism. The debates and positions are examined in some detail because these original contributions are too often caricatured in the massive secondary literature that has sprung up in response to them. My assessment of their arguments is from the vantage point of philosophy of science, and I find that sometimes that vantage point provides worthwhile insights, and sometimes it is useless. (It will be shown, for example, that though many of Terence Hutchison's contributions in his 1938 tract, *The Significance and Basic Postulates of Economic Theory*, were technically incorrect from a philosophical perspective, his larger contribution – the introduction of positivist language and thought into economic methodology – is of great importance.) These studies will aid us in our assessment of the strengths and limitations of using the philosophy of science in understanding economic methodology.

In the latter half of each of the chapters on economic methodology, related themes are treated. The content of these varies widely. In Chapter 6, I argue that the usual criticisms of Austrian economics (a branch of economics which has certain affinities with Robbins's methodological views) have thus far proven unsuccessful, primarily because they proceed by assuming the validity of a rival epistemological or methodological system (e.g. positivism or falsificationism) then 'proving' that the Austrian system does not meet the qualifications of their presumptively true system. That chapter concludes with some suggestions of the form that a legitimate critique of Austrian methodology might take. In Chapter 7, I review some recent attempts to test the rationality assumption, and conclude that it is indeed untestable, at least as currently stated. In Chapters 8 and 9, some recent contributions to the secondary literature, which seem destined someday to be accorded the status of 'original contributions', are reviewed and evaluated: Lawrence Boland's defense of Friedman's instrumentalism, Stanley Wong's critique via the method of rational reconstruction of Samuelson's revealed preference theory, and Wilber and Harrison's introduction of the pattern model of scientific explanation. These chapters conclude with a potpourri of opinions on current issues and alternative methodological schemas, as well as an interaction with some of whom I think are the best contemporary contributors to the methodological literature. What is *not* attempted is a comprehensive survey of current thinking in methodology. And again, the unifying theme is the vantage point from which I began – the chapters on philosophy of science which provide a common framework for interpretation and assessment.

An apt, if cynical, characterization of methodological study is that it is the systematic categorization of unanswerable questions. There are a number of questions that are referred to obliquely throughout this work that are best placed in the category of, if not unanswerable, then certainly unsettled. I mention them now because they are omnipresent, and because a person's response to them is perhaps the crucial determinant of his or her beliefs concerning the importance and function of methodology, and perhaps one's vision of the nature of science itself.

First, what is the best way to go about the study of methodology?

Is there a single approach, or a plurality?

Next, is methodology essentially a prescriptive discipline, a descriptive one, or both? Note that this question itself can be posed either descriptively (What has been the role of methodology?) or prescriptively (What should it be?).

Finally, what is the best response to the perennial problem of theory choice? The problem arises because, in many significant instances in science, there are no objective criteria according to which competing theories may be compared, ranked, and evaluated; in a phrase, there is no algorithm of choice. Part of our task is to show that the theory choice problem is a real one in economics; the real question is, however: How do we respond to it?

All of these questions have been broached by the growth of knowledge theorists. I offer some views on each of them in the last chapters of the book.

PART ONE

TWENTIETH CENTURY PHILOSOPHY OF SCIENCE

2

Logical Positivism

The Vienna Circle

In 1922, the physicist and philosopher Moritz Schlick was appointed professor of the philosophy of inductive science at the University of Vienna. Three years later he organized a Thursday evening discussion group of philosophically-minded mathematicians and scientists. Though its membership varied over time, the group met regularly for the next eleven years, and through the efforts of its members a new philosophy was born. The philosophy became known as logical positivism and the group took for itself the label, the Vienna Circle. Some of the more significant members over the years included Rudolf Carnap, Herbert Feigl, Phillip Frank, Kurt Gödel, Hans Hahn, Karl Menger (the economist's son), Otto Neurath, and Friedrich Waismann.

Though the logical positivists were confident that their new analyses constituted 'an altogether decisive turning point in philosophy',[1] they also acknowledged that many earlier thinkers influenced their work. Those mentioned included most of the European philosophers in the empiricist tradition, anyone who made a contribution to symbolic logic or axiomatics, and finally, any thinker who showed anti-metaphysical or anti-speculative tendencies in his work.[2] Three philosophers, however, stand out as having had a truly significant influence on the development of logical positivism: Ernst Mach, Bertrand Russell, and Ludwig Wittgenstein. Mach's theory of elements, which proposed that all phenomena (even psychical) could be reduced to complexes of sensations, and his dismissal of the idea of a 'thing-in-itself' behind one's sensations of an object as metaphysics, laid a strong positivist foundation upon which the logical empiricists could build. Bertrand Russell's path-breaking efforts (in conjunction with Alfred North Whitehead in their *Principia Mathematica*) in the development of symbolic logic and in the application of that logic to empirical investigations supplied the logical tools of analysis that were to differentiate the logical positivists from their earlier empiricist predecessors. And Wittgenstein's monumental *Tractatus logico-philosophicus*, which was actively discussed within the Vienna Circle in 1926, had a profound influence on the group's development. According to Joergen Joergensen, an historian of the logical positivist movement,

> it contained a series of important discoveries as well as a wealth of new philosophical views, the grounds for and consequences of which were often barely indicated and so left to be worked out in full by its readers . . . it led, in the course of the twenties, to the crystallization of the philosophical view characteristic of the Vienna Circle, to which Wittgenstein himself did not belong.[3]

The year 1926 also marked the entrance of Rudolf Carnap to the Circle. His 'theory of constitution', which is contained in written form in his *Der logische Aufbau der Welt* (1928), was of special importance in the formulation of the group's views. The aims of the movement were dramatically and brashly proclaimed in the pamphlet 'Wissenschaftliche Weltauffassung: Der Weiner Kreis' in 1929; in the following year the periodical *Erkenntnis*, edited by Hans Reichenbach and Rudolph Carnap, began publication. Through the 1930s a group of monographs collectively entitled *Einheitswissenschaft* (Unified Science) were published, and in 1938 the *International Encyclopedia of Unified Science* began publication in Chicago. The 1930s witnessed an expansion of the logical positivist movement beyond the confines of the Vienna Circle. With this expansion came divergences of opinion over certain issues: for example, in 1935 Rudolf Carnap proposed that confirmability rather than verifiability be used as a criterion of cognitive significance, and further that some new name other than positivism be used to describe the movement's program to avoid confusion between their ideas and those of earlier positivists like Comte and Mach.[4] The deaths of Hahn in 1934 and Schlick in 1936 (the latter was murdered by an insane student), and the disruptions which accompanied the onset of the Second World War led to a disintegration of the Vienna Circle by the late 1930s. The positivist tradition had a strong and continuing influence on the philosophy of science and the separate disciplines, however, an influence which extended well beyond the small group of intellectuals who met weekly to discuss philosophy in Vienna.

The Logical Positivist Program

Members of the Vienna Circle felt that they had discovered the true task of philosophy, which was to analyze knowledge statements with the aim of making such propositions clear and unambiguous. As Moritz Schlick stated in the lead article of the first issue of the journal *Erkenntnis*, '. . . philosophy is that activity through which the meaning of statements is revealed or determined'.[5] The new philosophy contrasted most sharply with the metaphysical systems of German speculative philosophy and post-Kantian idealism; indeed, one of its major critical contributions was the demonstration that all metaphysics is meaningless. Logical positivism, however, also differed from earlier forms of positivism in its use of *logical analysis* for the clarification of problems and assertions. (This difference is the major reason why Carnap preferred the label 'logical empiricism' to 'logical positivism'.) The aim of philosophy, then, is logical analysis; and its subject matter is the empirical or positive sciences.

> We have characterized the *scientific world-conception* essentially by *two features*. *First* it is *empiricist and positivist*: there is knowledge only from experience, which rests on what is immediately given. This sets the limits for the context of legitimate science. *Second*, the scientific world-conception is marked by the application of a certain method, namely *logical analysis*. The aim of scientific effort is to reach the goal, unified science, by applying logical analysis to the empirical material.[6]

The logical positivist program asserted that only meaningful statements were to be permitted scientific consideration and accorded the status of knowledge claims. Meaningfulness (or cognitive significance) was strictly defined as being attributable only to those statements which are either analytic (tautologies or self-contradictions) or synthetic (factual statements which may be verified or falsified by evidence). By this criterion, metaphysical statements are neither analytic nor subject to empirical test, so must be deemed meaningless, expressing emotional stances or 'general attitudes towards life'.[7] This does not mean that such propositions are false, as is emphasized by Moritz Schlick, founder of the Vienna Circle.

> The denial of the existence of a transcendent external world would be just as much a metaphysical statement as its affirmation. Hence the consistent empiricist does not deny the transcendent world, but shows that both its denial and affirmation are meaningless.
> This last distinction is of the greatest importance. I am convinced that the chief opposition to our view derives from the fact that the distinction between the falsity and the meaninglessness of a proposition is not

observed. The proposition 'Discourse concerning a metaphysical external world is meaningless' does *not* say: 'There is no external world,' but something altogether different. The empiricist does not say to the metaphysician 'what you say is false,' but 'what you say asserts nothing at all!' He does not contradict him, but says 'I don't understand you.'[8]

Nor does it mean that metaphysical statements can have no influence on our lives, for clearly when tied to beliefs they can. Such propositions cannot, however, be accorded the status of knowledge claims. As A. J. Ayer, a leading contemporary positivist, succinctly puts it: 'Metaphysical utterances were condemned not for being emotive, which could hardly be considered as objectionable in itself, but for pretending to be cognitive, for masquerading as something that they were not.'[9]

The next task before the logical positivists was to offer some objective criterion for distinguishing between analytic, synthetic, and meaningless statements. The analytic-synthetic distinction seemed to pose no difficulties; the problems lay in separating legitimate synthetic statements from metaphysical assertions. One early solution became known as the verifiability principle: a statement has meaning only to the extent that it is verifiable. Verifiability implies testability, since one must be able to test whether a synthetic assertion is true or false. Carl Hempel observes that the testability criterion of the most conservative and dogmatic logical positivists was quite strict: a sentence had empirical meaning only if it was capable, at least in principle, of complete verification by observational evidence, and such evidence was restricted to what could be observed by the speaker and his fellow beings during their lifetimes.[10] The testability criterion was modified considerably as time progressed; we will see that much effort was devoted to this question during the 1930s and 1940s by such eminent philosophers as Popper, Carnap, Ayer, and Hempel. However, a heavy reliance on observational evidence characterized almost all of the logical positivist efforts at specification of criteria of cognitive significance.

The insistence on the primacy of physical data had a number of implications. The most important concerned the status of theoretical terms. No one had ever observed atoms, protons, or magnetic fields; were statements positing their existence therefore to be considered nonsense expressions?

That position was in fact supported by physicist Ernst Mach, who viewed scientific theories positively as useful, economical tools for the representation and classification of phenomena, but who granted no independent existential status to theoretical entities and further called for the eventual elimination of theoretical terms from the language of science. Mach advances this position in his *Popular Scientific Lectures*:

> it would not become physical science to see in its self-created, changeable, economical tools, molecules and atoms, realities behind phenomena, forgetful of the lately acquired sapience of her old sister, philosophy, in substituting a mechanical mythology for the old animistic or metaphysical scheme, and thus creating no end of suppositions problems. The atom must remain a tool for representing phenomena, like the functions of mathematics. Gradually, however, as the intellect, by contact with its subject matter, flows in discipline, physical science will give up its mosaic play with stones and will seek out the boundaries and forms of the bed in which the living stream of phenomena flows. The goal which it has set itself is the *simplest and most economical* abstract expression of facts.[11]

A similar approach was taken by a contemporary of the logical positivists, the American physicist Percy W. Bridgman. He developed the position known as operationalism, which asserts that the definition of any concept in science is no more than the set of measurement operations which can be performed on it. He states this early on in his classic, *The Logic of Modern Physics*, 'In general, we mean by any concept nothing more than a set of operations; *the concept is synonymous with the corresponding set of operations.*'[12] If one adopts the operational approach, then one must dismiss as meaningless concepts which cannot be defined by a set of operations: 'if we remember that the operations to which a physical concept are equivalent are actual physical operations, the concepts can be defined only in the range of actual experiment, and are undefined and meaningless in regions as yet untouched by experiment'. Bridgman is fully aware of the consequences of his view, and at times sounds like a member of the Vienna Circle in his portrayal of how operationalism could change scientific thought:

> To adopt the operational point of view involves much more than a mere restriction of the sense in which we understand 'concept', but means a far-reaching change in all of our habits of thought, in that we shall no longer permit ourselves to use as tools in our thinking concepts of which we cannot give an adequate account in terms of operations.
> . . .
> I believe that many of the questions asked about social and philosophical subjects will be found to be meaningless when examined from the point of view of operations. It would doubtless conduce greatly to clarity of thought if the operational mode of thinking were adopted in all fields of inquiry as well as in the physical.[14]

Turning to the logical positivists themselves, no unified approach to the status of theoretical terms is in evidence. Some were as unabashedly phenomenalist as Mach and Bridgman, believing that only propositions about observable phenomena should be granted the status of knowledge. The early Carnap of *Der logische Aufbau der Welt* seems close to this view, but later he revised his position to one in which theoretical terms have partial meaningfulness to the extent that such terms can be partially interpreted into an observation language. It will be seen later that this view, further elaborated upon by Carnap and Hempel, came to dominate more recent positivist thought.

Primacy of physical evidence thus permeated the logical positivist approach to science. In addition to its influences on questions of cognitive significance and on the special problems posed by the use of theoretical terms in science, the stress on observability led the logical positivists to a belief in the methodological unity of all scientific endeavor. Otto Neurath first introduced the term 'unity of science'; Carnap attributes the unity thesis to the new logic employed by the logical positivists.

> Thus, with the aid of the new logic, logical analysis leads to a *unified science*. There are not different sciences with fundamentally different methods or different sources of knowledge, but only *one* science. All knowledge finds its place in this science and, indeed, is knowledge of basically the same kind; the appearance of fundamental differences between the sciences are the deceptive result of our using different sub-languages to express them.[15]

By implication, the social sciences no less than the natural sciences are concerned with observable phenomena; thus approaches to the social disciplines which rely on such devices as, say, subconscious motivations or introspective states of mind for the explanation of social phenomena can be accused of metaphysical speculation. This view is concisely summarized by A. J. Ayer: 'the scale and diversity of the phenomena with which the social sciences dealt made them less successful in establishing scientific laws, but this was a difficulty of practice, not of principle: they too were concerned in the end with physical events'.[16] Belief in the methodological unity of science led Neurath and Carnap to explore possibilities of the development of a physicalist language in which metaphysical propositions would by definition be nonexistent. This was to lead Carnap to his later work on the semantics of empiricist languages. Discussions of the physicalist thesis (so dubbed by Neurath) and of other related concepts took place as the 1930s progressed.

It should not be imagined that work done by members of the

Vienna Circle was carried out in isolation; during the same period both individuals and other groups outside of Vienna were engaged in investigations which complemented, elaborated upon, or challenged those done by the logical positivists. In America, operationalists and pragmatists had developed philosophical positions which paralleled in many respects those of the Vienna Circle, though members of the latter group were unaware of those American contributions until sometime in the 1930s. In 1928 a group which took the title Gesellschaft fur Wissenschaftliche Philosophie was formed in Berlin, important members of which included Hans Reichenbach, Alexander Herzberg, Walter Dubislav, and Carl G. Hempel. Other groups included the Lwow–Warsaw group in Poland (Alfred Tarski was the most influential participant, his exchanges with Gödel and Carnap led to his formulation of the semantic conception of truth), the Munster group in Germany, and the Uppsala School in Sweden.[17]

Notes

1   Moritz Schlick, 'The Turning Point in Philosophy,' trans. by David Rynin in A. J. Ayer (ed.), *Logical Positivism* (Glencoe, Ill.: The Free Press, 1959), p. 54.
2   Hans Hahn, Otto Neurath, and Rudolf Carnap, 'Wissenschaftliche Weltauffassung: Der Wiener Kreis,' in Otto Neurath, *Empiricism and Sociology*, trans. by Paul Foulkes and Marie Neurath, edited by Marie Neurath and Robert S. Cohen (Dordrecht, Holland: D. Reidel, 1973), p. 304.
3   Joergen Joergensen, *The Development of Logical Empiricism. International Encyclopedia of Unified Science*, Vol II, No. 9 (Chicago: University of Chicago Press, 1951), pp. 27–28. Joergensen became affiliated with Carnap, Neurath, and others during the 1930s.
4   Rudolf Carnap, 'Testability and Meaning,' *Philosophy of Science*, III (1936), p. 244, 2, pp. 245 and *passim*.
5   Schlick, 'Turning Point...,' loc. cit., p. 56.
6   Hahn, Neurath and Carnap, 'Der Wiener Kreis,' loc. cit., p. 309.
7   The expression is attributable to Carnap. See his 'The Elimination of Metaphysics Through Logical Analysis of Language,' trans. by Arthur Pap, in A. J. Ayer (ed.), op. cit., p. 78.
8   Moritz Schlick, 'Positivism and Realism,' trans. by David Rynin, in A. J. Ayer (ed.), op. cit., p. 197.
9   'Editor's Introduction,' in A. J. Ayer (ed.), op. cit., pp. 10–11.
10 Carl Hempel, 'The Empiricist Criterion of Meaning,' in A. J. Ayer (ed.), op. cit., p. 110.
11 Ernst Mach, *Popular Scientific Lectures*, trans. by Thomas J. McCormack, (Chicago: Open Court Publishing Co., 1895), p. 206. Philosopher Israel Scheffler characterizes this position as eliminative fictionalism, contrasting it with instrumentalist fictionalism, which grants no independent status to theoretical terms but would not call for their elimination, and pragmatism, which admits any term into science which has a use in prediction or theoretical simplification. See his 'The Fictionalist View of Scientific Theories,' in Baruch Brody (ed.), *Reading*

in the Philosophy of Science (Englewood Cliffs, NJ: Prentice-Hall, 1970), pp. 211–22.

12 Percy Bridgman, *The Logic of Modern Physics* (New York: MacMillan, 1927), p. 5.

13 Ibid, p. 7.

14 Ibid, pp. 30–1.

15 Rudolph Carnap, 'The Old and the New Logic,' trans. by Isaac Levi, in A. J. Ayer (ed.), op. cit., p. 144.

16 'Editor's Introduction,' in A. J. Ayer (ed.), op. cit., p. 21.

17 Joergensen gives a detailed listing of related movements and individuals. See Joergensen, op. cit., pp. 48–60.

3

The Positivist Tradition Matures –
The Emergence of Logical Empiricism

Introduction

The logical positivists of the Vienna Circle broke new ground in philosophy, and believed that their unique synthesis of 'the new logic' and empiricism held great promise for clarifying and solving previously intractable problems in philosophy and the special sciences. As often happens, a premature enthusiasm led certain logical positivists to issue declarations which in retrospect seem indicative of, at best, a sublime naiveté, and at worst, a dogmatic fanaticism. From the mid-1930s through the mid-1950s, however, a more sophisticated positivist stance emerged, one less radically empiricist than logical positivism. Philosophers whose names could be associated with what we will call logical empiricism, or mature positivism, include A. J. Ayer, Richard Braithwaite, Rudolf Carnap, Carl Hempel and Ernest Nagel, though this listing is not meant to be exhaustive.

While many problems were considered by philosophers of science during the period,[1] three are examined below. They are:

1. The search for a criterion of cognitive significance,
2. The status, structure, and function of theories and theoretical terms,
3. The nature of scientific explanation.

These three areas are mutually dependent,[2] and are separated here only for expository purposes. Before beginning our analysis of logical empiricism, some general observations need to be made.

First, it is not always evident who should be included in the mature positivist camp. Philosophers like Ayer, Carnap, and Hempel are uncomprisingly positivistic, but others are more difficult to classify. Neither Braithwaite nor Nagel (unlike the first three) was ever associated with positivist organizations like the Vienna Circle or the Berlin group, and both have been more cautious than most logical empiricists in their pronouncements. Karl Popper is an especially interesting case. He is known for his strenuous attacks against the Vienna Circle in the 1930s and would never consider himself a positivist, yet in 1959 Ayer wrote 'the affinities between him and the positivists whom he criticized appear more striking than the divergencies'.[3] Since no unified positivist view crystallized during the period, what follows is a discussion of selected recurrent issues and themes which occupied philosophers of science from the mid-1930s to, roughly, the mid-1950s.

Though we end our survey of the modern positivist epoch in the mid-1950s, the reader should not conclude that all positivist analysis ceased at that time. The mid-1950s was selected as the admittedly arbitrary dividing line between modern and contemporary philosophy of science because it was then that certain positivist assumptions, models, and doctrines came under steady, severe, and ultimately telling criticism. That story is told in later chapters; it is mentioned now as weak justification for the choice of the mid-1950s as a convenient, if simplistic, dividing line between the modern and contemporary periods.

The Search for a Criterion of Cognitive Significance

Remembering that the basic starting point for the positivist position is that only analytic and synthetic propositions have cognitive significance, we may ask: How can one tell whether a nonanalytic statement is synthetic (and thereby a knowledge statement) or nonsensical? The answer lies in the concept of testability: a proposition is meaningful only to the extent that it may be subjected to empirical test. Making this testability criterion concrete has been a major problem in the philosophy of science, however, with no formulation of it ever surviving unscathed.

We saw in the last chapter that certain members of the Vienna Circle believed that a sentence had to be capable, at least in principle, of complete verification by observational evidence to be considered empirically meaningful. By the mid-1930s, however, it was evident that this criterion was unnecessarily strict, for it rules out as meaningless statements of universal form (for example, 'All ravens are black.') which are often used in the specification of general scientific laws. Such statements are not conclusively verifiable (and thus lack cognitive significance) because one exception could falsify them, and no number of verifying instances can guarantee that such a counterinstance will not be found.

A criterion of meaning that excludes general laws from the universe of cognitively significant hypotheses is clearly incompatible with a philosophical position which desires to analyze the statements of science; this was Karl Popper's point when he wrote that 'positivists, in their anxiety to annihilate metaphysics, annihilate natural science along with it'.[4] It was Popper who suggested that the falsifiability of a proposition rather than its verifiability be the 'criterion of demarcation' for distinguishing scientific from non-scientific statements.[5]

This criterion has the advantage of admitting statements of universal form as cognitively significant; it fails, however, to accept affirmative existential hypotheses as meaningful. As Ayer wrote, 'One can say that there are no abominable snowmen, for this could be falsified by finding them; but one cannot say that there are abominable snowmen, for this could not be falsified; the fact that one had failed to find any would not prove conclusively that none existed.'[6]

In *Language, Truth and Logic* (1936), Ayer formulated his own, more liberal verifiability criterion. Known as 'weak verifiability', it asserts that a sentence has empirical import if 'some experimental propositions (he later changed this phrase to 'observation statements') can be deduced from it in conjunction with other premises without being deducible from those other premises alone'.[7] Both the verification and falsification principles were rejected as criteria of cognitive significance because they were too strict. Weak verifiability must also be rejected, but because it is too lax: it can be formulated so that any sentence whatever can be granted significance. Hempel provides an example:

> Thus, e.g., if S is the sentence 'The absolute is perfect,' it suffices to choose as a subsidiary sentence 'if the absolute is perfect then this apple is red' in order to make possible the deduction of the observation sentence 'This apple is red,' which clearly does not follow from the subsidiary hypothesis alone.[8]

Two final approaches to the testability problem are found in the work of Rudolf Carnap. One way of distinguishing between synthetic and nonsense sentences is to construct an empiricist language whose structure in itself rules out the formation of non-meaningful statements; translatability into the empiricist language would then serve as the criterion of cognitive significance. Carnap suggests this approach in his 'Testability and Meaning' (1936); Hempel praises it as a theoretically viable solution to the problem of constructing a criterion of meaning.[9] Unfortunately, efforts to construct a workable empiricist language have proven unsuccessful,[10] and thus most logical empiricists have embraced instead Carnap's alternative notion of confirmation.

Joergen Joergensen notes that Rudolf Carnap, while at a congress in Paris in 1935, 'had stressed the importance of distinguishing between "truth" and "confirmation" (Bewahrung): while truth is an absolute concept independent of time, confirmation is a relative concept, the degrees of which vary with the development of science at any given time'.[11] The difference between confirmation and verification is made explicit in 'Testability and Meaning' (1936).

> If verification is understood as a complete and definitive establishment of truth then a universal sentence, for example, a so-called law of physics or biology, can never be verified, a fact which has often been remarked. Even if each single instance of the law were supposed to be verifiable, the number of instances to which the law refers – for example, the space-and-time-points – is infinite and therefore can never be exhausted by our observations which are always finite in number. We cannot verify the law, but we can test it by its single instances. . . . If in the continued series of such testing experiments no negative instance is found but the number of positive instances increases then our confidence in the law will grow step by step. Thus, instead of verification, we may speak here of gradually increasing *confirmation* of the law.[12]

The notion of confirmation soon became widely accepted as providing a workable approach to the questions of demarcation and theory evaluation. Hypotheses were deemed scientific if they were testable; test instances confirmed or disconfirmed hypotheses; and hypotheses could be ranked according to their degree of confirmation relative to the available evidence. Further studies in later decades expanded on these themes:

1. Hempel and others have tried to define what counts as a confirmation instance, offering conditions which must be satisfied by an acceptable confirmation function.[13]
2. Several logical 'paradoxes of confirmation' have been discovered, work on which intensified in the 1960s. The first, the 'paradox of the raven', was pointed out by Hempel in 1945. Simply stated, it notes that the statement 'All ravens are black' is logically equivalent to the statement 'All non-black things are non-ravens.' We are faced with the counterintuitive result that a nonblack object, for example, a white shoe, counts as a con-

firming instance of the statement 'All ravens are black.'[14]

3. Carnap and others have done work on the nature of probability and inductive inference in an attempt to make concrete the notion of degree of confirmation of an hypothesis.[15]

4. Lastly, other criteria for the evaluation of hypotheses were proposed, and the emphasis shifted from the demarcation of scientific and nonscientific statements to the evaluation of competing theories.

Cognitive significance cannot well be construed as a characteristic of individual sentences, but only of more or less comprehensive systems of sentences (corresponding roughly to scientific theories). A closer study of this point suggests strongly that, much like the analytic–synthetic distinction, the idea of cognitive significance, with its suggestion of a sharp distinction between significant and non-significant sentences or systems of such, has lost its promise and fertility as an explicandum, and that it had better be replaced by certain concepts which admit of differences in degree; such as the formal simplicity of a system; its explanatory and predictive power; and its degree of confirmation relative to available evidence. The analysis and theoretical reconstruction of these concepts seems to offer the most promising way of advancing further the clarification of the issues implicit in the idea of cognitive significance.[16]

Thus we observe that the logical positivist's apparently straight-forward program for distinguishing the legitimate knowledge statements of science from meaningless metaphysical utterances was greatly transformed by later philosophers of science who nonetheless considered themselves firmly within the positivist tradition.

The Status, Structure, and Function of Theories and Theoretical Terms

In their attempts to develop a criterion by which to separate legitimate synthetic propositions from nonsense assertions, the logical positivists discovered that a certain class of terms – theoretical – posed a particularly intractable problem. They were used in all branches of science, yet they often were not amenable to explicit definition in terms of observables. It may be recalled that Ernst Mach believed that theoretical terms were at best useful, mnemonic devices for the organization of observational data, which should eventually be eliminated from science. Such a view was rejected by most logical empiricists of the 1940s and 1950s, however, who subscribed to the 'hypothetico-deductive' (H-D) model of the structure of a theory which emerged in the writings of

Carnap and Hempel. That model not only describes the structure of theories, but provides answers to the questions of the status and functions of theories, as well.

In the early 1930s, the dominant view maintained that all theoretical terms were reducible to assertions about phenomena in the observation or protocol language, which was described as a physicalist language, that is, a thing-language, in which objects are defined according to their observable properties.[17] At first, explicit definition of theoretical terms by way of observation terms was required, such definitions being called correspondence rules and being of the form

$$\text{Def. } Qx = (Cx \supset Ex)$$

that is, x has the property of Q if under test condition C it exhibits a response of E.[18] It was shown by Carnap, however, that to require correspondence rules to be explicit definitions was too restrictive.[19] He proposed instead that correspondence rules take the form of 'reduction sentences', which offer only a partial rather than a complete specification of the entity in question and which are of the form

$$Cx \supset (Qx = Ex)$$

that is, if object x is under test condition C, it has property Q if and only if it exhibits a response of kind E.[20] In a review article, Carl Hempel notes that Carnap later rejects this approach as well, and that philosophers eventually settled on the notion that theories be provided with a 'dictionary' or an 'interpretative system', which contains not definitions 'but statements to the effect that a theoretical sentence of a certain kind is true if and only if a corresponding empirical sentence of a specified kind is true'.[21] In comparing interpretative systems with reduction sentences, the two approaches share the same two characteristics which distinguish reduction sentences from explicit definitions, but additionally,

> an interpretative system need not provide an interpretation – complete or incomplete – for each term in theoretical vocabulary *individually*. In this respect it differs from a set of definitions, which specifies for each term a necessary and sufficient condition, and from a set of reduction sentences, which provides for each term a necessary and a – usually different – sufficient condition. It is quite possible that an interpretative system provides, for some or even all of the terms in V, no necessary or no sufficient condition in terms of V (Basic vocabulary), or indeed neither of the two. . .[22] (emphasis added)

By the above account, the formal structure of a theory is nothing more than that of a mechanical calculus, or a hypothetico-deductive system. A theory contains axioms, or primitive sentences, and theorems, or derivative statements. The axioms may refer to either observables or theoretical entities. The system gains empirical meaningfulness only when the system is given some empirical interpretation by means of interpretative sentences.[23] This occurs when some of the sentences of the theory, usually the derived ones, are translated into the observation language. Implicit in this view is that theories are to be judged as entire systems: the fact that there is no complete (or incomplete, for that matter) definition for every theoretical term is no reason to dispute a theory.

Few views have had more widespread support among modern positivists than this H-D model of the structure of scientific theories. In the opening pages of his *Scientific Explanation* (1953), Richard Braithwaite suggests that theories are hierarchical in structure.

> The propositions in a deductive system may be considered as being arranged in an order of levels, the hypotheses at the highest levels being those which occur only as premisses in the system, those at the lowest level being those which occur only as conclusions in the system, and those at intermediate levels being those which occur as conclusions from deductions from higher-level hypotheses and which serve as premisses for deductions of lower-level hypotheses.[24]

Higher-level hypotheses will often refer to theoretical entities, while lower-level hypotheses (i.e. deduced consequences of the theory) describe observable phenomena and are the propositions which may be tested against reality for purposes of evaluating a theory.[25] And Ernest Nagel, in his *The Structure of Science: Problems in the Logic of Scientific Explanation* (1961), states that scientific theories have three components: an 'abstract calculus', 'a set of rules that in effect assign an empirical content to the abstract calculus', and a model for explicating the abstract calculus.[26]

The H-D model explicitly addresses the problems of a theory's structure. In addition, it provides a solution to the troubling question of the status of theoretical terms. Since statements which make reference to nonobservable entities are now permitted in scientific discourse, the cognitive significance of such statements cannot rest on the possibility of directly testing each assertion, otherwise statements containing theoretical terms would be deemed meaningless. The present view circumvents this problem by allowing sentences containing theoretical terms to gain meaningfulness indirectly: even though theoretical terms may not be directly expressible in an observation language, they are accorded cognitive significance in instances of the successful confirmation of the theory in which they are embedded. Theories as a whole are tested by comparing their deduced consequences (predictions) with the data; it does not count against a theory if all of its terms cannot be given empirical counterparts via correspondence rules; indeed, it is generally the case that certain terms will be undefined or only partially defined in terms of the observation language.

The H-D model also turns the old realist–instrumentalist controversy into a moot debate. Realists claim that theoretical terms must refer to real entities, and that theories which do not are false. Instrumentalists are agnostic on the point, for they insist that theories are only instruments, that as such it is incorrect to speak of theories as being either true or false, and that the only relevant questions that can be asked regarding theories concern their adequacy. If each is carefully stated, either realism or instrumentalism can be made consistent with the H-D model of theoretical structure. For this reason, Nagel ends his chapter on the cognitive status of theories by leaving the choice between the two up to the reader.

> It is therefore difficult to escape the conclusion that when the two apparently opposing views on the cognitive status of theories are each stated with some circumspection, each can assimilate into its formulations not only the facts concerning the primary subject matter explored by experimental inquiry but also all the relevant facts concerning the logic and procedures of science. In brief the oppositions between these views is a conflict over preferred modes of speech.[27]

The implications we have drawn from the H-D model regarding the status and functions of theories and theoretical terms directly conflict with certain earlier, less sympathetic interpretations of the role of theories in science. Ernest Mach may be characterized as an 'eliminative fictionalist': he viewed theories as useful, heuristic fictions for organizing data that should nonetheless eventually be eliminated from science. This contrasts starkly with Carl Hempel's position in 'The Theoretician's Dilemma' (1958), in which he emphasizes the many positive functions of theories:

1. They allow generality in the specification of scientific laws.
2. They possess 'a certain formal simplicity' which allows the use of 'powerful and elegant mathematical machinery'.
3. They can serve the practical function of allowing the scientist to discover interdependencies among observables.
4. They are convenient and fruitful heuristic devices, often serving an explanatory function of their own.[28]

While many may accept Hempel's arguments that theories are useful and should not be eliminated in science, others might still insist that, whenever possible, theoretical terms should be replaced with terms that make reference to the immediate objects of phenomenal reality. This approach has many variants and has been termed physicalism, descriptivism, phenomenalism, and, in the particular form espoused by Bridgman, operationalism. Bridgman's thesis has been criticized by philosophers from within and without the positivist camp: Hempel, Nagel, and Rom Harré are among those who find the approach lacking.[29] The arguments brought against such strictly empirical accounts, with particular attention given to operationalism, include the following:

1. Any such approach could not resolve the problem of the explicit definition of theoretical terms; science as we know it would be eliminated or trivialized if the tenets were consistently applied.
2. All perception, even 'immediate experience', involves interpretation and ordering; there is no 'autonomous language of bare sense contents'.[30] (We will see that this argument has implications for the viability of logical empiricism, as well.)
3. In the case of operationalism, a single concept would have had to be considered two concepts if it could be defined by two separate sets of operations.
4. There is no way to decide which operational definitions are useful and which are not. In the extreme, this could lead to the unsatisfactory result that 'any random hook-up of equipment and sequence of operations defines an empirical concept'.[31]

We see, then, that though later positivists still preferred that science be intimately tied to observable phenomena, they allowed a far more substantial role for theories and theoretical terms than did their predecessors.

The Nature of Scientific Explanation

At the end of the last century and for the first few decades of the present one, the dominant view held that theories do not explain phenomena but are instead only economical and eventually eliminable tools for the organization of complexes of sensations; that establishing correlations among phenomena is all that science can and should do; and that only metaphysicians would try to go beyond the phenomena themselves in search of 'ultimate explanations'. In Auguste Comte's succinct prose, 'The true Positive spirit consists in substituting the study of the invariable Laws of phenomena for that of their so-called Causes, whether proximate or primary; in a word, in studying the *How* instead of the *Why*.'[32]

In short, Comte, Mach and other early positivists gave no role to explanation in science, as we understand the word.[33] This somewhat counterintuitive approach to scientific explanation was eventually replaced in modern positivist analyses by what have been called the 'covering-law models' of scientific explanation, which were developed in a paper by Hempel and Paul Oppenheim, and later elaborated upon by Hempel.

Hempel and Oppenheim advanced an account of what later came to be called the deductive-nomological (D-N) model of scientific explanation in a 1948 paper entitled 'Studies in the Logic of Explanation'. In that work, the authors proposed that every valid explanation is composed of two parts, an explanandum and an explanans. 'By the explanandum, we understand the sentence describing the phenomenon to be explained (not that phenomenon itself); by the explanans, the class of those sentences which are adduced to account for the phenomenon.'[34] Further, the explanans contains two subclasses: sentences comprising a list of antecedent conditions which must obtain, and sentences representing general laws. If an explanation is to be sound, four logical and empirical 'conditions of adequacy' must also be fulfilled.

I   Logical conditions of adequacy
    (R1) The explanandum must be a logical consequence of the explanans; in other words, the explanandum must be logically deducible from the information contained in the explanans, for otherwise, the explanans would not constitute adequate grounds for the explanandum.
    (R2) The explanans must contain general laws, and these must actually be required for the derivation of the explanandum. We shall not make it a necessary condition for a sound explanation, however, that the explanans must contain at least one statement which is not a law . . .
    (R3) The explanans must have empirical content, i.e., it must be capable, at least in principle, of test by experiment or observation. . . . the point deserves special mention because . . . certain arguments which have been offered as explanations in the natural and in the social sciences violate this requirement.
II Empirical condition of adequacy.
    (R4) The sentences constituting the explanans must be true.[35]

The D-N account, then, asserts that any legitimate scientific explanation must be expressible in the form of a deductive argument in which the explanandum, or sentence describing the event to be explained, is a valid, logical consequence of a group of sentences called the explanans. The deductive nature of explanation is stressed; if the initial conditions along with the general law(s) obtain, the phenomenon described by the explanandum *must* occur. This logical necessity is due to the restriction that only laws of universal form are permitted in scientific explanations.[36] If laws of a statistical nature are allowed, only a certain likelihood of the occurrence of the event described by the explanandum can be maintained.[37]

Further qualifications and observations provided the basis for more investigation in the 1950s. As Hempel and Oppenheim admit, the concept of 'a general law' is not unproblematical. Other philosophers offered alternative formulations of that key concept in response.[38] The authors also emphasized that many explanations in science, because they make use of statistical laws, cannot be adequately accounted for by the D-N model. Hempel accordingly developed a second 'inductive-probabilistic' (I-P) covering-law model to describe that type of explanation. In the I-P model the explanans, comprised now of sentences describing the requisite initial conditions along with *statistical* laws, 'confers upon the explanandum-statement a high logical, or inductive, probability'.[39]

Not all aspects of the covering-law approach to explanation enjoyed universal support: two assertions made by Hempel regarding his models were to engender much debate in the 1960s. The first of these concerns the so-called symmetry of explanation and prediction. Explanation and prediction are structurally symmetrical, the only difference between them being a temporal one: in the case of an explanation, the phenomenon described in the explanandum has already occurred, whereas in the case of a prediction, it is in the future. This implies that every explanation must be a potential prediction, or, as Hempel puts it, 'It may be said, therefore, that an explanation is not fully adequate unless its explanans, if taken account of in time, could have served as a basis for predicting the phenomena under consideration.'[40] This view was to be thoroughly contested by Michael Scriven.

The second assertion that came to be widely contested is that the two covering-law models, between them, adequately describe almost all legitimate explanation that occurs in both the natural and social sciences:

Our characterization of scientific explanation is so far based on a study of cases taken from the physical sciences. But the general principles thus obtained apply also outside this area. Thus, various types of behaviour in laboratory animals and in human subjects are explained in psychology by subsumption under laws or even general theories of learning or conditioning; and while frequently, the regularities invoked cannot be stated with the same generality and precision as in physics or chemistry, it is clear, at least, that the general character of those explanations conforms to our earlier characterization.[41]

This is true even for 'motivational explanations' of human behavior, for motives can be considered among the antecedent conditions, and as such, 'there is no formal difference on this account between motivational and causal explanations'.[42] In addition, not all motivational explanations are in fact legitimate explanations, for that method of explanation 'lends itself to the facile construction of ex-post facto accounts without predictive force', a procedure which 'frequently deprives alleged motivational explanations of their cognitive significance'.[43] We will see that challenges of these views have been accompanied by alternative models of scientific explanation.

One final point: in the D-N and I-P models of explanation, it is assumed that the sentences contained in the explanans are true. In the last section, it was observed that the indirect testability approach to the status of theoretical terms (i.e. theoretical terms gain cognitive significance indirectly when the theories in which they are embedded are confirmed) was compatible with either an instrumentalist or realist approach to the status of theories. Clearly, the covering-law models of explanation are in conflict with the instrumentalist interpretation of theories. If one is an instrumentalist, one cannot claim an explanatory role for theories; and if one adheres to the covering-law models of explanation, one can emphasize the importance of prediction in science (as Hempel and Oppenheim surely do), but one cannot say that theories are neither true nor false but only instruments.

A Representative Logical Empiricist

In the last chapter we reviewed the main tenets of logical positivism, which was a strong-willed and confident synthesis of empirical and analytic philosophies that promised nothing less than to rid philosophy and the positive sciences of all traces of speculative idealism and metaphysics. By the mid-1930s it was evident that such claims were unrealistic, and over the next twenty years a more cautious and moderate positivism, logical empiricism, emerged, one which nonetheless was able to offer a fairly complete and formally pleasing account of the nature of scientific enterprise. If such an animal existed, a 'representative logical empiricist' of the mid-1950s might offer the following characterization of the structure, nature, and function of science and scientific theories.

The relationships and phenomena investigated by both the natural and social sciences can often be represented formally by axiomatic hypothetico-deductive structures known as theories. In their formal state, such structures have no empirical import, which can only be achieved when certain of the symbols in the hypothetico-deductive system are given an empirical interpretation via correspondence rules.

Implied by this hypothetico-deductive model of the structure of theories is the weak requirement that only some of the terms need have empirical counterparts. This is necessary because theoretical terms, which are used extensively in science, defy explicit interpretation into the neutral observation language. Rather than attempting to rid science of such terms, as some early positivists and operationalists suggested, the current view recognizes the essential role played by theoretical terms and thus urges retention of them. As such, the following modifications of earlier positivist views are necessary.

First, the individual statements contained in a theory need not be tested separately; rather, the entire theory can be tested by checking to see if its observable deduced consequences correspond to reality. This rids science of the necessity of checking each synthetic statement of science for its cognitive value, a task which seems hopeless, anyway, given the problems encountered up until this time with the designation of an adequate testability criterion. That theories must to some extent be supported by evidence is the new criterion of cognitive significance; in addition, alternative non-empirical criteria for theory evaluation should be investigated and logically stated. To reiterate, cognitive significance now is to be applied as a tool of theory choice, rather than a means for distinguishing between meaningful and meaningless statements.

If we insist on retaining theoretical terms in science, what is their status? While the question of cognitive significance once turned on the testability of assertions, the present view allows theoretical terms to gain meaningfulness through the partial interpretation of such terms and by invocation of the indirect testability thesis: though theoretical terms need not be expressible directly in terms of the observation language, their meaningfulness is not thereby denied, for they are accorded cognitive significance in instances of the successful confirmation of the theory in which they are embedded. Whether or not theoretical terms make reference to 'real' entities (the old realist–instrumentalist controversy) is a moot question; what counts is whether the hypotheses which contain them are confirmable and confirmed.

Finally, we follow Hempel in asserting that the goal of science is explanation, and deny the naive view that theories can only describe but not explain phenomena. However, in centuries past men have offered explanations for phenomena which should not be considered scientific; for example, by 'explaining' bodily functions in terms of vital forces (entelechies), or natural disasters in terms of animistic spirits. To avoid such metaphysical excesses, the current view considers legitimate only those explanations which can be reconstructed in the form of either a deductive argument (following the deductive-nomological covering-law model) or a highly probable inductive argument (following the inductive-probablistic covering-law model). A corollary of that view, which further ensures the legitimacy of our explanations, is that explanation and prediction are logically symmetrical, the only difference between them being temporal.

Thus ends our representative account of the scientific enterprise. On that account, science is a cumulative and rational affair. Its goal is explanation, which is rigorously defined. Its theories are axiomatic systems, parts of which make reference to observable phenomena. It allows (and, in fact, embraces) the existence of theoretical terms in the language of science, but insists that theories still 'return to the data' by requiring that they meet the (albeit somewhat anemic) criterion of confirmation. It is a substantially weaker offspring, when compared to its hardy logical positivist forebearers, but it is also a more logically cohesive, formally pleasing, and judicious account of the scientific process.

That the logical positivists must be kept separate from their more circumspect followers has not always been noticed by critics of 'positivism'. The worst of such critics select various extreme statements made by logical positivists, easily refute them, then claim to have shown that modern positivism cannot be maintained. Such exercises are of little value and, worse, add confusion to topics already sufficiently complex to warrant clarity from discussants. In the next chapter it will be shown that the later variants of positivism are not immune from criticism; indeed, the 1950s witnessed a 'revolutionary crisis' of sorts within the philosophy of science as the complaints against positivism mounted. But these complaints were directed against the doctrines and models of a mature positivism, and thus share little in common with critiques which, due to poor scholarship on the part of antagonists, attempt to destroy logical empiricism by attacking the remains of its predecessor.

Notes

Parts of this chapter are taken from my paper, 'Positivist Philosophy of Science and the Methodology of Economics,' *Journal of Economic Issues*, vol. 14 (March 1980), pp. 53–76.

1. The areas I have chosen to investigate are those that will be useful in our later discussions of economic methodology. Many topics have been omitted or are only mentioned in passing; two examples are Hans Reichenbach's contributions (he studied the individual physical sciences for their philosophical implications), and the work of Carnap, Tarski, and others in linguistic analysis – the study of syntax, semantics and pragmatics. See Hans Reichenbach, *Philosophical Foundations of Quantum Mechanics* (Berkley and Los Angeles: University of California Press, 1944); Rudolf Carnap, *The Logical Syntax of Language* (first published 1934), trans. by Amethe Smeaton (New York: Harcourt, Brace, 1937), *Introduction to Semantics* (Cambridge: Harvard University Press, 1942), *Formalization of Logic* (Cambridge: Harvard University Press, 1942), and *Meaning and Necessity: A Study in Semantics and Modal Logic* (Chicago: University of Chicago Press, 1947); and Alfred Tarski, *Logic, Semantics, Metamathematics* (Oxford: Clarendon Press, 1956).

2. For an argument that all three hinge on one's conception of the structure and function of theories, see Frederick Suppe's superlative 'Criticial Introduction,' *The Structure of Scientific Theories*, 2nd edn. (Urbana, Ill.: University of Illinois Press, 1977), pp. 1–241.

3. This view may have been tenable in 1959, but in view of Popper's later work and subsequent developments in the philosophy of science, it is quite unconvincing today.

4. Karl Popper, *The Logic of Scientific Discovery* (first published 1934), translated edn. (New York: Harper and Row, 1959), p. 36.

5. Ibid., pp. 40–2.

6. A. J. Ayer, 'Editor's Introduction,' in A. J. Ayer (ed.), *Logical Positivism* (Glencoe, Ill.: The Free Press, 1959), p. 14.

7. A. J. Ayer, *Language, Truth and Logic* (first published 1936), 2nd edn. (New York: Dover, 1946), p. 39.

8. Carl Hempel, 'The Empiricist Criterion of Meaning,' in A. J. Ayer (ed.), *Logical Positivism*, p. 115.

9. Rudolf Carnap, 'Testability and Meaning,' *Philosophy of Science*, vol. 3 (1937), section 4; Hempel, 'Empiricist Criterion. . .,' op. cit., pp. 116–18.

10. Carnap worked extensively in this area; see note 1 and also his *Foundations of Logic and Mathematics, International Encyclopedia of Unified Science*, Vol. I, no. 3 (Chicago: University of Chicago Press, 1939). Popper has criticized attempts to understand the growth of scientific knowledge via construction of theoretical languages. Thus, in the English edition preface to *Logic*, he states, 'I do not think that the study of the growth of knowledge can be replaced by the study of linguistic usages, or of language systems' (p. 16).

11. Joergen Joergensen, *The Development of Logical Empiricism, International Encyclopedia of Unified Science*, Vol. II, no. 9 (Chicago: University of Chicago Press, 1951), p. 73.

12. Carnap, 'Testability and Meaning,' loc. cit., p. 425.

13. Carl Hempel, 'Studies in the Logic of Confirmation,' *Mind*, vol. 54 (1945), sections 8 and 9.

14. Ibid., sections 4–6.

15. See Rudolph Carnap, *Logical Foundations of Probability* (Chicago: University of Chicago Press, 1950), and *The Continuum of Inductive Methods* (Chicago: University of Chicago Press, 1952). For more recent studies, see Rudolf Carnap and R. C. Jeffrey (eds), *Studies in Inductive Logic and Probability*, Vol. I (Berkeley: University of California Press, 1971).

16. Hempel, 'Empiricist Criterion . . .,' op. cit., p. 129. For discussions of the viability of the analytic–synthetic distinction, see W. V. O. Quine, 'Two

Dogmas of Empiricism,' in *From A Logical Point of View* (Cambridge: Harvard University Press, 1953); and F. Suppe, 'Critical Introduction,' op. cit., pp. 67–80.

17. Neurath had at first argued for a phenomenalist language, that is, a sense-datum language which provides a direct characterization of experience. But Carnap's physicalist language won out. See Otto Neurath, 'Sozilogie in Physikalismus,' *Erkenntnis*, vol. 2 (1931), pp. 393–431; cf. Carnap, *Logical Syntax*, op. cit. For Neurath's recantation, see his 'Protocol Sentences,' translated by George Schick, in A. J. Ayer (ed.), op. cit., pp. 199–208.

18. The notation is Hempel's. See his 'The Theoretician's Dilemma,' in Herbert Feigl, Grover Maxwell, and Michael Scriven (eds), *Minnesota Studies in the Philosophy of Science*, Vol. II (Minneapolis: University of Minnesota Press, 1958), p. 50.

19. Carnap, 'Testability and Meaning,' loc. cit., sections 7 and 8. Specifically, disposition terms (terms which express the disposition of one or more objects to react in a specified manner under specified conditions) do not admit of explicit definition. See Hempel's discussion in his 'Empiricist Criterion. . .,' op. cit., pp. 118–22.

20. Again, see Hempel, 'Dilemma...,' op. cit., p. 51.

21. Ibid., p. 72. The term 'dictionary' was first used by Norman R. Campbell in his *Physics: The Elements* (Cambridge: Cambridge University Press, 1920).

22. Hempel, 'Dilemma...,' op. cit., pp. 71–2.

23. In recent literature, 'correspondence rules' is used more frequently and considered synonomous with 'interpretative sentences'.

24. Richard Braithwaite, *Scientific Explanation* (first published, 1953) (Cambridge: Cambridge University Press, 1959), p. 12.

25. Ibid., pp. 12–21.

26. Ernest Nagel, *The Structure of Science: Problems in the Logic of Scientific Explanation* (New York: Harcourt, Brace and World, 1961), p. 90.

27. Ibid., p. 152.

28. Hempel, 'Dilemma...,' op. cit., pp. 67–77.

29. For example, see Carl Hempel, 'A Logical Appraisal of Operationalism,' *Scientific Monthly*, vol. 79 (1954), pp. 215–20; Nagel, *Structure*, pp. 117–29; and Rom Harré, *The Philosophies of Science: An Introductory Survey* (London: Oxford University Press, 1972), pp. 74–8, 97.

30. Nagel, *Structure*, p. 121.

31. Harré, *Philosophies of Science*, p. 97.

32. August Comte, *A General View of Positivism*, trans. by J.H. Bridges, in Monroe Beardsley (ed.), *The European Philosophers from Descartes to Nietzsche* (New York: The Modern Library, 1960), p. 745. See also Gertrude Lenzer (ed.), *Auguste Comte and Positivism: The Essential Writings* (New York: Harper Torchbooks, 1975). The cited passage is not among those Professor Lenzer chose to include in her work.

33. It is only in relation to later positivist thought that the ideas of Comte and Mach should be grouped together. Comte, who coined the word positivism, argued for a search for laws rather than causes; Mach, a practicing physicist, influenced the Vienna Circle more directly with his theory of elements and his views on the mnemonic, economizing functions of theories.

34. Carl Hempel and Paul Oppenheim, 'Studies in the Logic of Explanation,' *Philosophy of Science*, vol. 15 (1948), pp. 135–75; reprinted in Herbert Feigl and May Brodbeck (eds), *Readings in the Philosophy of Science* (New York: Meridith Corporation, 1953), p. 321.

35. Ibid., pp. 321–2.

36. Ibid., p. 338.
37. Hempel and Oppenheim acknowledge that, because certain scientific laws are statistical rather than universal, their present study does not cover all the possible types of legitimate scientific explanations. Ibid., p. 324.
38. Ibid., pp. 337–50; A. J. Ayer, 'What Is a Law of Nature?' and Richard Braithwaite, 'Laws of Nature and Causality,' both in Baruch Brody (ed.), *Readings in the Philosophy of Science* (Englewood Cliffs, N.J.: Prentice-Hall, 1970), pp. 39–63. Braithwaite's article is drawn from his book, *Scientific Explanation*.
39. Carl Hempel, 'Explanation and Prediction by Covering Laws,' in Bernard Baumrin (ed.), *Philosophy of Science*: The *Delaware Seminar*, Vol. I (New York: Wiley, 1963), p. 110.
40. Hempel and Oppenheim, 'Logic. . .,' op. cit., p. 323.
41. Ibid., p. 325.
42. Ibid., p. 328.
43. Ibid., p. 328.

4

The Philosophical Attack on Logical Empiricism

Introduction

The positivist tradition within the philosophy of science underwent numerous transformations in its development from the early writings of Comte and Mach, through the radical empiricism of the Vienna Circle, to the more recent and circumspect contributions of Carnap, Hempel, Braithwaite, and Nagel. The bold claims of early positivism are absent in the later formulations. There still exists a heavy emphasis on observation, prediction, and the incorrigibility of data, but the crucial importance of theory is acknowledged, a step unthinkable in any strictly empirical system of thought. Due to such modifications, the logical empiricism of the 1950s seemed capable of providing a rigorous, robust, and firm epistemological and methodological foundation for analyses of the structure, function, and nature of science. But that assessment was soon to change.

A symposium on the structure of scientific theories was held in the late 1960s, and the papers presented there were gathered in a volume edited by Frederick Suppe. The first edition of the collection in the early 1970s contained a long introduction on the development of twentieth century philosophy of science by the editor; in 1977 a second paperback edition was published which included an Afterword. Suppe ends his chapter entitled 'Swan Song for Positivism' in the Afterword with the following words:

> To conclude, virtually all of the positivistic program for philosophy of science has been repudiated by contemporary philosophy of science. The Received View has been rejected, as have its treatments of explanation and reduction. . . Also the importance of induction and confirmation is coming to be sharply downgraded in contemporary philosophical thinking

about the scientific enterprise and the knowledge it provides. Positivism today truly belongs to the history of the philosophy of science, and its influence is that of a movement historically important in shaping the landscape of a much-changed contemporary philosophy of science.[1]

The changes that have taken place within the philosophy of science in the last three decades are dramatic, revolutionary, and consequential. In this chapter, some of the more telling criticisms brought against positivism are documented. For expository convenience, the tripartite division of subject areas begun in the preceding chapter is again followed.

Though the arguments discussed below were all advanced by philosophers in the 1950s and 1960s, some of them had first been made years earlier. Of the early critics of positivism, the most renowned is Sir Karl Popper, whose persistent and persuasive railings against positivism began while the Vienna Circle was still meeting, and continues into the 1980s. His first book, *Logik der Forschung* (1934; translated as *The Logic of Scientific Discovery*, 1959), which was published when he was only thirty-two, contains forceful arguments against 'inductivism', the alleged incontrovertibility of data, and other positivist beliefs, arguments that were to emerge again in the attacks against a more mature positivism.

Most economists recognize Popper's name and correctly identify him with the notion of falsifiability. Probably fewer realize that he rejects positivism, and still fewer are aware of his strong sympathies with classical liberalism.[2] His work is sufficiently complex and significant to warrant a separate chapter, but because he played such a central role in the critique of positivism, the overlap between such a chapter and this one would be too great. Accordingly, I will detail Popper's contributions in this chapter. Of course, Popper was not the only critic of positivism, and other philosophers are mentioned as well.

Popper is not solely a critic, he is a builder, too: in his terms, his work contains both refutations and conjectures. As an architect of systems, he again is a pivotal figure, because many philosophers (particularly those in the growth of knowledge tradition treated in the next chapter) take Popper as their starting point. The discussions of his contributions therefore treat both his critical and positive contributions. To make those discussions more comprehensible, four crucial aspects of Popper's thought should be highlighted at the outset.

1. The Growth of Knowledge – The central problem of epistemology is that of the growth of knowledge, and it can be

fruitfully studied by examining the growth of scientific knowledge. Popper has little use for philosophical approaches that lie outside of the rationalist tradition. He also rejects the views of linguistic philosophers who argue that all of the problems of philosophy reduce to the problem of linguistic usage, or the meaning of words.

2. Fallibilism – Objective truth, in Alfred Tarski's formulation as correspondence to facts, exists, but we have no criterion for knowing when we have reached the truth. Criteria do exist, however, which may allow us, 'if we are lucky', to recognize error. This latter rescues Popper from skepticism.

3. Anti-inductivism – A related view is the rejection of attempts to formulate an inductive logic by which the truth or high probability of a universal statement can be inferred from the truth of a number of singular statements. A universal theory can be shown to be false, but never proven to be true. As a result, all knowledge is conjectural.

4. Critical Rationalism – The way in which knowledge progresses is a twofold process: bold conjectures are advanced, and they are met by attempted refutations in which critical and severe tests are proposed and carried out. This is a trial and error process, and the hope is that we can learn from our mistakes. The penultimate rule of rational (and thus scientific) discourse is to subject every belief to critical scrutiny.[3]

These four initial conceptions underlie many of Popper's pronouncements; their enunciation now may aid the reader in understanding what will be said about him later.

Confirmation, Induction, and Popper's Methodological Falsificationism

One tenet of positivist analysis which was retained in all of the various forms of positivist philosophy of science is the firm belief that the nonanalytic statements of science must have empirical content which must be, at least in principle, testable. Neither verifiability nor falsifiability were successful criteria of testability; later positivists were able to settle on the notion that *theories* could be assessed according to their strength of confirmation relative to the available evidence.[4] This measuring of the strength of arguments is the primary task of inductive logic: just as the task of deductive logic is to discover whether deductive arguments are valid or invalid, inductive logic attempts to rank the relative strengths of confirmation of inductive arguments. A clearly formulated inductive logic is essential if we wish to be able to tentatively choose among competing hypotheses on the basis of their relative degrees of confirmation and disconfirmation.

Problems of Confirmation

Constructing and justifying an inductive logic has not proved to be a simple task. A number of problems and paradoxes have been discovered by philosophers throughout the years, of which we will mention three: the paradox of the raven, Goodman's paradox, and Hume's problem of induction.

The paradox of the raven was first raised by Carl Hempel in the 1940s and concerns the question: What is to count as a confirming instance in test situations? Hempel notes

> Thus, we shall agree that if A is both a raven and black, then (A) certainly confirms S_1: '(X) (Raven (x) $\supset$ Black (x)', and if D is neither black nor a raven, D certainly confirms S_2:

$$(x) \ (\backsim \text{Black} \ (x) \supset \backsim \text{Raven} \ (x) \ ).$$

> Let us now combine this simple stipulation with the equivalence condition: since S_1 and S_2 are equivalent, D is confirming also for S_1, any object which is neither black nor a raven. Consequently, any red pencil, any green leaf, any yellow cow, etc., becomes confirming evidence for the hypothesis that all ravens are black.[5]

What are we to make of this paradox? Hempel claims that we should accept it, that its paradoxical nature 'is not objectively founded, it is a psychological illusion' based on 'a misleading intuition'.[6]

> One source of misunderstanding is the view, referred to before, that a hypothesis of the simple form 'Every P is a Q' such as 'All sodium salt burns yellow', asserts something about a limited class of objects only, namely, the class of all P's. This idea involves a confusion of logical and practical considerations: Our interest in the hypothesis may be focused upon its applicability to that particular class of objects, but the hypothesis nevertheless asserts something about, and indeed imposes restrictions upon, *all* objects. . .[7]

Other philosophers of science have not accepted the paradox and have suggested alternative approaches to the problem of what is to count as a confirming instance.[8]

The next problem, labeled the Goodman paradox or the new riddle of induction, was introduced by Nelson Goodman in 1953; his treatment of it is found in his *Fact, Fiction and Forecast* (1955).

Goodman believes that the true problem of induction is neither that of justification (to be taken up next), nor Hempel's paradox of the raven, but rather the question: How are we to know which regularities are projectible?[9]

A system of inductive logic should be capable of assigning inductive probabilities to arguments, and such probabilities will be based on past observations of regularities. Inductive logic thus projects observed regularities into the future. But there is a problem here: not all observed regularities are *projectable*, some are only accidental or spurious correlations. A workable system of inductive logic must project only projectable observed regularities into the future.

That this is no simple matter is the point of the Goodman paradox. Let us choose a regularity that all would agree is projectable: that emeralds are green. The following argument should then have a high inductive probability:

> All observed emeralds have been green.
> ───────────────────────────────
> The next emerald to be observed will be green.

Define a new color word 'grue' in the following way – any object x is 'grue' if x is green before time t and x is blue after time t. We get the curious result that the presence of a regularity in identical phenomena depends on the descriptive machinery of the language employed.

> consider our case of emeralds. All those examined before time t are green; and this leads us to expect, and confirms the prediction, that the next one will be green. But also, all those examined are grue; and this does not lead us to expect, and does not confirm the prediction, that the next one will be grue. Regularity in greenness confirms the prediction of further cases; regularity in grueness does not. *To say that valid predictions are those based on past regularities, without being able to say which regularities, is thus quite pointless.* (emphasis added)[10]

Proposed solutions to the riddle posed by Goodman rest on the ability to distinguish between 'lawlike and accidental sufficient conditions'.

The traditional problem of induction, or Hume's problem, concerns our ability to *justify* inductive inferences. This problem has been stated in a number of different ways: What is the justification for the belief that the future will be largely like the past? What is the justification for inductive inferences? Can the claim that a universal theory is true be justified by assuming the truth of a certain number of test or observation statements?[11] Hume's answer to any of these formulations is clear: no rational justification of induction is possible. His proof is as follows.

Rational justifications are of two kinds: deductive or inductive. No deductive justification of induction is possible, 'since it implies no contradiction that the course of nature may change'.[12] We are left then with an inductive justification of induction, which might take the form:

> Arguments with high inductive probability have given us true conclusions from true premises in the past.
>
> ---
>
> Such arguments will give us true conclusions from true premises most of the time.

As Hume notes, arguments such as these 'must be evidently going in a circle and taking for granted which is the very point in question'.[13] Many attempts to solve Hume's problem have been proposed; since the Vienna Circle, the problem of justifying *probabilistic* induction has also occupied the attention of philosophers.[14]

Popper's Methodological Falsificationism

All of the arguments above concern our ability to justify or implement an inductive logic which could determine the relative strengths of arguments (or hypotheses) based on their confirmation by evidence. The *desirability* of formulating an inductive logic is unquestioned in the above treatments. Karl Popper take the opposite position, believing that a preoccupation with highly probable hypotheses is exactly the worst way to approach science. Science advances by bold conjectures and critical refutations, not by repeated attempts at confirmation of hypotheses; indeed, theories with the highest empirical content are those with the lowest probability.

Popper's beliefs about confirmation, his understanding of the actual history of science, and his prescriptions regarding scientific methods are all interdependent. An exposition of his views is made all the more difficult by the fact that Popper's beliefs have changed over time.[15] Fortunately, the philosopher has been so concerned that posterity understand the evolution and substance of his views that he has written prolifically on both subjects, and the interested reader should have little problem delving further.

While still in his teens in Vienna, Popper was exposed to a myriad of significant and powerful theories: Einstein's theory of relativity, Marx's theory of history, Freud's psychoanalytic theory, and Alfred Adler's individual psychology. At first impressed with these innovative ideas (he even practiced social work under Adler for a time with children in the working-class districts of Vienna), Popper later became dissatisfied with the latter three. The source of his uneasiness was something that advocates of the theories considered their strongest point: explanatory power.

> I found that those of my friends who were admirers of Marx, Freud, and Adler, were impressed by a number of points common to these theories, and especially by their apparent *explanatory power*. These theories appeared to be able to explain practically everything that happened within the fields to which they referred. The study of any of them seemed to have the effect of an intellectual conversion or revelation, opening your eyes to a new truth hidden from those not yet initiated. Once your eyes were thus opened you saw confirming instances everywhere: the world was full of *verifications* of the theory.[16]

Unlike the theories of Marx, Freud, and Adler, Einstein's theory *forbad* certain results; and indeed, among the forbidden results are some that everyone before Einstein would have expected. This led Popper to his famous emphasis on falsifiability: since confirming instances (verifications) are easy to find, they should count only if they are the result of genuine attempts to refute, or falsify, a theory; good theories make risky predictions; legitimate tests are serious attempts at falsification.[17]

Around 1927 Popper developed a solution to the problem of induction. Like most such solutions, his involved a restatement of the problem. The restatement and Popper's reply are given in a recent article:

> Can the claim that an explanatory universal theory is true or that it is false be justified by 'empirical reasons'; that is, can the assumption of the truth of test statements justify either the claim that a universal theory is true or the claim that it is false?
>
> To this problem, my answer is positive: Yes, *the assumption of the truth of test statements sometimes allows us to justify the claim that an explanatory universal theory is false.*[18]

Popper emphasized that a universal theory could never be proven true, or verified, and hence he was critical of the verificationists of the Vienna Circle. Popper later suggested falsifiability as a demarcation criterion for separating the statements of science from all others. He has consistently and adamantly insisted that falsifiability is not just another criterion of cognitive significance for distinguishing *meaningful* from *meaningless* statements, an interpretation given his demarcation criterion by members of the Circle. His criterion separates *scientific* from *nonscientific* statements; that statements may be nonscientific yet still meaningful is accepted by Popper.[19]

Hume's understanding of the problem of induction includes a psychological evaluation: though induction cannot be rationally justified, reasonable people still expect the future to resemble the past; put another way, though we cannot *prove* universal theories to be true, we still believe them to be true. That the origins of such beliefs are 'habit and custom', and ultimately based on an individual's *experience*, was Hume's thesis; and empiricists ever since have emphasized that observations of the phenomenal world are the source of theories. In analyzing Hume's problem of induction, Popper ultimately rejects the notion that our theories are 'read out of the data', since all observation presupposes a prior framework: 'the instruction, "Observe!" is absurd' unless one is told *what* to observe.[20]

Scientific theories begin as bold conjectures, as solutions to troubling problems. They are considered scientific if they can be subjected to severe and critical tests; a scientific theory is falsifiable. Those theories that can be more severely tested, that forbid more, are said to have higher *empirical* content, and are preferred. Theories with high content that survive repeated attempts at refutation are considered corroborated. Significantly, a well-corroborated theory is not more probable: probability and content vary inversely; science seeks improbable theories which are capable of surviving critical tests. On these grounds, Popper rejects the confirmationist goal of discovering theories which have high inductive probabilities.[21]

Popper's ideas here involve some subtleties that warrant further attention. First, it now seems clear that the technical disputes between Carnap and Popper on induction were mostly verbal – Carnap never construed induction as a form of inference from data to the truth or high probability of some universal statement.[22] Next, Popper's invocation that scientists search for improbable theories encounters adversity when it is realized that the most improbable theories are also those which are the most likely to be false. Do we really want to multiply the number of theories with high content (low probability), if most of them are false? The problem cannot be resolved by suggesting that scientists search for *true* theories, for as a fallibilist Popper holds that, though we may reach the truth, we can never know that we have. If we cannot recognize truth even when we have found it, in what sense can we say that we search for truth?

Popper has proposed a solution to these problems, and his response involves the notion of verisimilitude. Popper believes that objective truth exists, and follows Tarski's definition of truth as correspondence to the facts. Because of Popper's fallibilism, however, when he says that scientists search for true theories, 'true' plays the role of a maxim or regulative principle. A more correct statement of scientific activity is that scientists seek theories that possess a high degree of verisimilitude, or truth likeness. Verisimilitude *combines* the notions of *truth* and *content*. Using a calculus proposed by Popper, scientists could in certain cases measure the verisimilitude of two theories, comparing them for relative truth content and falsity content.[23]

It turns out that verisimilitude is not an operational notion; its role, like truth, is that of a regulative principle. Its importance in Popper's system of thought is that it permits us to avoid the dilemma brought on by the compatibility of falsity and high content.[24]

Now let us return to Popper's methodological falsificationism. Theories are tested against, and can be falsified by, basic statements or singular statements. These basic statements must not refer merely to random single occurrences; they must refer to *reproducible* effects and must themselves be capable of testing. Since this 'empirical basis' which is used for the testing of theories is itself open to test and modification, its acceptance at any time is provisional or conventional. In this Popper opposes the positivist notion that data are incontrovertible.[25]

What happens when a theory is falsified by a crucial test? Such occurrences should not be viewed despairingly, since they force scientists to reassess the theory, auxiliary assumptions, initial conditions, data – in sum, everything connected with the test. Something will be modified, and hopefully the theory will be improved. However, not every modification of a theory is an improvement. In fact, any falsified theory can be saved by various conventionalist stratagems – adding ad hoc hypotheses, modifying definitions, questioning the acumen of the experimenter or theoretician whose findings contradict the theory. To avoid this, we must state our methodological rules clearly, and our conditions for rejection of the hypothesis must be set up *in advance* of the test. While this involves the risk that we may reject a true hypothesis, it is a risk that must be taken if we are to avoid ad hocery.[26] (This is the view expressed in Popper's *Logic of Scientific Discovery* (1934). More recently he admits to situations in which dogmatism may be allowed, particularly if a theory is new and not yet adequately formulated.[27])

Popper's system is itself a bold and inspiring conjecture about the nature and progress of scientific knowledge. Its emphasis on criticism and objectivity is flattering; its stress on the tentativeness of all knowledge is appropriately circumspect. But there are questions to be raised. Is Popper's characterization of his opponents, the inductivists, fair and accurate? Does his history of science square with the facts? More specifically, does history reveal a sort of 'permanent revolution' of the kind Popper approvingly describes, or have scientists more usually attempted to confirm (rather than reject) hypotheses? Is there a distinction between bold, revolutionary science, and a more usual, mundane, 'normal' science? Popper claims that theories are tested against data; what about cases in which theories are tested against each other? And will Popper's prescriptions really lead to the growth of scientific knowledge?

These and other questions brought against both Popper and his opponents have led to a whole new tradition within the philosophy of science: the growth of knowledge analyses, which will be investigated in the next chapter. Since methodological pronouncements must always involve some combination of descriptive accuracy and prescriptive force, the answers to such questions are of some interest for this study.

Theories and Theoretical Terms

According to logical empiricists a theory's structure is nothing more than an abstract, uninterpreted hypothetico-deductive calculus. A theory gains empirical import when certain of its terms are given an observational interpretation via correspondence rules. Since not all theoretical terms are directly expressible in terms of observables, they gain meaning indirectly: their deduced consequences are compared against reality (the indirect testability thesis), and if the theory is confirmed, the terms employed within the theory gain 'partial meaningfulness'. This account has two important implications. First, only an entire theory (or hypothesis), and not each of its constituent parts, need be tested against evidence. And second, the debate between the realists and instrumentalists (the former argue that theoretical terms refer to actual entities; the latter are agnostic regarding such ontological debates, view theoretical terms as neither true or false, but nevertheless insist on their retention in scientific discourse for pragmatic reasons) over the status of theoretical terms is effectively sidelined, for both the realist and instrumentalist interpretation can be made consistent with the partial interpretation approach.[28]

The Dissolution of the Theoretical–Nontheoretical Distinction
The viability and usefulness of the above account depends on our ability to clearly distinguish theoretical from nontheoretical terms. More to the point, unless a body of nontheoretical terms can be

separated out, the status of theoretical terms and of theories becomes ambiguous since no observational interpretation is then possible. The notion that theories are structured as abstract hypothetico-deductive systems remains, but its usefulness may be questioned if there is no way to provide an abstract calculus with any empirical import.

That a straightforward distinction between theoretical and non-theoretical terms was possible seemed evident to logical empiricists. The distinction was traditionally drawn on observational grounds: nontheoretical terms can be expressed in the neutral observation language, while theoretical terms need not be so definable. This approach assumes, in good positivist style, that knowledge of what is meant by 'observation' and 'observation terms' is unproblematical; there is a 'protocol domain' consisting of 'brute atomic facts' which are describable in a 'neutral observation language', the existence and recognition of which poses no trouble for any competent observer. These intuitively pleasing beliefs came under sustained attack in post-positivist philosophy of science.

What sorts of problems exist with the observable/nonobservable dichotomy as a means for separating nontheoretical from theoretical terms?

First, it is clear that there is no one-to-one correspondence between theoretical terms and nonobservables on the one hand, and nontheoretical terms and observables on the other. As philosopher Hilary Putnam argues, a distinction drawn along such lines must be viewed as 'completely broken-backed', because

(A) If an 'observation term' is one that cannot apply to an unobservable, then there are no observation terms.
(B) Many terms that refer primarily to what Carnap would class as 'unobservables' are not theoretical terms; and at least some theoretical terms refer primarily to observables.
(C) Observational reports can and frequently do contain theoretical terms.
(D) A scientific theory , properly so-called, may refer only to observables. (Darwin's theory of evolution, as originally put forward, is one example.)[29]

Next, various philosophers argue that there can be no sharp distinction between what is observable and what is not. Richard Grandy notes this in his introduction to *Theories and Observation in Science* (1973).

There are, however, arguments against the tenability of any distinction between observable and unobservable objects. The explanation of an unobservable entity appeals to the difference between observing an object directly and merely observing its effects. But if one considers the fact that seeing any object involves photons reflected from (or emitted by) the object impinging on the retina of the observer, the notion of directly observing begins to lose its intuitive clarity. There seems to be only a slight difference of degree between directly seeing and observing through a magnifying glass, and only a slight difference between using a magnifying glass and using a microscope or telescope. . . . But if observability is merely a matter of degree, then there seems to be no plausible way of drawing a sharp line on this basis between objects which do and objects which do not exist.[30]

The assumption implicit in the positivist view that observation can be 'neutral' or independent of all theorizing has also met strong resistance. *Any* observation requires both *selection* and *interpretation* by the observer, and such activities will be colored by the observer's prior theoretical framework, which incorporates such intangible qualities as interests, perspectives, past experiences, and anticipations regarding results. The attack on the concept of neutrality and objectivity in data *selection* is eloquently stated by James Feibelman.

Data, then, are not just anything observed unless, that is, we take observation to involve some kind of discrimination. For no one observes the whole world but only some part of it which has been selected for that purpose. The problem of analyzing observation is complicated by the fact that in every object or event there is more observable than lies within the power of any one observer to detect. Existence is everywhere dense, and it is only the untrained observer who would doubt the force of the difficulty.
. . .
What confronts the observer is usually a choice of facts. Events have a way of outstripping observations and there is a richness to existence that compels a selection.[31]

The case against neutral data *interpretation* was made by Norwood Hanson in his classic treatise *Patterns of Discovery* (1958). The point being emphasized is that two scientists observing the 'same' phenomenon may still interpret it differently due to their unique perspectives.

. . . in Kohler's famous drawing of the Goblet-and-faces we 'take' the same retinal/cortical/sense-datum picture of the configuration; our drawings might be indistinguishable. I see a goblet however, and you see two men staring at one another. Do we see the same thing? Of course we do. But then again we do not.
. . .
To say that Tycho and Kepler, Simplicius and Galileo, Hooke and

Newton, Priestley and Lavoisier, Soddy and Einstein, Debroglie and Born, Heisenberg and Bohm all make the same observations but use them differently is too easy. It does not explain controversy in research science. Were there no sense in which they were different observations they could not be used differently. . . . . There is a sense, then, in which seeing is a 'theory-laden' undertaking.[32]

Popper should also be included on the list of philosophers who have denied that observation is prior to theorizing.[33] Thomas Kuhn and Paul K. Feyerabend extend this line of thinking in arguing that many disagreements between advocates of competing theories occur because scientists use the same words to refer to actually different phenomena. The differences are determined by the theoretical frameworks held by the disputants; different frameworks lead to different observations.[34]

While the above arguments attempt to establish that either observation or the meanings of terms are theory-dependent, others propose that even the facts themselves are theory-dependent, since what counts as a fact depends on one's prior theoretical framework. Philosopher Rom Harré goes farther and claims that no public domain of 'brute, atomic facts' exists.

The only facts which seem genuinely independent of any scientific theory are those of the present experiences of touch, taste, smell, hearing and sight that each individual scientist is currently experiencing. But such facts are not, of course, public facts, they are private to each individual. So we have the dilemma that, if facts are truly independent of theory they are private and do not form part of the public domain of knowledge; if they are public facts they are affected by all sorts of influences particularly from previous knowledge and upon which their exact form and our confidence in them depend. At least for science, there are no brute facts.[35]

Whatever one thinks of the individual arguments advanced above, it must be granted that any distinction between theoretical and nontheoretical terms based on our ability to distinguish theoretical terms, on the one hand, and terms which refer via a neutral observation language to a protocol domain of brute, atomic, unique facts, on the other, has been called seriously into doubt. Is there, perhaps, another way to draw the theoretical/nontheoretical distinction? While this is an open question, at least one philosopher, Peter Achinstein, thinks not.

I have considered the widespread doctrine that there exists a fundamental distinction between two sorts of terms employed by scientists. On one view the distinction rests upon observation; on another, upon conceptual organization, theory-dependence, or conjecture; still other criteria are precision and abstractness. What has been shown is not that divisions are impossible but that, using any one of these criteria, many distinctions will emerge; these will be fairly specific ones applicable only to certain classes of terms employed by the scientist; and each will be different, so that a term classified as observational (or theory-dependent, and so forth) on one criterion will be non-observational (or theory-independent, and so forth) on another. In short, none of these labels will generate the very broad sort of distinction so widely assumed in the philosophy of science.[36]

The Philosophical Response

The criticisms outlined above cover a wide range of subjects. What kinds of responses have they elicited?

Some philosophers, like Israel Scheffler, grant the cogency of some of the arguments advanced above, but fear that an over-emphasis on the subjective aspects of science can have dire consequences. As he states in the preface to *Science and Subjectivity*: 'The overall tendency of such criticism has been to call into question the very conception of scientific thought as a responsible enterprise of reasonable men.'[37] He attempts in that book to meet some of the challenges of the critics, and to reconstruct an 'epistemology of objectivity'.[38]

Acknowledging the power of the criticisms, others have modified their approaches to the questions of the structure of theories and the status of theoretical terms. One general type of modification is the employment of a taxonomic schema. For example, Hempel suggests that since theoretical terms can refer variously to objects, properties of objects, collective nouns, quantities of objects, forces, or other nonsimilar phenomena, they should be classified according to the general type of phenomena to which they make reference.[39] This view, supported also by Grandy and Achinstein, requires that more attention be paid to the way in which specific sciences use their theoretical terms.[40] A taxonomy of theories has also been suggested by Anatol Rapoport.[41]

Another general approach calls for broader and less restrictive definitions of theories and theoretical terms. Thus Michael Scriven urges that terms employed in science be defined loosely in terms of *indicators* and *indicator clusters*, which would entail 'giving paradigm examples, contrasts, and explicitly approximate or conditional definitions'.[42] Achinstein, in listing six very general conditions which he feels are characteristic of most theories, takes a similar approach to the definition of the structure of theories. Commenting on Achinstein's work, Frederick Suppe has the following to say:

Upon looking at the theories actually employed in science, some authors have been so impressed by the diversity of theories encountered and the functions they perform that they despair of ever providing a comprehensive analysis of theories which displays deep properties common to all theories.

Achinstein provides a particularly good example of such a skeptical position.[43]

Finally, some writers take an entirely new approach to the question of the role of theories in science. For thirty years, positivist philosophers of science had restricted their domain of inquiry regarding theories to the 'context of justification': they examined rationally reconstructed models of the ideal structure of fully-developed theories. In particular, they viewed the study of the discovery and emergence of theories (which was labeled the 'context of discovery') as of interest only to historians and psychologists and not as a proper topic of investigation for epistemologists and philosophers of science.[44] Suppe details the rejection of the view that only the context of justification should be analyzed in the philosophy of science.

Long before the verdict was in on such issues as the observational-theoretical distinction, a small number of philosophers of science had come to the conclusion that Reichenbach's thesis that epistemology is concerned only with the context of justification was wrong; in particular, it was very wrong for science. Rather, science was viewed as an ongoing social enterprise with common bonds of language, methodology, and so on. Full epistemic understanding of scientific theories could only be had by seeing the dynamics of theory-development, the acceptance and rejection of theories, the choosing of which experiments to perform, and so on. To understand a theory was to understand its use and development. . . Thus the context of discovery was held to be a legitimate and essential concern of epistemology. This, of course, requires rejection of Reichenbach's doctrine that philosophy of science only is concerned with the context of justification. With this rejection it no longer is plausible to maintain that an adequate analysis of theories will be a rational reconstruction of fully developed theories; for this reason, the Received View is inadequate and to be rejected. Rather, what is required is an analysis of theories which concerns itself with the epistemic factors governing the discovery, development, and acceptance or rejection of theories. . .[45]

The new concern with the context of discovery is reflected in the work of Hanson, Toulmin, Kuhn, Popper, Lakatos, Feyerabend, and others; again, some of these approaches will be reviewed in the next chapter.

To conclude, logical empiricists believe that scientific theories are structured as hypothetico-deductive systems in which certain non-theoretical terms are given an empirical interpretation, and theoretical terms gain partial meaning according to the strength of the confirmation of the theories in which they are imbedded. Both the structure of theories and the status of theoretical terms, then, depend crucially on the possibility of a distinction between theoretical and nontheoretical terms. The positivist attempt to draw that distinction along observational lines met substantial opposition in contemporary philosophy of science. Broader definitions for theories and theoretical terms, and various classification systems for each have been suggested as modifications. A more drastic alternative is to examine the discovery and emergence of theories, to emphasize the context of discovery in addition to the context of justification. One implication shared by these various criticisms is that theories and their constituent elements make up a more complex area of investigation than imagined by positivist philosophy of science, and that as such, a multiplicity of approaches to their study may enhance our understanding of their structure, function, and status in science.

A Note on the Realist–Instrumentalist Controversy

Acceptance of the positivist account of the status of theoretical terms eliminated the instrumentalist–realist debate as an important controversy in the philosophy of science: since meaning for theoretical terms was supplied by the results of indirect testing, whether one viewed those terms as making real references was immaterial, a matter of personal choice.

The partial interpretation thesis depends on the possibility of distinguishing between theoretical and nontheoretical terms; as shown above, the viability of that approach is open to doubt. This permits a renewed examination of the relative merits of the instrumentalist and realist theses as a possibly fruitful area of investigation.

The most attractive feature of instrumentalism is that it allows one to avoid a number of questions that seem to have no answers. For example, it is well known that many powerful theories contain terms that make reference to entities that may or may not exist. How can we ever know whether such entities *really* exist? Though such a question may be troubling for a realist, the instrumentalist can simply respond: it does not matter. What matters is how well a theory performs the tasks for which it was developed. Again, it is well known that for any set of data, an infinite number of theories can be developed to explain them. Which is the 'true' theory? Instrumentalists need not concern themselves with the question. For them, theories are only instruments; it is meaningless to speak of instruments as being either true or false; instruments can only be judged for their adequacy, given some task to perform. While metaphysicians worry about truth, instrumentalists stress the practical, applied side of science; they are the master technicians.[46]

Opponents of instrumentalism raise a number of objections. They point out that, though we may never *know* whether a theory is true or false (which is an essential part of Popper's fallibilism), a theory nonetheless *is* true or false, and that to ignore the issue of truth is bad philosophy. Imre Lakatos is acrimonious as well as insistent on the point:

> . . . some conventionalists did not have sufficient logical education to realize that some propositions may be true whilst being unproven; and others false whilst having true consequences, and also some which are both false and approximately true. These people opted for 'instrumentalism': they came to regard theories as neither true nor false but merely as 'instruments' for prediction. Conventionalism, as here defined, is a philosophically sound position; instrumentalism is a degenerate version of it, based on a mere philosophical muddle caused by a lack of elementary logical competence.[47]

Karl Popper opposes instrumentalism for a number of reasons. His primary objection is that instrumentalism allows scientists to abandon the search for truth. Popper acknowledges that sometimes all we want from our theories are computational devices; that some theories *are* best perceived as only instruments. But a more basic goal of science is explanation, and as such we also need theories that offer ever fuller explanations of the phenomena we study. Instrumentalism must be rejected because it does not urge scientists to practice a critical methodology; it is satisfied with high correlation and does not push the scientists to search for more detailed explanations. Popper also criticizes instrumentalism for abandoning falsification: if theories are neither true nor false, how can they be falsified? By avoiding the rigors of critical, potentially falsifying tests, instrumentalists can always preserve their theories. In cases of failure, they can claim that the theory should not have been applied to the situation in question.[48]

Another philosopher argues, however, that instrumentalism need not lead to the ad hoc immunizing of theories. Jerzy Giedymin notes that because instrumentalism places no constraints on theories other than predictive adequacy, it allows the theory proliferation which both Popper and Feyerabend (among others) seem to consider so essential to the progress of science.

> In their articles referred to in my analysis both Popper and Feyerabend evaluate epistemological and methodological doctrines from the point of

view of whether and how much these doctrines encourage criticism. They also regard the existence and development of rival theories as essential to criticism, to the emergence of new problems and thus to the progress of science. So did instrumentalists, except that they also advocated suspension of assertion and greater tolerance towards alternative theories . . . Have the differences between instrumentalism and their own philosophy not been overstated by both Popper and Feyerabend? Now the classical concept of truth plays a paramount role in Popper's philosophy. This is a major difference. The same does not apply, however, to Feyerabend's views most of which – their anarchistic coloring excepting – had been anticipated by the instrumentalist tradition.[49]

Despite such claims, it seems that most contemporary philosophers of science, whether positivist of post-positivist, reject instrumentalism, Stephen Toulmin being a prominent exception. In his list of six conditions which he feels are characteristic of most theories, Peter Achinstein still includes the condition that proponents must believe a theory is true, or at least plausible.[50] And Frederick Suppe, in his recent attempt to forecast the direction of future work in the philosophy of science, predicts a movement towards 'a metaphysical and epistemological realism'.[51]

In conclusion, most philosophers of science today have adopted some brand of realism in their analyses of the status of theories and theoretical terms. Realism is viewed as preferable to instrumentalism because the former urges that scientists seek ever fuller explanations while the latter is content with correlation. Instrumentalism under this interpretation is a conservative methodology which can be used to preserve the status quo: one need never ask whether a theory is true or false, as long as it meets to some extent the criterion of (predictive) adequacy. Given another interpretation, however, instrumentalism can be a liberal methodology, since it would not reject new theories on any grounds other than predictive adequacy. A liberal methodological synthesis of realism and instrumentalism is possible: one could *prefer* more to less realistic theories, but not *require* theories to be realistic. Such a synthesis is equivalent to adding realism (however defined) to the list of criteria by which theories are evaluated. A similar synthesis on the epistemological level is not possible, however, since instrumentalists deny ontological status to theoretical entities while realists affirm it.

The Nature of Scientific Explanation

The Covering-Law Models Challenged

Most logical empiricists accepted the two 'covering-law' models as adequate characterizations of explanation as it takes place in science. The deductive-nomological (D-N) model, developed by Hempel and Oppenheim, requires that the explanandum statements be logically deducible from the explanans, which includes statements expressing initial conditions and at least one general law of universal form. The inductive-probabilistic (I-P) model, developed by Hempel, represents those explanations in science whose statements refer to highly probable statistical laws rather than universal ones; as such, the explanandum statement may be inferred with a high degree of probability from the explanans. Implicit in the covering-law models is the symmetry thesis: any legitimate explanation is a potential prediction, because the only difference between explanation and prediction is temporal. Finally, any alleged explanation which cannot be reconstructed to fit one of the two above models is suspect: the covering-law models exhaust the universe of all legitimate explanation in the physical sciences, and nearly all in the social sciences.

The above approach, it should be remembered, is a considerable advance over earlier positivist ideas concerning explanation: many nineteenth century positivists denied that explanation took place at all in science, or equated explanation with correlation. The goal of the covering-law models is to reintroduce the notion of explanation in science, but to do so in a sufficiently cautious manner that illegitimate pseudo-explanations are avoided. The optimal analysis of explanation, then, would involve enough restrictions on the definition of explanation that metaphysical or 'ultimate' explanation would be ruled out, but that would be sufficiently lax to allow those explanations which scientists traditionally accept as legitimate. Do the covering-law models accomplish this? Recent work in the philosophy of science supports a negative response to that question: the D-N and I-P models have generally been found to be too restrictive in their characterization of what is to count as a legitimate explanation, thereby excluding many types of explanations which are considered legitimate by scientists.

Two early criticisms should be dealt with first. The first concerns the definition of 'general law.' A clear definition of that term is essential to the covering-law models, since each requires that a general law be referred to in the explanans. If one cannot tell whether a statement expresses a general law, it will be difficult to separate legitimate from pseudo-explanations.

Looking at D-N explanation, it might be imagined that true statements of universal form (e.g. 'All robins' eggs are greenish-blue,' 'All metals are conductors of electricity.') express general laws. That a general law be expressible as a statement of universal form is necessary but not sufficient, however, since such statements can also express 'accidental generalizations' (e.g. 'All the coins in my pocket are nickels.') which we would not want to accept as general laws. In their original paper, Hempel and Oppenheim discuss the possibility of distinguishing laws of nature by their universal scope and purely qualitative predicates, but admit that some law-like statements make assertions about finite classes of objects and that 'the problem of an adequate definition of purely qualitative predicates remains open'.[52] A. J. Ayer suggests that the distinction lies in differences in one's attitude toward laws of nature and statements of fact, and R. B. Braithwaite focuses on the nature of the evidence which one can adduce for law-like statements.[53] What seems to be the most adequate description of a law of nature, however, is suggested by Nelson Goodman. In the first chapter of *Fact, Fiction and Forecast*, that philosopher notes laws can, while accidental generalizations cannot, support both counterfactual conditionals (i.e. 'If A had occurred, B would have occurred.') and subjunctive conditionals (i.e. 'If A should occur, B will occur').[54] Two additional criteria, suggested by Hempel, are that laws can serve as bases for explanations, and that laws are often (but not always) supported by an existent theoretical structure.[55]

The symmetry thesis, that every explanation must be a potential prediction, also drew fire from various quarters. Perhaps the most famous debate is that which occurred at a seminar on the philosophy of science at Delaware in the early 1960s, with Hempel and Michael Scriven being the main protagonists. A careful reading of their exchanges could lead one to believe that those philosophers are actually discussing two different concepts. In his article, Hempel backs off from his earlier position (i.e. that every explanation must be a potential prediction) and insists that his is a purely logical analysis of the structure of scientific explanation. Given one of the covering-law models, Hempel simply states that the structure of an explanation (which refers to events taking place in the past) and that of a prediction (which refers to events taking place in the future) are symmetrical in terms of the inductive or deductive *inferability* of the explanandum from the explanans.[56] In particular, the symmetry does *not* pertain to the 'assertability per se' of the explanandum, as was pointed out by Adolf Grunbaum at the seminar.

> they (Hempel & Popper) do not claim that every time you are entitled to assert, on some grounds or another, that a certain event will occur in the past, you are also entitled to say that the same kind of event will occur in the future. Being concerned with scientific understanding, Popper and Hempel said that there is temporal symmetry not of assertability per se but of assertability on the strength of the explanans.[57]

If Hempel's analysis of the symmetry of explanation and prediction seems counterintuitive, it is because it is a logical analysis of an argument's structure, and is not, as Hempel himself notes, 'the same sort of thing as writing an entry on the word explanation for the *Oxford English Dictionary*'.[58] The only concession which Hempel makes in his paper is that some predictions do not entail explanations.[59]

Scriven, for his part, accepts that Hempel is arguing only the symmetry of inferability,[60] but stresses that such logical analyses should not mislead people into believing that all explanations can be potential predictions. He particularly emphasizes those asymmetrical cases in which the explanandum can be explained in terms of prior states, but in which such knowledge does not allow prediction of the explanandum. Evolutionary theory offers one example; another, taken from sociology, demonstrates that while it may be possible to explain a suicide by reference to certain antecedent conditions, prior knowledge that those conditions hold does not enable one to predict suicides.

> We have no difficulty in finding *the* explanation, although the facts available before the event were not enough to permit us to tell what would happen. Indeed, it may be that the chances in advance were very strongly against the actual outcome, and we would therefore have been entitled to make a well-founded scientific prediction of the event's non-occurrence.[61]

It is clear, then, that Hempel and Scriven are talking beyond each other; the former is concerned with the logical structure of explanation, the latter with the way explanation actually takes place in science.

More significant than either of the above debates is the question of whether the covering-law models provide an adequate character-ization of scientific explanation. Hempel's assertion that the two models cover virtually all legitimate forms of explanation in science has already been noted. But during the late 1950s and through the 1960s, this assertion was challenged, particularly by those who felt that the covering-law models were inaccurate characterizations of explanation as it took place in the social and historical sciences.

Certain critics have claimed that the so-called 'teleological' mode of explanation is legitimate but does not fit into the pattern of either covering-law model. What is a teleological explanation? There are at least two types: motivational explanation and functional explanation. The former involves cases in which purposive behavior or voluntary actions occur; it is argued in such cases that the antecedent conditions comprising the explanans are motives which cannot be linked to the explanandum in any direct causal way. Thus, the suicide example is a specific instance of a more general phenomenon, which has been described by Donald Davidson:

> generalizations connecting reasons (that is, motives) and actions are not, and cannot be sharpened into, the kind of law on the basis of which accurate predictions can reliably be made. If we reflect on the way reasons determine choice, decision, and behavior, it is easy to see why this is as, what emerges, in the *ex post facto* atmosphere of explanation and justification, as *the* reason frequently was, to the agent at the time of the action, one consideration among many, *a* reason. Any serious theory for predicting action on the basis of reasons must find a way of evaluating the relative forces of various desires and beliefs in the matrix of decision; it cannot take as its starting point the refinement of what is to be expected from a single desire.[62]

Note that Davidson's position is antithetical both to the cover-law models and Scriven's argument that we can, *ex post facto*, find *the* explanation of a phenomenon with relative ease. Hempel, for his part, clings to the necessity of predictive power for motivational explanations, which seems to miss Davidson's point that, *by their very nature*, such explanations do not generally provide predictions. Thus Hempel and Oppenheim claim:

> A potential danger of explanation by motives lies in the fact that the method lends itself to the facile construction of *ex post facto* accounts without predictive force. It is a widespread tendency to 'explain' an action by ascribing it to motives conjectured only after the action has taken place. While this procedure is not in itself objectionable, its soundness requires that (1) the motivational assumptions in question be capable of test, and (2) that suitable general laws be available to lend explanatory power to the assumed motives.[63]

Hempel would therefore disallow motivational explanations which do not meet the above criteria from the realm of legitimate explanation.[64]

The other type of teleological explanation is functional: characteristics of an organism (in biology), a society (in anthropology, political science, or sociology), or some other physical or temporal phenomenon are explained by reference to certain ends or purposes which the characteristics are said to serve. Nagel provides an example from botany: 'The function of chlorophyll in plants is to enable plants to perform photosynthesis.' Many such explanations found in biology are translatable into nonteleological ones, Nagel notes approvingly.[65] He is much less comfortable with functional explanation in the social sciences, however; 'function' is rarely adequately defined (he lists six common approaches), and the limits between institutions and functions are often vague.[66] For his part, Hempel would disallow any explanation that could not be reformulated so as to make reference to general laws or theories.[67]

A variety of other modes of explanation have been suggested for the social and historical sciences. Whether or not the method of 'intuitive understanding' (Verstehen) is an adequate approach to scientific understanding in sociology or anthropology was hotly debated in earlier decades.[68] In the 1940s, historian R. G. Collingwood suggested that one of the principle tools of analysis for the historian is the re-experiencing in thought of the historical situation under examination.[69] Genetic explanation, in which only necessary (but not sufficient) conditions for the occurrence of historical events are described, has been defended by historian W. B. Gallie.[70] The key question in all of this is whether any of the above types of explanation should be considered legitimate. Positivist philosophy of science would answer: in general, no; not unless such 'explanation-sketches' could be reformulated according to the criteria set out in the covering-law models.

It is not clear in the literature whether or not the ability to support reliable predictions is a criterion under the covering-law models. It seems to be in the Hempel–Oppenheim piece (in the form of the symmetry thesis), but not in Hempel's later exchanges with Scriven. In any case, many explanations in the social sciences (as well as in some natural sciences, like biology or geology) cannot support reliable predictions, and thus *may* not be considered legitimate. It does not seem that much can be concluded from the debate as it now stands. Counterexamples which may or may not satisfy the covering-law models have been enumerated; but even if it were conclusively shown that a vast majority of explanations in the social sciences did not fit the covering law requirements, such counterexamples could be dismissed by logical empiricists as illegitimate. As long as one *defines* explanation in terms of the covering-law models, counterexamples that do not fit the models carry little weight.

Philosopher Sylvain Bromberger takes another approach which is far more costly for the covering-law models: he offers examples of 'explanations' which fit the covering-law models but which clearly do not qualify as legitimate explanations. In his famous article 'Why-Questions', Bromberger argues specifically against the 'Hempelian Doctrine' that explanation involves a deduction of an explanandum from an explanans. One of his counterexamples involves a famous monument (as he mentions, such examples 'are easily multiplied').

> There is a point on Fifth Avenue, M feet away from the base of the Empire State Building, at which a ray of light coming from the tip of the building makes an angle of θ degrees with a line to the base of the building. From the laws of geometric optics, together with the 'antecedent' condition that the distance is M feet, the angle θ degrees, it is possible to deduce that the Empire State Building has a height of H feet. Any high school student could set up the deduction given actual numerical values. By doing so, he would not, however, have *explained* why the Empire State Building has a height of H feet, nor would he have *answered* the question 'Why does the Empire State Building have a height of H feet?', nor would an exposition of the deduction be the explanation of or answer to (either implicitly or explicitly) why the Empire State Building has a height of H feet.[71]

Bromberger concludes that the satisfaction of the conditions laid down in the D-N model is necessary, but not sufficient, for a casual explanation to occur. He attempts to delineate sufficient conditions[72]; Suppe, however, is unimpressed with that effort, concluding that 'Bromberger's attempt to salvage the D-N model fails, and counterexamples such as the flagpole case [or Empire State Building case] remain'.[73]

The I-P model has also been a subject of criticism, though of a different sort. A number of philosophers have noted that statistical arguments can be used to explain events which have a low probability; Hempel's requirement that the explanandum of a statistical argument have high probability is therefore too restrictive.[74] This is clearly in line with Popper's assertions that scientists should not seek for highly probable hypotheses; that the most interesting hypotheses are the ones with the highest empirical content and which therefore are least probable.

Popper's analysis of explanation in science provides another example of his apparent similarities to, but in actuality real differences from, the positivist view. In his *Logic of Scientific Discovery* (1934), Popper develops a deductive model of explanation that is indistinguishable from Hempel's D-N model,[75] yet his view of explanation is radically different from that put forth by the covering law theorist. For Popper, explanation is the major goal of science, a point he uses against the instrumentalists. It is crucially important that scientists constantly seek to overthrow the theories that exist; critical testing must be a never-ending activity. The idea of compiling a group of well-established deductive and inductive explanations is antithetical to Popper's vision of how science advances. The I-P model in particular would not be well received in the Popperian camp.

Thus, a number of serious doubts have been raised concerning the adequacy of the covering-law models for describing all the types of explanation that occur in science. As in the case of the H-D model of the structure of a theory, the problem is not that such models are useless for the understanding of certain types of theories or explanations, for both the H-D model and the covering-law models have obvious fruitful applications. The problem lies in the logical empiricist claim that any explanation or theory which cannot be rationally reconstructed to fit one of the models is somehow deficient. Positivists have traditionally made such claims in an effort to separate nonscience from science and to provide a clear, empirical basis for the scientific enterprise. As such, their motivation may be admired. But their prescriptions cannot be accepted if by that acceptance many branches of science are excluded; and that point has provided the motivation for the scores of critics of the positivist view who have written in the last thirty years.

Alternative Models of Scientific Explanation

As in the case of the H-D model of the structure of scientific theories, alternative models of scientific explanation have surfaced within the critical literature. Few critics charge that the covering-law models are useless for the description of certain kinds of explanation in science; the claim is, rather, that some explanations involve something quite different from the deduction of an explanandum statement from an explanans, that the covering-law models are only one of many forms of legitimate scientific explanation.[76] What other types of explanatory models exist? Mary Hesse favors a model in which explanation can be viewed as 'a metaphoric redescription of the domain of the explanandum'.[77] She offers an example of that approach in which a primary and a secondary system or domain are utilized:

> In a scientific theory the primary system is the domain of the explanandum, describable in observation language; the secondary is the system, described either in observation language or the language of a familiar theory, from which the model is taken: For example, 'Sound (primary system) is propagated by wave motion (taken from a secondary system)'; 'Gases are collections of randomly moving massive particles'.[78]

Hesse admits that not all explanations are metaphoric and lists other conditions which must be met if a metaphoric explanation is to be considered legitimate, but concludes that metaphoric explanation is a useful supplement to the 'deductive' (covering-law) models.

the metaphoric view does not abandon deduction, but it focuses attention rather on the interaction between metaphor and primary system, and on the criteria of acceptability of metaphoric descriptions of the primary system, and hence not so much upon the deductive relations that appear in this account as comparatively uninteresting pieces of logical machinery.[79]

In an early work, R. Harré distinguishes between two types of models which aid our understanding, stating that

> understanding is gained either by our finding an illuminating analogy to the phenomena whose character we do not understand, or by 'exposing a hidden mechanism' the workings of which inevitably result in the phenomena that required explanation.[80]

The models which Harré describes in that work include micromorphs, which are scale model replicas of reduced size, and paramorphs, which are employed by describing processes which have analogies to the processes to be explained. In later work Harré expands his taxonomy of models, however, to include homeomorphs (a family of models that includes three genera, of which micromorphs are a species; in all homeomorphs the phenomena to be explained are 'equal to their source', that is, no analogies are used), paramorphs (where reasoning by analogy takes place), and an ill-defined third group, which he labels protomorphs ('Members of this genera are related to homeomorphs and paramorphs roughly as lamprey are related to fish.').[81]

In addition to providing alternative models of how explanation can take place in science, certain philosophers stress that explanation must go beyond a simple, logical deduction; that it must somehow involve an increase in understanding. Harré argues this when he states that explanations 'must enable us to understand'; Michael Scriven is more verbose but his message is the same:

> The task of explanation is the integration of 'new' phenomena (whether subjectively or objectively now makes no difference) into the structure of knowledge. Typically, this consists in fitting these phenomena into a pattern with which we are already familiar.
> . . .
> The key notion behind that of explanation, and hence that of cause, is understanding. It must not be thought of purely as a subjective feeling; the feeling is only something associated with it. . . Understanding is integrated, related knowledge; more generally – so that the definitions will apply to the understanding possessed by machines, animals, and children – it is the capacity to produce the appropriate response to novel stimuli within a certain range or field.
> . . .
> Models, from analogies to axiomatizations, are the key to understanding.[82]

Thus, alternative forms of scientific explanation have often been accompanied by broader and less rigorous definitions of explanation in the sciences.

Summary

The case against positivist philosophy of science is now completed and may be summarized.

1. The logical empiricists of the 1950s settled on confirmation as a means for assessing the acceptability of hypotheses, and went about trying to construct an inductive logic by which the relative strengths of competing hypotheses could be judged. Though many advances in the logic of confirmation were made, certain fundamental questions remain unanswered. Hume's problem of induction stands as intractable as ever; various paradoxes of confirmation provide additional obstacles. The value of making statements that have a high inductive probability has been challenged: Popper and his followers assert that the most interesting statements in science have a high empirical content and, therefore, a low inductive probability.

2. Logical empiricists believed that theoretical terms gain at least partial meaningfulness if some (not all) of the terms in the theories in which they are embedded have empirical counterparts in the observation language and if the deduced (predicted) consequences of the theories can thereby be tested and are confirmed. But this view requires that it is possible to isolate and then interpret certain nontheoretical terms into a neutral observation language; that theoretical and nontheoretical terms are independent and can be distinguished on observational grounds. A number of criticisms of that position have emerged, including the following:

   a. No hard division between theoretical terms and nonobservables, on the one hand, and nontheoretical terms and observables, on the other, can be drawn.

   b. It is not always clear whether a phenomenon is observable or not; degrees of observability exist.

   c. Observation is not neutral; any observation requires both a selection of the data to be observed and an interpretation of that data by the observer.

   d. The meaning of observation terms (and, indeed, *all* terms) is influenced by the theoretical framework from which they originate.

   e. Finally, the existence of 'brute, atomic facts' which are independent of the linguistic framework by which they are defined is questionable.

The above arguments when taken together undercut the foundations of the logical empiricist approach to theories and the status of theoretical terms which presupposes that a distinction between theoretical and nontheoretical terms can be drawn on observational grounds. They also lead to a renewed examinaton of the realist-instrumentalist debate.

3. The deductive-nomological (D-N) and inductive-probablistic (I-P) covering-law models of scientific explanation were once thought to be sufficient for the description of all the legitimate types of explanation existent in science. Any explanation that could not be reconstructed to fit one of the two argument forms was suspected of being a pseudo-explanation. By the symmetry thesis, every explanation, if taken account of in time, must also be capable of being a prediction.

In later writings, it is not clear whether the symmetry between explanation and prediction is simply a logical attribute of the structure of explanation or a pragmatic requirement that must be met if an explanation is to be considered legitimate. There are examples in the natural and social sciences of explanations which cannot support reliable predictions. At least *some* of them would not be considered legitimate by the covering law theorists; alternatively, the existence of such counterexamples has caused some to question the adequacy of the covering-law models.

More damaging for the covering-law models are the counter-examples pointed out by Bromberger (arguments that fit the covering-law models but which clearly cannot count as expla-nations) and Salmon, Jeffrey, and Greeno (in which perfectly good statistical explanations violate the I-P requirement that the general law invoked has a high inductive probability). Whatever one thinks of the strengths of the various arguments adduced against the covering-law models, the direction of current research is toward a broader definition of scientific explanation and a concomitant attempt to devise alternative or supplemental models by which to describe explanation as it takes place in science.

Notes

1 Frederick Suppe, 'Afterword,' in Frederick Suppe (ed.), *The Structure of Scientific Theories*, 2nd edn (first published, 1973) (Urbana, Ill.: University of Illinois Press, 1977), p. 632.

2   His book *Conjectures and Refutations: The Growth of Scientific Knowledge*, 2nd edn (first published, 1963) (New York: Basic Books, 1965) is dedicated to Hayek; in its introduction, Popper considers the following to be a proper formulation of the essential question of political theory: 'How can we organize our political institutions so that bad or incompetent rulers (whom we should try not to get, but whom we so easily might get all the same) cannot do too much damage?' (p. 25). For a fuller statement of Popper's liberalism, see his *The Open Society and Its Enemies*, (first published, 1944) (Princeton, N.J.: Princeton University Press, 1950).

3   The only statement that Popper feels should not be subjected to criticism and possible rejection reads: 'All of my views must be subject to criticism and possible rejection.' This aspect of critical rationalism has been discussed and criticized by a number of philosophers; such debates try to get at a formulation of rationality which is neither paradoxical nor self-contradictory. For a discussion of these issues, see W. W. Bartley, 'Rationality versus the Theory of Rationality,' in Mario Bunge, (ed.), *The Critical Approach to Science and Philosophy* (Glencoe, Ill.: The Free Press, 1964), pp. 3–31; W. W. Bartley, *The Retreat to Commitment* (New York: Knopf, 1962); J. W. N. Watkins, 'Comprehensively Critical Rationalism,' *Philosophy*, vol. 44 (1969), pp. 57–62; J. W. N. Watkins, 'C.C.R.: A Refutation,' *Philosophy*, vol. 46 (1971), pp. 56–71; Noretta Koertge, 'Bartley's Theory of Rationality,' *Philosophy of Social Science*, vol. 4 (1974), pp. 75–81.

4   Through this and later sections, the terms 'hypothesis' and 'theory' will be used interchangeably unless otherwise noted.

5   Carl Hempel, 'Studies in the Logic of Confirmation,' reprinted in Baruch Brody (ed.), *Readings in the Philosophy of Science* (first published, 1945) (Englewood Cliffs, N.J.: Prentice-Hall, 1970), p. 391.

6   Ibid., p. 396.

7   Ibid., p. 396.

8   See, for example, the articles by Nelson Goodman, Richard Grandy, and J. W. N. Watkins in Baruch Brody (ed.), op. cit., pp. 427–38.

9   Nelson Goodman, *Fact, Fiction and Forecast*, 2nd edn (first published, 1955) (New York: Bobbs-Merrill, 1965), pp. 59–72.

10 Ibid., p. 82.

11 A nice survey of some of the problems facing and accomplishments attained in the field of inductive logic is Brian Skyrms, *Choice and Chance: An Introduction to Inductive Logic*, 2nd edn (Encino, Calif.: Dickenson Publishing, 1975).

12 David Hume, *An Inquiry Concerning Human Understanding* (first published, 1748) (Indianapolis: Bobbs-Merrill, 1955), p. 49. Hume's argument is contained in Section IV of the *Inquiry*; our presentation is faithful to Hume's argument though not to his terminology.

13 Ibid., p. 50.

14 Skyrms, op. cit., pp. 30–56, mentions four general types of solution to Hume's problem. Suppe, op. cit., pp. 624–31 reviews the literature concerning probabilistic induction.

15 Lakatos distinguishes three Poppers (Popper$_0$, Popper$_1$ and Popper$_2$) in his 'Falsification and the Methodology of Scientific Research Programmes,' in I. Lakatos and A. Musgrave (eds), *Criticism and the Growth of Knowledge* (Cambridge, England: Cambridge University Press, 1970), p. 181; it was he who coined the phrase 'methodological falsificationist'.

16 Karl Popper, 'Science: Conjectures and Refutations,' in *Conjectures and Refutations*, pp. 34–5. The article presents a brief intellectual autobiography; for a fuller treatment, see his 'Autobiography of Karl Popper,' in Paul Schilpp (ed.), *The Philosophy of Karl Popper* (La Salle, Ill.: Open Court, 1974), pp. 3–181.

17   Popper, 'Science: . . .,' op. cit., pp. 36–7.
18   Karl Popper, 'Conjectural Knowledge: My Solution to the Problem of Induction,' in *Objective Knowledge: An Evolutionary Approach* (Oxford: The Clarendon Press, 1972), p. 7.
19   Karl Popper, *The Logic of Scientific Discovery* (Eng. transl., 1959), 2nd edn (first published, 1934) (New York: Harper Torchbooks, 1968), sections 4–6; 'Science: . . .,' op. cit., pp. 40–1; 'The Demarcation between Science and Metaphysics,' in *Conjectures and Refutations*, pp. 253–92.
20   Popper, 'Science: . . .,' op. cit., pp. 42–8; 'Conjectual Knowledge . . .,' op. cit., pp. 3–9, 22–9.
21   Popper, *Logic*, sections 31–46; 'Truth, Rationality, and the Growth of Scientific Knowledge,' in *Conjectures and Refutations*, pp. 215–20.
22   The details of the debate are fully examined in Alex C. Michalos, *The Popper – Carnap Controversy* (The Hague: Martinus Nijhoff, 1971).
23   Popper, 'Truth, Rationality. . .,' op. cit., pp. 223–36).
24   For an excellent discussion, see Robert Ackermann, *The Philosophy of Karl Popper* (Amherst, Mass: University of Massachusetts Press, 1976), pp. 87–92.
25   Popper, *Logic*, sections 7, 10, 11, 25–30.
26   Ibid., sections 19–22.
27   Ackermann, op. cit., pp. 30–1 and citations listed there.
28   See Suppe (ed.), op. cit., pp. 29–36; the introduction and articles by J. J. C. Smart and Grover Maxwell in Richard Grandy (ed.), *Theories and Observation in Science* (Englewood Cliffs, N.J.: Prentice Hall, 1973); and Ernest Nagel, *Structure of Science*, pp. 129–52.
29   Hilary Putnam, 'What Theories Are Not,' in Richard Grandy (ed.), op. cit., p. 113. Similar arguments are found in Peter Achinstein, *Concepts of Science: A Philosophical Analysis* (Baltimore: Johns Hopkins Press, 1968), Chapter 5. For dissenting views and qualifications, see Suppe (ed.), op. cit., pp. 80–6; and Richard C. Jeffrey, 'Review of Putnam,' in Grandy (ed.), op. cit., pp. 124–8.
30   Richard Grandy, 'Introduction,' in Grandy (ed.), op. cit., p. 3.
31   James K. Feibelman, *Scientific Method* (The Hague: Martinus Nijhoff, 1972), p. 50.
32   Norwood R. Hanson, *Patterns of Discovery* (Cambridge: Cambridge University Press, 1958), pp. 12, 19.
33   Popper, *Logic*, sections 28–30; 'On the Sources of Knowledge and Ignorance,' in *Conjectures and Refutations*, pp. 21–4; 'Science. . . .,' op. cit., pp. 42–8.
34   Kuhn speaks of a 'gestalt-switch', an entire reorientation to a phenomenon under study, which is brought about by a change in one's theoretical framework. Feyerabend insists that the meaning of each term in science is dependent on the theory in which it is used. See Thomas Kuhn, *The Structure of Scientific Revolutions*, Vol. II, no. 2, *International Encyclopedia of Unified Science*, 2nd enlarged edn (first published, 1962) (Chicago: University of Chicago Press, 1970), Chapter 10; Paul K. Feyerabend, 'Explanation, Reduction and Empiricism,' in H. Feigl, G. Maxwell, and M. Scriven (eds), *Minnesota Studies in the Philosophy of Science*, Vol. III (Minneapolis: University of Minnesota Press, 1962), pp. 28–97.
35   Rom Harré, *Philosophies of Science*, pp. 43–4. Similar arguments can be found in Kuhn, *Structure*, p. 126 passim; and Feibelman, *Scientific Method*, p. 51 passim.
36   Achinstein, *Concepts of Science*, p. 199.
37   Israel Scheffler, *Science and Subjectivity* (New York: Bobbs-Merrill, 1967), p. v.
38   Ibid., chapter 5.
39   Carl Hempel, 'On the "Standard Conception" of Scientific Theories,' in M. Radner and S. Winokur (eds), *Minnesota Studies in the Philosophy of Science*, Vol. IV (Minneapolis: University of Minnesota Press, 1970), pp. 142–63.

40   See Grandy, op. cit., p. 15; and Achinstein, op. cit., Chapters 2–4.
41   Anatol Rapoport, 'Various Meanings of "Theory"', *American Political Science Review*, vol. 3 (1958), pp. 927–88.
42   Michael Scriven, 'The Philosophy of Science,' *International Encyclopedia of the Social Sciences*, vol. 14 (1968), p. 85.
43   Suppe (ed.), *Structure*, p. 120.
44   Hans Reichenbach was the first to use the terms 'context of discovery' and 'context of justification'. See his *Experience and Prediction: An Analysis of the Foundations and the Structure of Knowledge* (Chicago: University of Chicago Press, 1938), pp. 6–7.
45   Suppe (ed.), op. cit., pp. 125–6.
46   Ibid., pp. 29–36; Nagel, *Structure of Science*, pp. 129–41; Popper, 'Three Views Concerning Human Knowledge,' in *Conjectures and Refutations*, pp. 107–114.
47   Imre Lakatos, 'History of Science and Its Rational Reconstructions,' in R. Buck and R. Cohen (eds), *P.S.A. 1970: In Memory of Rudolf Carnap. Boston Studies in the Philosophy of Science*, Vol. VII (Dordrecht, Holland: D. Reidel, 1971), p. 95.
48   Popper, 'Three Views. . .,' op. cit., pp. 107–14.
49   Jerzy Giedymin, 'Instrumentalism and Its Critique: A Reappraisal,' in Cohen, Feyerabend and Wartofsky (eds), *Essays in Memory of Imre Lakatos*, XXXIX, *Boston Studies in the Philosophy of Science* (Dordrecht, Holland: D. Reidel, 1976), pp. 179–80.
50   Achinstein, *Concepts of Science*, p. 122.
51   Suppe (ed.), op. cit., pp. 716–28.
52   Hempel and Oppenheim, 'Logic of Explanation,' op. cit., p. 23.
53   See A. J. Ayer, 'What Is a Law of Nature?' and R. B. Braithwaite, 'Laws of Nature and Causality,' both in B. Brody (ed.), op. cit., pp. 39–63.
54   Goodman, op. cit., Chapter 1.
55   Carl Hempel, *Philosophy of Natural Science* (Englewood Cliffs, N.J.: Prentice Hall, 1966), pp. 56–8.
56   Hempel, 'Explanation and Prediction by Covering Laws,' in B. Baumrin, (ed.), *Philosophy of Science: The Delaware Seminar*, Vol. I (New York: Wiley, 1962), pp. 125–31.
57   Adolf Grunbaum, 'Temporally Asymmetric Principles, Parity between Explanation and Prediction and Mechanism versus Teleology,' in B. Baumrin (ed.), op. cit., p. 74.
58   Hempel, 'Explanation and Prediction. . .,' op. cit., p. 126.
59   Ibid., pp. 119–20.
60   Michael Scriven, 'The Temporal Asymmetry of Explanations and Predictions,' in B. Baumrin (ed.), op. cit., p. 102.
61   Scriven, 'The Philosophy of Science,' op. cit., p. 88.
62   Donald Davidson, 'Actions, Reasons and Causes,' *Journal of Philosophy*, vol. 60 (1963), p. 697.
63   Hempel and Oppenheim, 'Logic of Explanation. . .,' op. cit., p. 16.
64   Ibid., pp. 16–19.
65   Nagel, *Structure of Science,* pp. 403–6.
66   Ibid., pp. 520–31.
67   Carl Hempel, 'The Logic of Functional Analysis,' in B. Brody (ed.), op. cit., pp. 121–43.
68   See, for example, Maurice Natanson, *Philosophy of the Social Sciences: A Reader* (New York: Random House, 1963).
69   R. G. Collingwood, *The Idea of History* (Oxford: Clarendon Press, 1946). Cf. W. H. Dray, 'Historical Understanding as Re-Thinking,' in B. Brody (ed.), op. cit., pp. 167–79.

70 W. B. Gallie, 'Explanations in History and the Genetic Sciences,' in B. Brody (ed.), op. cit., pp. 150–66. But note Brody's warnings in his Introduction to Part I, p. 6.

71 Sylvain Bromberger, 'Why-Questions,' in B. Brody (ed.), op. cit., p. 71.

72 Ibid., Sections 6, 7, 8.

73 Suppe (ed.), op. cit., p. 622.

74 See, for example, the articles by Salmon, Jeffrey, and Greeno in W. Salmon (ed.), *The Foundations of Scientific Inference* (Pittsburgh: University of Pittsburgh Press, 1966).

75 Popper, *Logic,* section 12.

76 This view is stated by Romano Harré in *An Introduction to the Logic of Sciences* (first published, 1960) (New York: St Martin's Press, 1967), p. 82. Cf. Mary Hesse, *Models and Analogies in Science* (Notre Dame, Indiana: University of Notre Dame Press, 1966), pp. 171–4.

77 Mary Hesse, op. cit., p. 171.

78 Ibid., pp. 158–9. Note that this approach requires the existence of a neutral observation language. But see her attempt to revitalize the concept of an observation language in which observational and theoretical predicates have 'elements both of empirical association in situations of easy empirical reference and of contextual relation with other predicates which co-occur or are co-absent'. 'Positivism and the Logic of Scientific Theories,' in Peter Achinstein and Stephen Barker (eds), *The Legacy of Logical Positivism: Studies in the Philosophy of Science* (Baltimore: The Johns Hopkins Press, 1969), p. 112.

79 Ibid., p. 174.

80 Harré, *Logic of the Sciences*, p. 82.

81 Rom Harré, *The Principles of Scientific Thinking* (Chicago: University of Chicago Press, 1970), p. 50. See especially Chapter 2, section 5.

82 Scriven, 'The Philosophy of Science,' op. cit., pp. 88–90.

5

Contemporary Philosophy of Science – The Growth of Knowledge Tradition

Introduction

In the last chapter, the erosion of a unified and defensible logical empiricist approach to the philosophy of science was detailed. Within certain of the traditional positivist categories of investigation, alternative models (e.g. of the structure of theories and the nature of scientific explanation) were proposed. However, it was also hinted that certain philosophers were simultaneously advancing alternative and radically new approaches to the philosophy of science, and it is some of those new developments that are the focus of investigation of this chapter.

An obvious but nonetheless essential point must be made right away – no single, unified approach has arisen in response to the failures of positivist philosophy of science. On the other hand, the disparate analyses which are examined in this chapter do have a number of common elements. First and foremost, contemporary philosophers of science see their job qua philosophers in a very different way than did their positivist predecessors. Whereas logical empiricists concerned themselves with the elaboration of universal models and procedural rules which they believed aptly characterized legitimate scientific practice, post-positivists emphasize the growth of knowledge over time, the dynamics of change within individual disciplines, and the actual practices of scientists. Universality is qualified by specificity; immutable verities are challenged by recognition of changing standards of investigation and patterns of thought; logical analysis is supplemented by and checked against the study of history.

But how does this affect methodology, one may well ask? In a sense, the new approach taken in philosophy of science can be conceived as asking the question: Is methodology possible? To be sure, that is an extreme characterization, but the seeds of such a question do exist within some of the analyses to follow. For once it is admitted that the history of science reveals a complex, interwoven tapestry, it becomes easier to question whether a static set of procedural rules for, say, the appraisal of theories or for the definition of appropriate theoretical structure has ever been or should ever be followed by scientists in their attempts to gain knowledge.

On the other hand, most observers would no doubt insist that scientific disciplines do in some sense 'progress', that the evolution of scientific knowledge does possess some 'rationality', at least in the long run. Such observations lead us directly into discussions of how such words as 'progress', 'rationality', and even 'science' are defined, but even more important for our purposes, they reopen the door to the possibility of a rational reconstruction of methodology itself.

It would be impossible to treat all the subjects hinted at above in this chapter: our interest is, after all, with methodology, and in particular with those methodological discussions which may have some implications for the practice of economics. However, it is just as impossible to try to sketch recent developments in philosophy of science and only talk about their methodological implications. Accordingly, what follows will not be an exclusively methodological analysis.

I have chosen to examine the works of three thinkers whose efforts I believe best exemplify recent currents in the philosophy of science. I begin with the work of Thomas Kuhn, whose *The Structure of Scientific Revolutions* (1970) in many ways initiated the recent 'revolution' in the philosophy of science. Because of that, and because much of what comes later is, in one way or another, a response to Kuhn's views, his book will be thoroughly reviewed, as will some of the criticisms of it which have emerged in the past fifteen years or so. Kuhn's work is significant for its influence on how historians characterize the growth of science, how philosophers of science view their own profession, and how history, philosophy, and sociology may be linked in studying science, all of which will be mentioned. But, of course, it is his methodological dictums that interest us most and that will be emphasized. Briefly put, Kuhn raises the question of whether rational canons of theory choice can be used in a logically compelling fashion during times of what he calls 'revolutionary science'. His answer is no, and he suggests that sociological studies of the values and norms of the scientific community may be of assistance in understanding how theory choice is effected in such periods.

Next we will look at the writings of Paul Feyerabend. The epistemological bases of Feyerabend's methodological views have been subjected to repeated criticism within the philosophy of science; as such, it would be remiss not to mention at least some of the more important complaints. However, of greater significance is his later methodological Dadaism, a delightfully devilish exercise whose point is to show that no methodological rules are sacrosanct; that the best methodology is nonmethodology. A total acceptance of Feyerabend's position closes the door to the possibility of rational methodology, at least according to most definitions of the term 'rational'.

A final vision of history, philosophy, and methodology is provided by Imre Lakatos. In his 'Falsification and the Methodology of Scientific Research Programmes' (1970), Lakatos offers a reconstruction of rational methodology which he claims avoids all the errors of his predecessors, is descriptively accurate, and has nontrivial prescriptive content.

It is perhaps unnecesary to add that this is not meant to be a comprehensive survey of contemporary work in the philosophy of science. Besides my professional incompetence to attempt such a task, it seems clear that an in-depth treatment of three philosophers whose work has obvious meaning for economists is preferable to a survey that would at best be sketchy and superficial.

Thomas Kuhn

The Structure of Scientific Revolutions
Thomas Kuhn's *The Structure of Scientific Revolutions* first appeared in 1962; a revised, enlarged edition with a Postscript was published in 1970, and that more recent version is the focus of our attention. Kuhn notifies his audience in the introduction that his work will challenge the usual positivist approach to the problem of the growth of science, since his interpretation gives a fundamental role to the history of science. He asserts further that an historical approach provides new answers to some old questions; in particular, the role of methodological prescription in science is seen in a new light.

> What aspects of science will emerge to prominence in the course of this effort? First, at least in order of presentation, is the insufficiency of methodological directives, by themselves, to dictate a unique substantive conclusion to many sorts of scientific questions. . . Observation and experience can and must drastically restrict the range of admissible scientific belief, else there would be no science. But they cannot alone determine a particular body of such belief. An apparently arbitrary element, compounded of personal and historical accident, is always a

formative ingredient of beliefs espoused by a given scientific community at a given time.[1]

Kuhn begins by defining two concepts which are essential to his analysis: 'normal science' and 'paradigm'.

> 'normal science' means research firmly based upon one or more past scientific achievements, achievements that some particular scientific community acknowledges for a time as supplying the foundation for its further practice.[2]

Normal science is the hallmark of science, it allows progress because the legitimate areas and methods of investigation are clearly spelled out. Normal science requires the existence of a paradigm, by which Kuhn means 'some accepted examples of actual scientific practice-examples which include law, theory, application and instrumentation together – [which] provide models from which spring particular coherent traditions of scientific research'.[3] The concepts of normal science and paradigm are intertwined, for the archetype of mature scientific activity is normal science research taking place within the framework provided by a paradigm. Kuhn even suggests that the existence of a paradigm and normal science are prerequisites for calling a field a science.[4]

What is the nature of normal science? Much of the research that practitioners of normal science engage in involves 'mopping up activities' which extend and articulate the paradigmatic structure assumed; in a phrase, it is 'an attempt to force nature into the preformed and relatively inflexible box that the paradigm supplies'.[5] Thus, normal science involves a highly restrictive sort of scientific activity. But there are advantages which accompany this narrowness of focus, for without it, the subtlety and depth of scientific investigation that also characterizes normal science would not be possible. Normal science does not seek to produce novelties; rather it is a 'puzzle-solving' activity – the scientist proceeds according to a well-specified set of rules; solutions are usually anticipated in advance; such activity tests the scientist's skill with the tools he employs; and a failure to reach a solution to a particular problem usually is taken more as a reflection of the scientist's competence than of the nature of the problem or methods used.[6] In addition, it is through 'doing' normal science that a scientist learns the methodological, quasi-metaphysical, theoretical, and instrumentational assumptions of his discipline; that is, those rules and values which are accepted within his own line of work. It is important to understand that little of that education is conscious; it occurs slowly, and over time, and is a result of scientific activity itself.

Though many scientists talk easily and well about the particular individual hypotheses that underlie a concrete piece of individual research, they are little better than laymen at characterizing the established bases of their field, its legitimate problems and methods. If they have learned such abstractions at all, they show it mainly through their ability to do successful research. That ability can, however, be understood without recourse to hypothetical rules of the game.[7]

Finally, though normal science is a cumulative enterprise, it has unintentional noncumulative effects. By its very nature, normal science leads its practitioners to awareness of anomalies, which are a prerequisite to new discoveries that ultimately can produce paradigm change.

Anomalies often take some time to be recognized and acknowledged. Additionally, they are often met with resistance, which serves a useful purpose in guaranteeing that 'scientists will not be lightly distracted and that the anomalies that lead to paradigm change will penetrate existing knowledge to the core'.[8] Small adjustments in a paradigm occur when new discoveries are able to handle the anomalous situation; such small changes usually only affect that group of specialists that works in the particular area where the anomaly is first discovered. But discoveries are not only sources of paradigm change. From time to time, a number of anomalies can emerge within a certain normal science tradition which precipitate a crisis such that much of the usual puzzle-solving activity breaks down. This has profound effects on the scientific community in question.

> Confronted with anomaly or with crisis, scientists take a different attitude toward existing paradigms, and the nature of their research changes accordingly. The proliferation of competing articulations, the willingness to try anything, the expression of explicit discontent, the recourse to philosophy and to debate over fundamentals, all these are symptoms of a transition from normal to extraordinary research.[9]

This extraordinary research sets the stage for the possibility of a scientific revolution, a 'gestalt-switch' in which a new paradigm emerges and a battle over its acceptability is joined.

Such a revolution does not follow automatically from the crisis situation. Normal science may successfully handle the apparent anomaly, or, on occasion, no new replacement that can solve the old problems is forthcoming. This points up an essential prerequisite for the possibility of a revolution: scientists never reject an old paradigm without coming up with a replacement; an alternative must exist for a revolution to take place. Such a view directly challenges the ideal of powerful falsifications by data, an ideal shared by positivists and Popper.

> No process yet disclosed by the historical study of scientific development at all resembles the methodological stereotype of falsification by direct comparison with nature. That remark does not mean that scientists do not reject scientific theories, or that experience and experiment are not essential to the process in which they do so. But it does mean – what will ultimately be a central point – that the act of judgement that leads scientists to reject a previously accepted theory is always based upon more than a comparison of that theory with the world. The decision to reject one paradigm is always simultaneously the decision to accept another, and the judgement leading to that decision involves the comparison of both paradigms with nature *and* with each other.[10]

If a new paradigm emerges, it differs from its predecessor in a number of ways. First, it provides answers to the anomalies that plagued the old one. Next, it often involves a new perception of which problems are relevant. And finally, methodological differences may emerge, since a paradigm also dictates the methods and standards of solution that are acceptable to the community. This can have profound consequences.

> As a result, the reception of a new paradigm often necessitates a redefinition of the corresponding science. Some old problems may be relegated to another science or declared entirely 'unscientific.' Others that were previously non-existent or trivial may, with a new paradigm, become the very archetypes of significant scientific achievement. And as the problems change, so, often, does the standard that distinguishes a real scientific solution from a mere metaphysical speculation, word game, or mathematical ploy. The normal-scientific tradition that emerges from a scientific revolution is not only incompatible but often actually incommensurable with that which has gone before.[11]

This potential incommensurability is the grounds for Kuhn's most controversial claim: that during periods of extraordinary research, the old rules for choosing between theories or hypotheses within a given normal-science tradition no longer apply. Because competing paradigms provide different world-views, dictate meanings for terms, and even affect the selection of data for testing, a rational resolution of the debate between such paradigms is unlikely. Certain criteria can be employed: a new paradigm is favored if it can solve the anomalies encountered by the older one, if it has more quantitative precision and can predict new phenomena, if it has certain aesthetic qualities or is supported by some of the more well-known members of the profession.[12] But because a new paradigm rarely emerges in a fully articulated form, such criteria are usually only applicable in retrospect. The implications of all of this for the rationality of scientific activity are devastating, for it seems that though debates over paradigms are usually couched in terms of evaluation via objective methodological standards, the decision to support one or the other is more often a question of (anathema of anathemas) *faith*.

> A decision between alternative ways of practicing science is called for, and in the circumstances that decision must be based less on past achievement than on future promise. The man who embraces a new paradigm at an early stage must often do so in defiance of the evidence provided by problem-solving. He must, that is, have faith that the new paradigm will succeed with the many large problems that confront it, knowing only that the older paradigm has failed with a few. A decision of that kind can only be made on faith.[13]

Given this analysis of the structure of scientific development, one final question remains: Is progress possible in science? Kuhn argues that there is little progress in pre-paradigmatic 'science', but that the development of a paradigm and the normal science that follows assure progress. (Since Kuhn's definition of progress employs the concepts of 'successful creative work' and scientific activity, this claim may be less controversial than it seems.) It is more difficult to assess whether progress takes place during times of revolution. Though new paradigms bring new areas and methods of investigation to light, the incommensurability of paradigms guarantees that certain old questions and methods will no longer be regarded as interesting. Kuhn states that a new definition of progress may be required, for if one assumes that progress means 'moving closer to the truth', it is impossible to tell whether such progress takes place because there are no meta-methodological standards by which to judge between competing paradigms. If one defines progress (rather emptily) as the 'evolution of the state of knowledge', one might be able to make a better case for the concept of revolutionary progress. Kuhn ends his analysis with the remarks that trying to evaluate such questions within his framework might be less than fruitful, that evolution rather than some sort of teleology may provide a better insight when one analyzes the progression of a discipline's thought.[14]

Some Criticisms of Kuhn
Though Kuhn's influence has spread far beyond the confines of the philosophy of science, some nonphilosophers who are acquainted with his work have not been aware of criticisms of his position. This

has the paradoxical (though hardly unusual, given the information lags that exist among disciplines) consequence that at present Kuhn's prestige is greater outside the philosophy of science than within it.

Some of the criticisms have been openly accepted by Kuhn and he has revised his views accordingly. This is most evident in his reconsideration of the use of the word paradigm in the light of Margaret Masterman's masterful piece, 'The Nature of a Paradigm', in which she shows that Kuhn used that term in no less than twenty-two distinct ways.[15] Kuhn pleads guilty to the charge of vagueness on this point, and attempts a reconciliation by defining two new concepts, exemplars (concrete, technical problem solutions which the students of a particular discipline encounter in gaining their professional education) and disciplinary matrices (the symbolic generalizations, models, values, commitments, and examplars shared by and which unite given scientific communities) which he feels capture most of the meanings formerly adduced to the single concept paradigm.[16] Other criticisms have not been accepted by Kuhn, but have provided topics for much fruitful debate over the last decade. Three of these are treated here. The first examines whether the conceptual framework developed in *The Structure of Scientific Revolutions* is *descriptively* accurate. The latter two involve the *normative* issues of whether Kuhn's interpretation of scientific activity during periods of normal science, on the one hand, and revolutionary science, on the other, can and do provide an adequate methodology for science.

1. Few of Kuhn's critics deny that something like normal science exists; many, however, dispute that philosopher's characterization of the activity. Popper, for example, thanks Kuhn for bringing to light the distinction between normal and revolutionary science (a distinction about which in the past he had 'at best been only dimly aware'), but goes on to deny that normal research is as prevalent in science as is demanded by Kuhn's analysis. Popper also rejects the idea that science can be characterized by long periods in which only one paradigm is dominant in each discipline. This should come as no surprise, since Popper has always stressed both the methodological need for and the historical reality of the constant criticisms of theories in science, a position which does not fit in well with Kuhn's 'puzzle-solving' description of normal scientific activity.[17] Finally, Popper believes that Kuhn errs in claiming that competing paradigms are incommensurable, since that would prohibit rational debate during periods of extraordinary science. For Popper, extraordinary science is the norm, but rational debate is neverthe-less always possible.

I do admit that at any moment we are prisoners caught in the framework of our theories; our expectations; our past experiences; our language. But we are prisoners in a Pickwickian sense: If we try, we can break out of our framework at anytime. Admittedly, we shall find ourselves again in a framework, but it will be a better and roomier one; and we can at any moment break out of it again.

The central point is that a critical discussion and a comparison of the various frameworks is always possible. It is just a dogma – a dangerous dogma – that the different frameworks are like mutually untranslatable languages.[18]

Paul Feyerabend, whose work like that of Lakatos has been heavily influenced by Popper, makes many of the same arguments as does his mentor. He begins his critique of Kuhn with a 'methodological fairytale' in which he proposes that science should be carried on by the proliferation of tenaciously held theories; then, on the basis of a number of examples, he suggests that that is in fact a historically accurate description of the way that science develops. Feyerabend feels that his criticisms do fatal damage to Kuhn's linear normal science–revolution–normal science model, since that model '*temporally separates* periods of proliferation and periods of monism'.[19]

Stephen Toulmin scores Kuhn for his distinction between normal and revolutionary periods. He argues that, not only has Kuhn drawn the lines too sharply in separating the two, but also that *no* revolution (scientific, political, or otherwise) can be accurately characterized in such a dichotomous manner: continuities always exist. Toulmin is aware that Kuhn may rejoin by noting that revolutions 'in the small' are also present in the *Structure* in which a paradigm change only affects a subgroup of a given discipline. But if Kuhn uses this device to cover gradual change, then his distinction between normal science (a period in which puzzle-solving, not gradual change, is supposed to occur) and revolutionary science loses much of its force.[20] In Toulmin's words,

> the 'absoluteness' of the transition involved in a scientific revolution provided the original criterion for recognizing that one had occurred at all. And, once we acknowledge that *no* conceptual change in science is ever absolute, we are left only with a sequence of greater and lesser conceptual modifications differing from one another in degree. The distinctive element in Kuhn's theory is thus destroyed, and we are left looking beyond it for a new sort of theory of scientific change.[21]

The conceptual scheme developed in *The Structure of Scientific Revolutions* has thus been slighted for its inability to handle (1) periods of normal science in which more than one paradigm exists; (2) nonrevolutionary periods in which fruitful debate and criticism rather than simple puzzle-solving accompany a dominant research tradition; and (3) the gradual shifts in paradigms which are common to such periods. Kuhn for his part insists that such periods occur less frequently historically than his critics might think, and that in any case, his framework is fully adequate for describing and analyzing them.[22]

2. The normal science–revolution–normal science progression advanced in *The Structure* is more than a descriptive device; as Kuhn freely admits, there are normative elements present in his analysis, as well.[23] One of these elements concerns the positive value of normal science. Normal research is praised by Kuhn for two reasons. First, normal science is the hallmark of science: it *more than anything else* is what distinguishes the scientific from the non-scientific. Second, normal science leads to revolutions, and thus ultimately to scientific development.

On few points is there more disagreement between Kuhn and his (mostly Popperian) critics than on this one. John Watkins draws the line between the two camps nicely.

> Thus we have the following clash: the condition which Kuhn regards as the normal and proper condition of science is a condition which, if it actually obtained, Popper would regard as *un*scientific, a state of affairs in which critical science had contracted into defensive metaphysics.[24]

Popper himself goes further than 'unscientific' in his characterization of normal science and its practitioners: for him, it is dangerous, dogmatic, even pathetic, and the normal scientist 'is a person one ought to be sorry for'.[25] Preferring 'revolution in permanence' to puzzle-solving as a credo for everyday scientific activity, Popper attacks normal science for insulating a ruling, dogmatic orthodoxy from critical scrutiny.

But what of Kuhn's second point, that normal science is beneficial because it leads to revolutions? To establish this point, Kuhn must show both that revolutions are beneficial and that normal science is a sure way to guarantee their occurrence. Feyerabend argues that Kuhn has shown neither. Since Kuhn admits (because of the incommensurability of competing paradigms) that it is illegitimate to speak of a paradigm change as progressive, Feyerabend notes that it seems strange that Kuhn would argue that normal science should be praised for its power to eventually bring about extraordinary research. But since Feyerabend himself prefers periods in which theory proliferation takes place, his major point is that there are more sure ways of guaranteeing periods of revolutionary science than Kuhn's. While Feyerabend would insist (like Kuhn) that no theory should be given up too easily (his principle of tenacity), he would also insist that the best way to avoid the dogmatic retention of unsuitable theories is by the acceptance of a 'principle of proliferation', which calls for the proliferation of theories.[26]

Thus we see that Kuhn's esteem for normal science as the methodological hallmark of science and the surest route to revolutionary research is not universally shared.

3. If many critics were unimpressed by Kuhn's salutary assessment of normal science, his comments on revolutionary science provoked an even greater outcry. The fear is that Kuhn's incommensurability thesis, if accepted, undercuts any objective, rational foundation for science. Critics maintain that Kuhnian revolutionary theory evaluation is little else than 'an intuitive or mystical affair', and that the growth of a new paradigm resembles something like the spread of an epidemic.[27]

Even if Kuhn's arguments led to an irrationalist view of the development of science, that would not in itself destroy the credibility of his position. To defeat Kuhn, strong arguments would have to be advanced to establish that incommensurable paradigms could be compared in some rational manner, something which Kuhn (according to his critics) denies. This, indeed, is the direction that most critics take.[28]

But most of this is beside the point, since Kuhn readily concedes that comparisons between paradigms are possible. His point is that the criteria invoked in such debates cannot give *conclusive* grounds for choice, and that therefore persuasion and the values of the scientific community must play a part in such discussions.

> To say that, in matters of theory-choice, the force of logic and observation cannot in principle be compelling is neither to discard logic and observation nor to suggest that there are not good reasons for favoring one theory over another.
> . . .
> To name persuasion as the scientist's recourse is not to suggest that there are not many good reasons for choosing one theory rather than another . . . These are, furthermore, reasons of exactly the kind standard in philosophy of science: accuracy, scope, simplicity, fruitfulness and the like. It is vitally important that scientists be taught to value these characteristics and that they be provided with examples that illustrate them in practice.
> . . .
> What I am denying then is neither the existence of good reasons nor that these reasons are of the sort usually described. I am, however, insisting

that such reasons constitute values to be used in making choices rather than rules of choice.[29]

Paul K. Feyerabend

We saw in the last chapter that the positivist faith in the possibility of distinguishing clearly the theoretical from the nontheoretical in science has been thoroughly challenged in contemporary philosophy of science. Critics argued that perceptions, the meanings of terms, even 'the facts' are all dependent on theories. In his early work, philosopher Paul K. Feyerabend doggedly pursued the implications of the 'theory-dependence thesis' to their logical conclusions. His results seem to undermine almost any place for rational discourse in science (especially in relation to positivism); because of this, philosophers were quick to respond critically to his analysis. In the last decade, this iconoclastic philosopher developed a position which differs radically from any we have encountered: it rests upon what he calls an anarchistic, or Dadaist, theory of knowledge. In what follows, the evolution of Feyerabend's methodological Dadaism is traced.

Feyerabend's Early Methodology

In his early writings, Feyerabend espouses an extreme version of the theory-dependence thesis, one that undermines two of the pillars of modern empiricism, the condition of meaning invariance and the consistency condition.

Feyerabend asserts that the meanings of both observational and theoretical terms are completely dependent on the theory in which they are embedded. As a consequence, any new theory that emerges to replace an old one will contain terms which are used in a different way from their previous usage; though the terms are the same, their meanings are not. The only cases in which two theories share terms that have the same meanings are trivial: they involve situations in which a new theory simply extends the classes used in an old theory. Feyerabend supports his claim with numerous historical examples of nontrivial theory replacement, and asserts that such examples render unacceptable the positivist belief in the condition of meaning invariance.[30]

Another tenet of modern empiricism which Feyerabend rejects is the consistency condition, which demands that new theories either contain or be consistent with well-established theories in their domain. Feyerabend first cites some historical examples of instances when the condition was fruitfully ignored; he then argues that the condition is inherently unreasonable.

It eliminates a theory not because it is in disagreement with the *facts*; it eliminates it because it is in disagreement with *another* theory . . . The only difference between such a measure and a more recent theory is age and familiarity. Had the younger theory been there first, then the consistency condition would have worked in its favor.[31]

Feyerabend admits that a counterargument exists: Why should scientists waste their time in endlessly adding new theories which do nothing more than re-explain the same facts, albeit with a different framework? It is common knowledge that an infinite number of theories can be provided to explain a given set of facts; a recognition of this leads directly to the consistency condition. Proponents of the consistency condition will consider a new theory only if it is also capable of explaining *novel* facts.[32] This later stipulation guarantees that proposed alternative theories are true advances over older theories.

This defense of the consistency condition depends crucially on the truth of the assumption of 'the relative autonomy of facts', which states that facts exist independent of theories. Since Feyerabend adheres to the theory-dependence thesis, he denies the relative autonomy of facts, which weakens the case for the consistency condition.

The final argument against the consistency condition is that it restricts the growth of empirical knowledge, whereas any tenable empiricist methodology should aim at increasing the empirical content of knowledge. Feyerabend's argument is straightforward, and again depends on the theory-dependence thesis. If facts are theory dependent, then the best way to increase the number of facts (and hence the empirical content of scientific knowledge) is to increase the number of alternative, mutually inconsistent theories. The key to scientific advance is the proliferation of theories.

> You can be a good empiricist only if you are prepared to work with many alternative theories rather than with a single point of view and 'experience'. This plurality of theories must not be regarded as a preliminary stage of knowledge which will at some time in the future be replaced by the One True Theory. Theoretical pluralism is assumed to be an essential feature of all knowledge that claims to be objective . . . Such a plurality allows for a much sharper criticism of accepted ideas than does the comparison with a domain of 'facts' which are supposed to sit there independently of theoretical considerations.[33]

In a later article, Feyerabend suggests that his principle of proliferation be supplemented with a principle of tenacity: ideas should be retained at times, even though the evidence or well-supported theories contradict it.[34] These two principles taken together seem to lead to a very strange sort of methodology: established theories should be challenged by an ever increasing number of alternatives which need not be well supported either theoretically or empirically. Such prescriptions were not well received by most philosophers. Since most of Feyerabend's case depends on the plausibility of the theory-dependence thesis, his critics have attacked that central doctrine.

The Philosophical Response
One of the most glaring weaknesses of Feyerabend's analysis is his adamant insistence that, except for trivial cases, any change in a theory will alter the meanings of all terms, observational and theoretical, in the theory. He defends this assertion by presenting a number of examples from the history of science, examples which are in general representative of a revolutionary type of change in which world-views, and hence meanings, do change. But clearly, counter-examples exist in which theories are altered but many meanings remain intact. Feyerabend's failure to retreat from his severe dichotomization of theory and meaning change (it is either trivial or revolutionary, on his account) weakens his position substantially. What is needed is an analysis which provides a means for recognizing and specifying the extent to which a given theory change affects the meanings of the terms employed.[35] All that Feyerabend has accomplished is to point out the limiting case and assert on the basis of a few examples that it is the only relevant case.

But let us accept for the moment Feyerabend's assertion that any nontrivial change in a theory will change the meanings of all of its constituent terms. What are the implications of such a position?

First, it is clear that on this account any term used in two different theories will have different meanings in those theories. If that is true, then two theories can never contradict each other, even if they seem to imply contradictory consequences.

> According to this approach, if I assert *p* and you assert *not-p*, we are not and cannot be disagreeing, because the terms in my assertion are *p-laden* and so mean one thing, whereas those in *not-p* are *not-p laden* and so mean another. *Not-p*, then is not the negation of *p*. In short, negation is impossible! On the other hand, if every assertion does not burden its terms with what is asserted, then which ones do and why? The answers are not forthcoming.[36]

In a like manner, agreement between theories can never be established. But if this is the case, how can two theories ever be considered as alternatives?

Not only is any disagreement impossible for proponents of two different theories but, for the same reason, so is any agreement. It will be impossible for theorists to agree even on a description of the data to be explained by their respective theories, for in such a description all the terms employed will depend for their meanings upon the given theory. But if there can be no agreement and no disagreement either, in what sense can two different theories be about the same thing? In what sense can two different theories be (as Feyerabend calls them) alternatives?[37]

Both of these arguments were advanced by Peter Achinstein; a third concerning the circularity (or impossibility) of empirical testing in a Feyerabendian world is attributable to Frederick Suppe.

If one attempts to test a theory by comparing its predictions with the results of observation, both the predictions and the observation report will have to be expressed in the same language, with the same meanings attached to descriptive terms. Suppose now that the theory's prediction – say P – disagrees with the results of observation; then the observation report must entail not-P. The prediction, P, however is part of the theory and its denial presumably alters the theory and hence changes the meaning of the descriptive terms in P. It follows, then, . . . that the desriptive terms occurring in P and not-P cannot have the same meanings. Hence no observation report is possible which could possibly disconfirm or falsify the theory. That is, the only observation reports which are relevant to testing the theory will be those which are consistent with the theory. All testing of theories thus is circular.[38]

Feyerabend attempted to answer some of the criticisms advanced above by showing how theories which share terms with dissimilar meanings can be compared; counterexamples have been provided by critics.[39] Few scientists would wish to accept that dissimilar theories can neither agree nor disagree with each other. Few would wish to accept that all empirical testing is circular. Yet these consequences follow from Feyerabend's extreme interpretation of the theory dependence of meanings. Additionally, these weaknesses in Feyerabend's analysis undercut much of the rationale behind his methodological principles of tenacity and of theory proliferation. Why follow any methodology if theories can neither agree nor disagree, nor be tested against evidence?

According to Suppe, Feyerabend's early methodological beliefs collapse under the weight of the above criticisms.[40] I think it is undeniable that Feyerabend's responses have not been sufficient to re-establish his earlier position. But in recent years it is evident that Feyerabend has no intention of providing an alternative methodology. His proclaimed purpose is rather to attack the notion that *any* rules-oriented methodology can ever be viable. A brief examination of *Against Method* (the title tells it all) supports this interpretation of Feyerabend.

Feyerabend's Dadaist Anti-Methodology

The opening sentence of *Against Method* states simply that '*anarchism*, while perhaps not the most attractive *political* philosophy, is certainly excellent medicine for *epistemology*, and for the philosophy of science'.[41] Why anarchy? The answer is simple. History in general is much richer, more varied, more many-sided, livelier, and more subtle than even the best methodologist can imagine; as such, it 'demands complex procedures and defies analysis on the basis of rules which have been set up in advance and without regard to the ever-changing conditions of history'.[42] A narrow-minded adherence to well-specified methodological rules does not bring progress. Rather, scientists should be 'unscrupulous opportunists' who feel no guilt in bending or even contradicting such rules whenever they see fit. The history of science lends clear support on this issue; many significant advances occurred only after methodological rules were cast aside. Even more important, it is often sound methodological practice to break the rules.

> given any rule, however 'fundamental' or 'necessary' for science, there are always circumstances when it is advisable not only to ignore the rule, but to adopt its opposite. For example, there are circumstances when it is advisable to introduce, elaborate and defend ad hoc hypotheses, or hypotheses which contradict well-established and generally accepted experimental results, or hypotheses whose content is smaller than the content of the existing and empirically adequate alternative or self-inconsistent hypotheses, and so on.
>
> There are even circumstances – and they occur rather frequently – when *argument* loses its forward-looking aspect and becomes a hindrance to progress. . . . And where arguments *do* seem to have an effect, this is more often due to their *physical repetition* than to their *semantic content*.[43]

Feyerabend thus defends in his book the thesis that methodological anarchism is a precondition of progress in science, that 'there is only *one* principle that can be defended under *all* circumstances and in *all* stages of human development. It is the principle *"anything goes"* '.[44]

Much of the rest of the book is dedicated to the illumination of these ideas, both by argument and by historical example. Thus he claims that the proliferation of hypotheses whose results contradict well-confirmed theories can advance knowledge. He defends this claim by reiterating the arguments against the consistency condition.[45] He also argues that there are times when political interference may be required to aid the advancement of science: it took intervention by the Chinese government to free that country from the domination of Western medical science which, in its infinite wisdom and self-confidence, had labeled all of the traditional Chinese medical practices superstitions which were no longer to be taken seriously.[46] Ad hoc hypotheses, whose proliferation has traditionally been viewed as the final, desperate maneuver of scientific charlatans, also have their role, for they can be used to give 'breathing space' to new theories which are generally not well specified or organized at their inception.[47] And finally, Imre Lakatos, to whom the book is dedicated, is praised for being 'an anarchist in disguise'.[48]

There is much, much more in this little book – Feyerabend is a lighthearted, opinionated, and scathing gadfly and his essay is a delight to read. His message is not complex: the world is a very complicated place, thus no simple rules should guide us in our exploration of it, and in fact, adherence to simple rules will prevent us from obtaining certain kinds of knowledge. But Feyerabend says it so much better:

> To sum up: wherever we look, whatever examples we consider, we see that the principles of critical rationalism (take falsification seriously; increase content; avoid ad hoc hypotheses; be 'honest' – whatever *that* means; and so on) and, a fortiori, the principles of logical empiricism (be precise; base your theories on measurements; avoid vague and unstable ideas; and so on) give an inadequate account of the past development of science and are liable to hinder science in the future. They give an inadequate account of science because science is much more 'sloppy' and 'irrational' than its methodological image. And, they are liable to hinder it, because the attempt to make science more 'rational' and more precise is bound to wipe it out. . . What appears as 'sloppiness,' 'chaos' or 'opportunism' when compared with such laws has an important function in the development of those very theories which we today regard as essential parts of our knowledge of nature. *These 'deviations,' these 'errors,' are preconditions of progress.*[49]

In his most recent work, Feyerabend extends his message further. The first section of *Science in a Free Society* (1978) is a restatement and clarification of some of the ideas found in *Against Method*: his is not a new method but the statement that all methodologies have their limits; the development of science combines reason and practice (he ultimately labels this 'the interactionist view', in which methodology serves as 'a guide who is part of the activity guided and is changed by it'); rationalism is only one tradition among many, so should not be used to judge other traditions; a plurality of traditions is not only reasonable, it is useful, and it is correct.[50] In the second section, he questions why science and the scientific world-view have been given so much prestige in modern society. He opens the section with the question, 'What's so great about science?'[51] In exploring the question, Feyerabend finds little that is great: scientists are as prejudiced, their opinions are as untrustworthy as anyone else's; but they are far more *dangerous*, because they are viewed as rational and objective. The arguments are numerous, too many to recount; but all are delightfully made. Note, for example, his discussion of a recent article, signed by 186 scientists, in which astrology is roundly denounced.

> Now what surprises the reader whose image of science has been formed by the customary eulogies which emphasize rationality, objectivity, impartiality and so on is the religious tone of the document, the illiteracy of the 'arguments' and the authoritarian manner in which the arguments are being presented. The learned gentlemen have strong convictions, they use their authority to spread these convictions (why 186 signatures if one has argument?), they know a few phrases which sound like arguments, but they certainly do not know what they are talking about.[52]

The third and final section contains responses to his critics; its title is 'Conversations with Illiterates'. His insults are intentional: the circumspect prose style of professional academics is just another trick used to fool the public (and themselves) into thinking that they are more 'rational', and therefore (by virtue of the high esteem given to the rationalist tradition) better.

It will be interesting to see how history treats Feyerabend. By challenging the authority and objectivity of science he most certainly has attacked one of the most fundamental assumptions of our age. His caricatures of the pompous academic should certainly appeal to *any* graduate student, as well as anyone whose views do not fit neatly within the prevailing professional divisions. They are probably less impressive to the 'layman' that Feyerabend takes such pains to extol: How many laymen have heard of P. K. Feyerabend? In any case, few philosophers of science have played the skeptic as well, and with such obvious relish.

Imre Lakatos

The most influential contemporary interpreter of Popper's critical rationalism was Imre Lakatos. His work is best viewed as a critical commentary on, and extension of, Popper's methodology. The originality of his creation (the methodology of scientific research

programs) and his later explorations in historiography earn him a
place of his own in the annals of the philosophy of science. His
sudden death in 1974 was a great loss to the profession.

The Methodology of Scientific Research Programs

In his *locus classicus*, 'Falsification and the Methodology of
Scientific Research Programmes' (1970), Lakatos attempts to show
that the rejection of the ideals of proven or highly probable
knowledge (which are the illusory goals pursued by those he labels,
respectively, justificationists and probabilists) need not force one to
accept either Kuhnian social psychology or skepticism. A third
alternative is falsificationism. There are at least three varieties of
falsificationism: dogmatic, naive methodological, and sophisticated
methodological falsificationism. Lakatos argues that many of
Popper's critics wrongly accused him of being a dogmatic falsificationist, when in truth his position as it evolved over the years
moved from naive toward sophisticated falsificationism. Lakatos's
positive contribution is to complete the program begun by Popper
by proposing a methodology of scientific research programs that
contains the best of Popper's insights (some of which, incidently,
agree with ideas propounded by Kuhn and Feyerabend) and that
enables a rational (as opposed to a sociological or nonrational)
reconstruction of methodology and of the growth of scientific
knowledge. His sophisticated methodological falsificationism, then,
not only lays down prescriptions by which science can proceed, it
also provides a basis for a descriptive rational reconstruction of how
scientific disciplines often evolve.[53]

Sophisticated methodological falsificationism recognizes that
theories do not exist in isolation; rather, they are part of a larger
and dynamic system. Within such a system, or research tradition,
theories are often undergoing modifications. Hypotheses are added,
revised, or deleted in accordance with: the range of problems the
research tradition is meant to cover, its success in doing so, the
relation of the present body of theories with the evidence, and so
forth. Because of this constant revision, it does not make sense to
talk of *a* theory; instead, the point of reference of methodological
discussion should be a *series* of theories 'where each subsequent
theory results from adding auxiliary clauses to (or from semantical
reinterpretations of) the previous theory in order to accommodate
some anomaly, each theory having at least as much content as the
unrefuted content of its predecessor'.[54] The role of methodologist is
to evaluate how research traditions change through time; the aim is
to discover whether such theory change and modification is either
progressive or degenerative.

Lakatos formulates a method for distinguishing whether a series of theories is progressing or degenerating; this method distinguishes between theoretical and empirical 'problemshifts'.

> Let us say . . . a series of theories is theoretically progressive (or 'constitutes a theoretically progressive problemshift') if each new theory has some excess empirical content over its predecessor, that is, if it predicts some novel, hitherto unexpected fact. Let us say that a theoretically progressive series of theories is also empirically progressive (or 'constitutes an empirically progressive problemshift') if some of this excess empirical content is also corroborated, that is, if each new theory leads us to the actual discovery of some new fact. Finally, let us call a problemshift progressive if it is both theoretically and empirically progressive, and degenerating if it is not. We 'accept' problemshifts as 'scientific' only if they are at least theoretically progressive; if they are not, we 'reject' them as 'pseudo-scientific' . . . We regard a theory in the series falsified when it is superceded by a theory with higher corroborated content.[55]

There is an implied continuity in science when it is viewed as a body of evolving theories; this continuity is real, and it is supported by what Lakatos calls a 'research program'. That program consists of two general sorts of methodological rules, namely, a negative heuristic (which indicates which paths of research are improper) and a positive heuristic (which indicates which research paths are legitimate). The negative heuristic disallows investigation of the 'hard core', the (by convention) irrefutable part of the research program, while the positive heuristic 'consists of a partially articulated set of suggestions or hints on how to change, develop the "refutable variants" of the research-program, how to modify, sophisticate the refutable protective belt'.[56] Significantly, the positive heuristic does not focus overly much on anomalies and 'refutation'; rather, it stresses modifications of the protective belt which would substantiate the assumptions implicit in the hard core. Whether or not alterations in the protective belt represent progressive or degenerating problemshifts can be determined by the rules outlined above, and the success of the research program will be judged accordingly. Any such evaluation clearly is a long-range affair; there is no 'instant rationality' by which to evaluate the success or failure of a research program.[57]

Lakatos's methodological position is unique in focusing the methodologist's attention on series of theories as they develop through time. The most important implication of this view is that theory evaluation cannot be instantaneous, since a whole system of theories in its historical evolution must be evaluated. The addition of a time dimension alters the nature of theory choice in a number of significant ways. First, the empirical side of science is given a long run characterization.

> The time-honoured empirical criterion for a satisfactory theory was agreement with the observed facts. Our empirical criterion for a series of theories is that it should produce facts. The idea of growth and the concept of empirical character are soldered into one.[58]

Next, there is a concomitant de-emphasis of the significance of refutation, though it still plays a role in science. This de-emphasis is due to the new stress placed on the modification of the auxiliary hypotheses within the protective belt which is undertaken to offer *support* to the evolving series of theories. As such, the importance of experimental testing for the binding refutation of any given hypothesis is greatly reduced. 'Relatively few experiments are really important', even crucial experiments are seldom recognized as such without the benefit of hindsight.[59] When evaluating a series of theories, the analog to refutation is the judgment of whether problemshifts are progressive or degenerating, that is, whether they anticipate novel facts, some of which are corroborated, or not.

His divergence from Popper is most evident in Lakatos's assessment of the importance of falsification in science. Tests are more often than not carried out to *support* rather than refute hypotheses in the protective belt; there are few decisive tests and no 'instant rationality'; even when a theory is falsified, it will not be rejected unless a suitable replacement exists.[60] Though Lakatos claims that Popper was heading in this direction in his later work, such a reduction of the sigificance of falsification is a clear-cut break from his mentor's views.

Finally, we discover in Lakatos some echoes of Feyerabend's principles of proliferation and tenacity. Since science progresses by the enunciation of research traditions which are judged by their 'excess empirical content', the proliferation of theories is beneficial.

> We are no longer interested in the thousands of trivial verifying instances nor in the hundreds of readily available anomalies: the few crucial excess verifying instances are decisive. . . . 'Theoretical pluralism' is better than 'theoretical monism': on this point Popper and Feyerabend are right and Kuhn is wrong.[61]

And because the evaluation of a research program must be based on evidence that is collected over a long period of time, scientists must be careful not to eliminate any particular research tradition too quickly. This is especially true for programs which are just developing.

> ... we must not discard a budding research programme simply because it has so far failed to overtake a powerful rival. ... As long as a budding research programme can be rationally reconstructed as a progressive problemshift, it should be sheltered for a while from a powerful established rival.[62]

Lakatos believes that his methodology of scientific research programs provides a program for the critical evaluation of competing scientific theories, a program which, though fully cognizant that there is not instant rationality and that therefore both justificationists and probabilists are wrong, nevertheless retains a *prescriptive* role for methodology and avoids what he perceives as the subjective quagmire of Kuhn's 'social psychology' or Feyerabend's Dadaism. Lakatos argues in a later paper that his model is also the preferred *descriptive* vehicle for the 'rational reconstruction' of science.[63] Lakatos thus understood that any successful methodology had to be acceptable on both prescriptive and descriptive grounds, and claimed to have produced a viable candidate. Whether he succeeded, and whether any methodology can attain such goals, are questions of paramount importance for methodology. They are addressed in the final section of this book.

Contemporary Philosophy of Science – A Dilettante's Review and Commentary

What, then, can be said about the philosophy of science in the last quarter century? Positivism as the epistemological–methodological foundation for philosophy of science is in decline, and may even be in eclipse: Frederick Suppe relegates even the most mature forms of the philosophy to the intellectual history of the discipline.[64] If positivism is dead, perhaps its death was one of a thousand qualifications, for it was modified often in the long history of its development. Whatever its present status, the vision of science held by positivists was both powerful and seductive, one that promised to banish the speculative and the unverifiable from the very language of science. And paradoxically, positivists came to value objective, dispassionate analysis with an almost irrational passion, and therein lay the seeds of their ruin.

In their haste to eradicate the flights of metaphysical fantasy, which they felt characterized the systems built by idealist philosophers, positivists became dogmatic in their refusal to allow any subjective, qualitative elements to enter into their rational reconstructions of science. That refusal artificially limited their analyses, and created gaps in their descriptions of science. They insisted on certainty in the use of terms – and many were not cognizant of the ways in which words can change meanings over time and across theories. They believed that theories and explanations in science were uniform, and always (if legitimate) translatable into a specified axiomatic form – and missed the rich and complex diversity of patterns of explanation and theorizing in science. And in their search for certain or probable knowledge – be that verifiable or falsifiable statements, or hypotheses that are probable to a high and numerically-specifiable degree – they failed to see that the most important decisions made in science, and these include choice over the very direction of science itself, are in the final analysis made by men who should be aware of their own fallibility, but who hopefully attempt to be rational anyway.

What alternatives are proposed by the 'growth of knowledge' critics of logical empiricism? Their most wide-ranging break with the earlier tradition lies in the suggestion that the scope of philosophy of science be greatly enlarged. The discipline should no longer be restricted to logical analyses of explanation, confirmation, and theory structure; it must also include investigations of the wide range of scientific activity as it exists within the separate disciplines. Ideas once relegated to the 'context of discovery' or 'external history' must be included when tracing the evolution of scientific thought within disciplines over time.

This broadening scope implies a drastic increase in the number and types of methods of investigation permissible within the philosophy of science. Critical roles for the history, sociology, and even psychology of science emerge; descriptive analysis must feed back on prescriptive. It would be unfair and inaccurate to claim that positivists were exclusively concerned with advancing prescriptive pronouncements about science. To be sure, most of their models defined what constituted 'legitimate' scientific activity. However, their positions shifted over the years, and many of those shifts (e.g. criteria of meaning as applied to theoretical terms) were predicated by recognition of the failure of their models to truly represent important elements of actual scientific practice. The major difference between more contemporary approaches and those of the positivists is that the former give *emphasis* to the role of (in particular) the history of science as a check against which to test the rational reconstructions of philosophers.

The proposed expansion of the philosophy of science into whole new domains has brought with it problems as well as prospects. The relationships among philosophy, sociology, and history are frighteningly complex, and their exploration is no task for the part-time scholar. Historiography becomes as important as methodology and history when it is recognized that one's perception of proper methods affects one's interpretation of history.[65] It is simple to proclaim that an interdisciplinary approach to the philosophy of science is best; it is much harder to produce an interdisciplinary study that is not dilettantish. I can remember my own enthusiastic response when I first read Institutionalist economists propose that economics become a more holistic discipline. I was delighted by the thought of breaking down the barriers among such disciplines as economics, political science, sociology, and anthropology, so that a true study of man, the social animal, could be undertaken. It was disappointing to discover that far fewer scientists actually attempted such studies than urged they be attempted, and that of those who did try, few succeeded.

It should be evident from the text of this chapter that while the approaches of the major growth of knowledge protagonists share such characteristics as are outlined above, there exist substantial differences among them in the details of their analyses. Each philosopher has a particular image of how science evolves (the historico-descriptive element); and each has a normative vision of the role of methodology with regard to the 'progress' of science. Significantly, the individual analyses often raise questions over the proper definition of such key terms as rationality and progress, questions which have yet to be successfully resolved.[66] In addition, the normative and descriptive elements are often inextricably intertwined, making it difficult to tell whether a particular writer is describing what is or prescribing what should be. Finally, there are differences in the answers which the three thinkers give to some very important questions.

For example, does (and should) scientific activity in any given field take place within a single theoretical framework, or many: is Kuhn's theoretical monism or Feyerabend's and Lakatos's theoretical pluralism more descriptively accurate (and normatively desirable)? Historically, both occur; they may even occur simultaneously (e.g. rival programs, each of which has its own normal science tradition). Similarly, each approach has its own distinct methodological strengths and weaknesses, which makes selection between them as prescriptive pronouncements unreasonable. It is clear that monism permits the intensive investigation of a particular subject which can lead to fruitful and sophisticated analysis. Monism can also lead to revolutions, if the scientists involved pay proper attention to the anomalies which may (or must, à la Kuhn) eventually surface as a result of their intense efforts. But if anomalies are generally ignored or 'patched up' with ad hoc, theory-saving devices, normal science can also become stagnant and dogmatic. Theoretical pluralism will seldom if ever lead to stagnation. Unfortunately, it is also hard to imagine an adherent of pluralism attaining the kind of indepth insights which are possible for his less well-rounded (but more 'normal'?) monistic opponent.

Does science change incrementally, or by explosive, discontinuous revolutions? I think that Toulmin is correct in criticizing Kuhn's rigid dichotomy between normal and extraordinary research: *no revolution is ever a complete transformation*. However, Kuhn's analysis is certainly adequate for handling epochs in which dramatic changes of emphasis occurred in relatively short periods of time, though his notion of micro-revolutions for handling smaller shifts fares less well. For incremental changes, Lakatos's view that long wars of attrition between competing research programs, in which changes in the protective belt can be judged in the long run as progressive or degenerating, seems promising. Other frameworks have been proposed for describing other types of change in science.[67] Whichever models of historical development gain prominence in the future, all must continue to look to the history of science for sources of justification and for impetus for modification.

Do terms in different theories share meanings, or are different theories by nature either incommensurable or incomparable? Feyerabend's extreme version of the theory dependence of all scientific terms seems to be as dogmatic as the notion of strict meaning invariance which is implicit in the positivist thesis of reduction. Kuhn's closeness to Feyerabend's views is understandable given his emphasis on revolutions (where paradigms are most likely to be incommensurable). Lakatos's views are similarly explicable given his stress on the gradual problemshifts which take place in a protective belt. When alternative research programs investigate roughly the same domain (e.g. as is the case for the Keynesian and Monetarist approaches to macro-theory and policy), some commensurability and comparability is possible. When groups differ on both methods and focus of investigation (as is the case in certain aspects of the controversy between 'the two Cambridges'), it is more likely that meanings given to words will vary, and also that choice between the approaches will be based on less than objective factors. In limiting cases where two programs share no points of contact (say, Keynesian theory and evolutionary theory), one may hold both views without being inconsistent. Whether that possibility exists within a single field is worth investigating. Finally, meaning variance over time needs greater study, especially by those interested in the history of thought. The failure to recognize that the meanings of words can change over time has been the root cause of much sloppy work in doctrinal history. Those historians who have ignored this seemingly trivial point have at times ended up criticizing or praising past authors for holding views which they did not and could not have possessed.[68]

There are, of course, many more questions. All are difficult; some may be unanswerable. That they exist is no reason to dismiss the growth of knowledge tradition, for it is a new research program which has yet to be fully articulated. Their persistence is another matter, yet even then they may be *instructive*, since they will define the limits of such analyses. How such anomalies are handled also provide insights about the scientific communities involved; that is to say, the tools of analysis can be used to study contemporary philosophy of science.

While all of the above is nothing more than the scribbling of a philosophical dilettante, one observation seems both true and pertinent. The growth of knowledge tradition has been given its honeymoon period, and critical analysis lies ahead. Economists who, having discovered that positivism is passé, too eagerly embrace the new tradition in philosophy may find themselves feeling as foolish as their predecessors (who insisted that economics probably is, and if not should be, a positivist discipline) should now feel. We are now in a position to examine the positivist period in economic methodology.

Notes

1 Thomas Kuhn, *The Structure of Scientific Revolutions. International Encyclopedia of Unified Science* Vol. II, no. 2, 2nd enlarged edn (Chicago: University of Chicago Press, 1970), pp. 1–2.
2 Ibid., p. 10.
3 Ibid., p. 10.
4 Ibid., pp. 21–2.
5 Ibid., p. 24.
6 Ibid., pp. 35–9.
7 Ibid., p. 47.
8 Ibid., p. 65.
9 Ibid., pp. 90–1.
10 Ibid., p. 77.
11 Ibid., p. 103.
12 Ibid., pp. 153–6.
13 Ibid., pp. 157–8.
14 Ibid., pp. 167–71.
15 Margaret Masterman, 'The Nature of a Paradigm,' in I. Lakatos and A. Musgrave (eds), *Criticism and the Growth of Knowledge* (Cambridge,

England: Cambridge University Press, 1970), pp. 59–89.

16 Kuhn, *Structure*, pp. 176–87. But see Dudley Shapere, 'The Paradigm Concept,' *Science* vol. 172 (1972), pp. 706–9, for a critical review.

17 Karl Popper, 'Normal Science and Its Dangers,' in I. Lakatos and A. Musgrave (eds), op. cit., pp. 52–5.

18 Ibid. p. 56.

19 Paul Feyerabend, 'Consolations for the Specialist,' in I. Lakatos and A. Musgrave (eds), op. cit., pp. 202–10, quote on p. 208.

20 Stephen Toulmin, 'Does the Distinction between Normal and Revolutionary Science Hold Water?', in I. Lakatos and A. Musgrave (eds), op. cit., pp. 39–47.

21 Ibid., p. 45.

22 Thomas Kuhn, 'Reflections on My Critics,' in I. Lakatos and A. Musgrave (eds), op. cit., pp. 249–59.

23 Ibid., p. 233.

24 John Watkins, 'Against "Normal Science",' in I. Lakatos and A. Musgrave (eds), op. cit., p. 28.

25 Popper, 'Normal Science. . .,' op. cit., p. 52.

26 Feyerabend, 'Consolations. . .,' op. cit., pp. 202–7.

27 Israel Scheffler, *Science and Subjectivity*, (New York: Bobbs Merrill, 1967), pp. 18, 78.

28 Ibid., pp. 82–9; Popper, 'Normal Science. . .,' op. cit., pp. 56–7.

29 Kuhn, 'Reflections. . .,' op. cit., pp. 234, 261, 262.

30 Paul K. Feyerabend, 'Explanation, Reduction and Empiricism,' in H. Feigl, G. Maxwell, and M. Scriven (eds), *Minnesota Studies*, Vol. III (1962), pp. 28–97; 'How to be a Good Empiricist – A Plea for Tolerance in Matters Epistemological,' in Baruch Brody (ed.), *Readings in the Philosophy of Science* (Englewood Cliffs, N.J.: Prentice-Hall, 1970), pp. 319–42. For his position on trivial theory change, see 'On the "Meaning" of Scientific Terms,' *Journal of Philosophy*, vol. 62 (May 1965), pp. 267–9.

31 Feyerabend, 'How To Be a Good Empiricist – A Plea for Tolerance in Matters Epistemological,' in Brody (ed.), op. cit., p. 328.

32 Ibid., p. 329.

33 Ibid., pp. 320–1.

34 Feyerabend, 'Consolations. . .,' op. cit., pp. 202–10.

35 This is suggested, for example, in Dudley Shapere, 'Meaning and Scientific Change,' in R. Colodny, (ed.), *Mind and Cosmos*, pp. 56–57. See also Frederick Suppe (ed.), *The Structure of Scientific Theories*, 2nd edn (first published, 1973) (Urbana, Ill.: University of Illinois Press, 1977), pp. 180, 200.

36 Peter Achinstein, *Concepts of Science: A Philosophical Analysis* (Baltimore: Johns Hopkins Press, 1968), p. 93.

37 Ibid., p. 96.

38 Suppe (ed.), op. cit., pp. 201–2. Suppe lists some other arguments in his discussion on pp. 199–206.

39 See Feyerabend, 'Reply to Criticism,' in R. Cohen and M. Wartofsky (eds), *Boston Studies in the Philosophy of Science*, Vol. II (New York: The Humanities Press, 1965), pp. 232–3. Cf. Achinstein, op. cit., pp. 93–5.

40 Suppe (ed.), op. cit., pp. 180, 643.

41 Paul K. Feyerabend, *Against Method: Outline of an Anarchistic Theory of Knowledge* (London: New Left Books, 1975), p. 17. I term his approach Dadaist because he states in footnote 12, p. 21, that he prefers the less serious minded and zealous Dadaists to anarchists: 'A Dadaist is utterly unimpressed by any serious enterprise and he smells a rat whenever people stop smiling and assume that attitude and those facial expressions which indicate that something important is about to be said.' Note also that anarchism is seen as an *antidote* to

an overemphasis on rationality in philosophy of science *today*: Feyerabend is not a proponent of continual chaos. See p. 22.

42   Ibid., pp. 17–18.
43   Ibid., pp. 23–4.
44   Ibid., p. 28.
45   Ibid., Chapter 3.
46   Ibid., pp. 50–1.
47   Ibid., pp. 93–8.
48   Ibid., Chapter 16. The essay is meant to be a letter to Lakatos, who was preparing a reply and who approved of the mocking dedication 'to Imre Lakatos: Friend, and fellow-anarchist'. The untimely death of Lakatos in 1974 prevented the completion of the project. Feyerabend discusses his relationship with Lakatos in *Science in a Free Society* (London: NLB, 1978), pp. 152–3, 184–5.
49   Feyerabend, *Against Method*, op. cit., p. 179.
50   Feyerabend, *Science*, op. cit., Section 1.
51   Ibid., p. 73.
52   Ibid., p. 91.
53   Imre Lakatos, 'Falsification and the Methodology of Scientific Research Programmes,' in I. Lakatos and A. Musgrave (eds), *Criticism and the Growth of Knowledge* (Cambridge, England: Cambridge University Press), pp. 91–116.
54   Ibid., p. 118.
55   Ibid., p. 118.
56   Ibid., pp. 132–5, quote on p. 135.
57   Ibid., p. 137, pp. 154–9.
58   Ibid., p. 119.
59   Ibid,. pp. 157–8.
60   Ibid., pp. 117–21, 151, 179–84.
61   Ibid., p. 155.
62   Ibid., p. 157.
63   Imre Lakatos, 'History of Science and Its Rational Reconstruction,' in Roger Buck and Robert Cohen (eds), *PSA 1970: In Memory of Rudolf Carnap. Boston Studies in the Philosophy of Science*, Vol. VIII (Dordrecht, Holland: D. Reidel, 1971), pp. 91–136. Other discussions of how history of science is or should be written include the comments by Kuhn, Feigl, Hall, and Koertge which follow Lakatos' paper; many articles in Roger Stuewer (ed.), *Minnesota Studies in the Philosophy of Science*, Vol. V (Minneapolis: University of Minnesota Press, 1970); I. Bernard Cohen, 'History and the Philosopher of Science,' in Suppe (ed.), op. cit., pp. 308–49; Peter Achinstein, 'A Reply to Cohen', ibid., pp. 350–60; Noretta Koertge, 'Rational Reconstructions' in R. Cohen, P. K. Feyerabend, and M. Wartofsky (eds), *Essays in Memory of Imre Lakatos. Boston Studies in the Philosophy of Science*, Vol. XXXIX (Dordrecht, Holland: D. Reidel, 1976), pp. 359–70; Marx Wartofsky, 'The Relation Between Philosophy of Science and History of Science,' ibid., pp. 717–38.
64   Suppe (ed). op. cit., p. 632.
65   For philosophers and historians on historiography, see Joseph Agassi, *Towards an Historiography of Science* (The Hague: Mouton, 1963), and any of the references from footnote 63. On interdisciplinary prospects, see Stephen Toulmin, "Scientific Strategies and Historical Change," in Cohen, Robert, and Wartofsky, Marx, (eds), *Philosophical Foundations of Science. Boston Studies in the Philosophy of Science*, Vol. XI (Dordrecht, Holland: D. Reidel, 1974), pp. 401–14.
66   For two examples not included in the text, see Toulmin, 'Scientific Strategies. . .,' op. cit., and Erman McMullin, 'Logicality and Rationality,' ibid., pp. 415–30.
67   See, for example, Dudley Shapere, 'Scientific Theories and Their Domains,' in

Suppe (ed.), op. cit., pp. 518–65.

68 Two examples will make this point quickly. Thomas Sowell's *Classical Economics Reconsidered* (Princeton, N.J.: Princeton University Press, 1974) corrects many errors made by later commentators who first gave modern definitions to terms used by classicals, and then criticized them for faulty analysis. And J. M. Keynes's erroneous claims that his views were anticipated by Malthus and other classical underconsumptionists is a paradigmatic example of poorly-done history of thought.

PART TWO

SOME ESSAYS ON POSITIVISM AND ECONOMIC METHODOLOGY

6

Robbins versus Hutchison – The Introduction of Positivism in Economic Methodology

Prior to Terence Hutchison's introduction of positivism in the late 1930s, the dominant methodological viewpoint in twentieth century economic thought stressed subjectivism, methodological individualism, and the self-evident nature of the basic postulates of economic theory.[1] This particular vision of the appropriate methods for economics is eloquently expressed in Lionel Robbins's classic tract, *An Essay on the Nature and Significance of Economic Science*. Though first published in 1932, his 1935 revision is a more comprehensive statement and will be the edition treated here. The marked contrast between the views of these two English economists makes Robbins's study a fitting starting point for our investigation of twentieth century methodological thought.

Robbins's Essay

In the opening chapters of Robbins's essay there is little that modern economists would view as controversial. Though his phrasing suggests an earlier period, many of his pronouncements ring a surprisingly familiar note. When one lists some of these, such as 'Economics is the science which studies human behavior as a relationship between ends and scarce means which have alternative uses',[2] or 'It follows that Economics is entirely neutral between ends; that, in so far as the achievement of *any* end is dependent on scarce means, it is germane to the preoccupations of the economist',[3] the source of the familiarity is revealed: these ideas form the substance of many opening chapters of contemporary introductory textbooks. Less conventional and consonant are his views on the status of what he calls 'the generalizations of economics'.

On the opening page of his work Robbins comments,

> The efforts of economists during the last hundred and fifty years have resulted in the establishment of a body of generalizations whose substantial accuracy and importance are open to question only by the ignorant or the perverse.[4]

Upon what foundations do these 'generalizations' rest? Taking as an example the concept that a price ceiling leads to an excess of demand over supply, Robbins asserts,

> It should not be necessary to spend much time showing that it cannot rest upon a mere appeal to "History". The frequent concomitance of certain phenomena in time may suggest a problem to be solved. It cannot by itself be taken to imply a definite causal relationship.[5]

Later he states, in reference to the same example,

> It is equally clear that our belief does not rest upon the results of controlled experiment. It is perfectly true that the particular case just mentioned has on more than one occasion been exemplified by the results of government carried out under conditions which might be held to bear some resemblance to the conditions of controlled experiment. But it would be very superficial to suppose that the results of these "experiments" can be held to justify a proposition of such wide applicability, let alone the central propositions of the general theory of value.[6]

If neither historical experience nor controlled experiment provides us with grounds for asserting the general propositions of economics, where then do such grounds exist? His answer is straightforward.

> The propositions of economic theory, like all scientific theory, are obviously deductions from a series of postulates. And the chief of these postulates are all assumptions involving in some way simple and indisputable facts of experience relating to the way in which the scarcity of goods which is the subject matter of our science actually shows itself in the world of reality. The main postulate of the theory of value is the fact that individuals can arrange their preferences in an order, and in fact do so. The main postulate of the theory of production is the fact that there are more than one factor of production. The main postulate of the theory of dynamics is the fact that we are not certain regarding future scarcities. These are not postulates the existence of whose counterpart in reality admits of extensive dispute once their nature is fully realized. We do not need controlled experiment to establish their validity: they are so much the stuff of our everyday experience that they have only to be stated to be recognized as obvious.[7]

These universally acknowledged facts of experience are combined with a number of subsidiary postulates (e.g. 'the condition of markets, the number of parties to the exchange, the state of the law . . .') to deduce the more complex applications of the theory.[8] In deference to historicists, he admits that these subsidiary assumptions are historico-relative, and notes that consequently great care must be taken in their application. The historicist claim that *all* the generalizations are historico-relative is rejected as unconvincing, and further, as politically motivated.[9] The 'behaviorist' claim that science should only deal with phenomena that are directly observable is also rejected, because the explanations which economists offer ultimately must refer to an individual's subjective valuation process, which is *understandable*, but not *observable*. Because of this, the procedures of a social science like economics 'can never be completely assimilated to the procedure of the physical sciences'.[10]

Robbins offers a coherent account of the status of terms used in economic theory: fundamental assumptions, which we know by immediate acquaintance, are combined with subsidiary hypotheses, which are varied and allow us to apply the theory to actual situations. But the fundamental assumptions mentioned (scarcity of goods, individual scales of valuation, the presence of more than one factor of production) do not include what is today considered perhaps *the* fundamental assumption: the assumption of rational conduct. Of what status is *homo economicus* in Robbins' system?

Robbins presents a detailed discussion of this point. He is quickly able to show that the conception of rational economic man does not imply psychological hedonism, nor that only money gains provides his motivation (the Smithian notion of net advantage is invoked), nor finally any notion of which actions are ethically appropriate.[11] Rationality does imply consistency in choice, however, in the sense that if A is preferred to B and B to C, A will be preferred to C. Is there any reason to believe that choice is always consistent? Robbins answers in the negative, providing examples of instances when choice may not be consistent. Thus he notes that means may be scarce in relation to ends, but the *ends* may be inconsistent; or, people may not know what the future holds, so may have to base their views on expectations; or again, people may not always understand the full implications of what they are doing. On the other hand, complete consistency in choice may itself be irrational if the time and attention required for it could be better used; in Robbins's delightful prose, 'the marginal utility of not bothering about marginal utility' may be a legitimate way to explain apparently inconsistent behavior.[12] Ultimately, Robbins asserts that the assumption of rational conduct, and with it the assumption of perfect foresight, are 'expository devices'; they are simplifying but unrealistic assumptions.

> The fact is, of course, that the assumption of perfect rationality in the sense of complete consistency is simply one of a number of assumptions of a psychological nature which are introduced into economic analysis at various stages of approximation to reality. The perfect foresight . . . is an assumption of a similar nature.
> . . .
> If this were commonly known, if it were generally realized that Economic Man is only an expository device – a first approximation used very cautiously at one stage in the development of arguments which, in their full development neither employ any such assumption nor demand it in any way for a justification of their procedure – it is improbable he would be such a universal bogey.[13]

Finally, Robbins examines the role of empirical studies in economics. Such studies attempt to give quantitative estimates of the scales of relative valuations existent at any given point in time. Any such studies may be of use for the short-term prediction of possible trends, but, and on this point he is adamant, they do not provide the grounds for discovering 'empirical laws'. Since this seems to be the goal of Wesley Mitchell and other practitioners of 'Quantitative Economics', he dismisses that work as futile. The proper uses of 'realistic' (empirical) studies are three in number: to check on the applicability of theoretical constructions to particular concrete situations, to suggest auxiliary postulates to be used with the fundamental generalizations, and to bring to light areas where pure theory can be reformulated or extended.[14] While the last of these seems to indicate a role for the empirical testing of theories, Robbins's emphasis is on the heuristic role of empirical studies, that of suggesting new problems for theory to solve.

Two final passages summarize Robbins's view of the nature and significance of economic inquiry, and provide a warning to future practitioners of the dismal science.

> By 'trying out' pure theory on concrete situations and referring back to pure theory residual difficulties, we may hope continually to improve and extend our analytic apparatus. But that such studies should enable us to say what goods must be economic goods and what precise values will be attached to them in different situations, is not to be expected. To say this is not to abandon the hope of solving any genuine problem of economics. It is merely to recognize what does not lie within the necessary boundaries of our subject matter.
> . . .
> Economists have nothing to lose by understating rather than overstating

the extent of their certainty. Indeed, it is only when this is done that the overwhelming power to convince of what remains can be expected to have free play.[15]

Lionel Robbins's methodological position may be restated as follows: The fundamental generalizations of economics are self-evident propositions about reality: ends are multiple and can be ordered; means and time are limited and capable of alternative application; knowledge of present and future opportunities may be incomplete or uncertain, so that expectations are important. To handle this last difficulty, the expository devices of rationality (consistency in choice) and perfect foresight are usually invoked as simplifying assumptions which are first approximations to reality. Finally, these basic postulates are combined with subsidiary postulates which reflect the actual conditions of the world to yield the applications of economic theory. Empirical studies are used to suggest plausible subsidiary postulates, and to check on the applicability of the theoretical framework to given situations. The collection of data to predict future constellations of valuations on the basis of past valuations may be of limited use in the short run, but it should not be imagined that such efforts will ever yield empirical 'laws' which share the necessity of the basic postulates.

We will see that all of these views will be challenged by Hutchison and other positivist economists. Before turning to Hutchison's critique, a few words must be said on the relation between Robbins and the 'Austrian' economists.

Robbins and the Austrians

Those familiar with the methodological views of Austrian economists will perceive a striking similarity between the writings of, say, Ludwig von Mises or Friedrich von Hayek, and the positions espoused by Robbins. The similarity is not illusory: Robbins had lectured in the 1920s at the Austrian Economic Society (Nationalökonomische Gesellschaft) in Vienna, which was founded by Mises, Hayek, Fritz Machlup, Oskar Morgenstern, and Hans Mayer; and Hayek taught the Austrian variant of marginalism at the London School of Economics in the 1930s. It thus comes as no surprise that Robbins should single out Mises, and in his second edition, Hayek, for special recognition for their contributions to his methodological monograph. Nor is it remarkable that Robbins's essay is replete with citations of Austrian contributors: reference to a Misesian interpretation of the causes of the business cycle; praise for Menger and Böhm-Bawerk who, unlike Gossen, Jevons, and Edgeworth ('to say nothing of their English followers'), avoided the error of linking value theory to psychological hedonism; reference to the marginal revolution as the 'Mengerian revolution', and so on.[16] I will not discuss here the extent to which the Austrian approach had entered into the corpus of English economic thinking prior to the upheavals wrought by Keynes and his followers. If Robbins's essay is representative of the prevailing methodological position of his time, the view that subjectivism and methodological individualism had entered the English economic orthodoxy of the early 1930s is supported.

Some may question why this study did not begin with one of the contributions of the Austrians. An obvious candidate is Mises's *Grundprobleme der Nationalökonomie* (first published in 1933; translated as *Epistemological Problems of Economics*, 1960), which Robbins approvingly cites in his second edition.[17] Contained in this early work is a rough explication of the 'science of human action' which would later emerge as the subject of Mises's monumental methodological treatise of the same name. However, much of Mises's early book is a *backward-looking* defense of praxeological thought, concerning itself with a critique of historicism and an analysis of the positions of Max Weber and other turn of the century social scientists. Robbins's essay was also selected because it quickly gained notoriety among English-speaking economists as an authoritative statement of the discipline's first principles, on a par with J. N. Keynes's earlier classic, *The Scope and Method of Political Economy* (1891).

Another pertinent question is why I have chosen not to affix some label to Robbins's position. Two which come to mind are rationalist and a priorist. Both are rejected, but for different reasons. The designation rationalist is easily dismissed for the simple reason that the term has different meanings in different contexts, and to apply it in yet another context would be no aid to clarity. A priorist may be somewhat less familiar to those untrained in philosophy; if novelty is a virtue, we could alternatively invoke Mises's still more obscure modifier, praxeological. There is precedence for such terms, in that both can be found in Mises's 1933 work. Furthermore, such economists as Robbins, Mises, Hayek, and Frank Knight all agreed that the fundamental axioms of economics are obvious and self-evident facts of immediate experience.

But all did not agree with Mises's particular (and perhaps peculiar) vision that economic science is praxeological, that the basic postulates of the discipline are necessary and unquestionable truths about the human condition; that the status of the fundamental axioms is that of synthetic statements that are a priori true. Nowhere in Robbins's essay can one find the term 'a priori'. And though he states that no one will deny the universal acceptability of the fundamental generalizations, he also admits that 'there may be room for dispute as to the best mode of describing their exact logical status'.[18] Frank Knight, in a bellicose review of Hutchison's work, argues in his critique that the 'basic postulates' of economics are known to us 'intuitively', but goes on to say that 'we neither know them a priori nor by one-sided deduction from data of sense observation'.[19] And Hayek, who also wrote extensively in the area of methodology, chose to treat the 'dangers of scientism' rather than analyze the logical status of the fundamental postulates. It may finally be mentioned that no unanimity exists today among later generations of Austrians regarding the status of those postulates.[20]

I might further add that a recent attempt to lump the Austrians, Robbins, and all of the nineteenth century writers on economic methodology under the common heading 'verificationist' is even less satisfactory for at least two reasons.

First, the choice of the term verificationist is unfortunate, since it is open to many interpretations. Within the philosophy of science, the verificationists were that small group within the Vienna Circle who believed that a sentence was cognitively meaningful if and only if it was capable, at least in principle, of complete verification by observational evidence. This criterion of cognitive significance was rejected by Carnap, Ayer, and other logical empiricists by the mid-1930s. Among economists, Machlup is one who discussed 'the verification problem', which for him referred to the question of whether the assumptions of economic theory (in particular the motivational assumption of maximizing behavior) need be independently testable and tested (He answered no). For Mark Blaug, verificationists include those economists who 'continually warned their readers that the verification of economic predictions was at best a hazardous enterprise' and who believed 'the purpose of verifying implications was to determine the applicability of economic reasoning and not really its validity'.[21] It seems strange that those who believe verification to be a 'hazardous enterprise' should be labeled verificationists, but even this aside, there is little consistency in his essay regarding usage of the terms verification, verificationist, and verifiability.[22]

Even more important, it would seem to reflect a certain modern-day chauvinism to lump together a diverse group of thinkers from earlier times simply because none of their writings endorse methodological principles which are dominant today. Senior, J. S. Mill, Cairnes, J. N. Keynes, Robbins, Knight, and the modern

Austrians take vastly different approaches to their subjects. They are alike on one point, however: none of them recommended that economists try to falsify their theories by subjecting them to empirical test. Their common ground, then, is that they failed to adhere to the language and intent of Popperian falsificationism. While that failure undoubtedly means that they are terribly out of step with current scientific thinking, it is no justification for lumping them all together as if no differences existed among them.

There is a further point. Later in this chapter it is suggested that Popper's methodological falsificationism may not be an applicable method for a social science like economics. If that controversial claim was ever established, economists might be interested in investigating in more detail the arguments made by methodologists who did not embrace falsificationism. The differences among such analyses would then have to be considered more significant than their similarity regarding falsificationism.

To return to our point of departure: There seems little to be gained by grouping together the methodological views of such diverse thinkers under the common labels of verificationist, a priorist, praxeological, etc. Such identifying procedures in this case do little to aid clear thinking. To simply note that Robbins's position contains elements of subjectivism, methodological individualism, and the belief that the basic postulates of economics are self-evident may be less concise than affixing a label to his views, but is also more accurate descriptively.

Hutchison's Introduction of Positivism

After completing his studies at Cambridge, Terence Hutchison served as a lecturer from 1935 to 1938 at the University of Bonn, Germany. While there, he studied the writings of members of the Vienna Circle, as well as those of other like-minded philosophers and scientists. Their proposals for constructing an objective and value-free foundation for the various sciences found a sympathetic reader in Hutchison. The necessity of making the sciences truly 'scientific' was not just a casual point for discussion among academics of the time. Indeed, the nationalistic hysteria, the sinister cult of irrationalism and power that was Hitler's Germany was reaching its apex as the young English economist pursued his studies, and it lent his work a certain urgency. The fruit of his labors was his 1938 volume, *The Significance and Basic Postulates of Economic Theory*. Though Hutchison does not specifically single out Robbins as the target of his criticisms, his book can be read as a point by point critique of Robbins's 'pseudo-scientific' methodology. Four points of criticism are treated here: the 'emptiness' of the 'propositions of pure theory'; the necessity of the assumption of 'perfect expectation' for the rationality postulate; the necessity of more extensive use of empirical techniques in economics; and the illegitimacy of using the 'psychological method' (or introspection) as grounds for asserting the fundamental postulates.

Hutchison states the goal of his book early on: it is not to engage in the old philosophical debates on methods which dominated economic methodology in years past, but to search for and make clear the foundations of modern economic theory. In order to do this, we must first realize that economics is a science, and as such it must appeal to fact; otherwise, we are engaging in 'pseudo-science'. What sets apart the empirical propositions of science from those of other intellectual endeavors is their testability, the fact that their truth or falsity must 'make a difference'.

> (I)f the finished propositions of a science, as against the accessory purely logical or mathematical propositions used in many sciences, including Economics, are to have any empirical content, as the finished propositions of all sciences except of Logic and Mathematics obviously must have, then these propositions must *conceivably* be capable of empirical testing *or be reducible to such propositions* by logical or mathematical deduction. They need not, that is, actually be tested or even be *practically* capable of testing under present or future technical conditions or conditions of statistical investigation, nor is there any sense in talking of some kind of 'absolute' test which will 'finally' decide whether a proposition is 'absolutely' true or false. But it must be possible to indicate inter-subjectively what is the case if they are true or false: their truth or falsity, that is, must make some conceivable empirically noticeable difference, or some such difference must be directly deducible therefrom.[23]

Having presented this principle for distinguishing the statements of empirical science from all others, we may now inquire as to the status of the propositions of pure economic theory. Hutchison posits three possible categories into which fall all the propositions encountered in economics. The first contains all statements having the form 'if p then q' in which q follows p by logical necessity; that is, q may be inferred deductively from p. In this category lie all propositions of pure theory. The next group of propositions follows the pattern 'since p then q'; in these cases, p is asserted empirically as true. To distinguish these 'propositions of applied theory' from their pure theory counterparts, we may note simply that 'in "propositions of pure theory" no empirical assertion as to the truth of p or q individually is made'.[24] This has the interesting implication that 'propositions of pure theory are independent of all facts, which can be of any conceivable kind without their consistency being affected'.[25] The third kind of proposition is that which makes inductive inferences; that is, 'if p then q' is asserted but is conceivably falsifiable, even if such falsification would be 'miraculous'.[26]

Hutchison next notes that science contains statements which are either conceivably falsifiable by empirical observation or are not. Those which are not so falsifiable are tautologies, and are thus devoid of empirical content. It follows, then, that the propositions of pure theory have no empirical content.

> The price of unconditional necessity and certainty of propositions of pure logic and mathematics (and of propositions of pure theory) is, therefore, complete lack of empirical content.[27]

The primary reason why the propositions of pure theory have no empirical content is that they are posed in the form of deductive inferences. In addition, two secondary arguments are advanced. First, while the postulates of pure theory seem to refer to real objects, they in fact are only 'relations between definitions – a "fact" of linguistic usage, if one likes'.[28] And second, the widespread use of the ceteris paribus clause robs even those propositions which may be making empirical claims of all empirical content.

> The ceteris paribus assumption makes out of an empirical proposition that is concerned with facts, and therefore conceivably can be false, a necessary analytical-tautological proposition. For a mathematical solution (by tautological transformation) the number of equations must be equal to the number of unknowns. The ceteris paribus assumption sweeps all the unknowns together under one portmanteau assumption for a logical "solution".
>
> . . .
>
> We suggest that the ceteris paribus assumption can only be safely and significantly used in conjunction with an empirical generalization verified as true in a large percentage of cases but occasionally liable to exceptions of a clearly describable type.[29]

Given that we have proven our case that the propositions of pure theory have no empirical content, we should not therefore imagine that they are of no use. Though they cannot tell us anything new about the world, they can call our attention to implications of our definitions and offer us a 'sharp clear-cut language' with which to approach the problems of economics. They also enable us to pass from one empirical synthetic statement, if asserted as true, to another.[30] Thus, though they are devoid of empirical content, the propositions of pure theory serve a pragmatic purpose in economic science.

The next topic which Hutchison takes up is an examination of the 'basic postulates' of economic science. He asserts correctly that scarcity alone is insufficient for establishing the rest of the deductions of economic theory, which also requires postulates concerning rational conduct, expectations, and equilibrium. In his analysis of these other postulates, Hutchison argues that the 'fundamental assumption' of maximizing behavior as well as the concept of market equilibrium are stripped of their force and significance unless they are accompanied by a further assumption of 'perfect expectation', and that the truth of this last assumption is certainly open to question.

The 'fundamental principle' of economic theory is that all agents maximize: households (or individuals) maximize utility, firms maximize profits. But our theory does not tell us *how* to maximize; rather, it assumes that agents not only strive to reach a maximum position, but are aware of how to reach it. Regarding this fundamental principle, then, our theory simply says 'it is "rational", "sensible", or "natural" to do this, assuming, presumably, that one knows how this can be done'.[31] But to make the assumption that one knows how to maximize requires that the maximizing agent has full information concerning both current and future prices, incomes, and tastes: what Hutchison calls 'perfect expectation'. This is clearly seldom the case in the real world, where the best one can do is to attempt to maximize 'expected returns'. Once one leaves the world of perfect expectations, error becomes possible.

> When an investor is called "stupid" or "irrational" it is not usually meant that the investor in question was deliberately aiming at less than the maximum return open to him, but that it was "stupid" of him to *expect* that he would maximize his returns that way.[32]

Note that neither 'correct' nor 'undisappointed' expectations are sufficient to guarantee a maximum position: they must be perfect.

> "Perfect", "correct", and "undisappointed" expectations appear often to have been used more or less interchangeably as a necessary or even defining characteristic of equilibrium. But in quite ordinary senses of the words, "undisappointed" expectations may well not have been "correct", and "correct" expectations may well not have been "perfect".
> . . .
> (I)f expectations are not perfect it is quite possible for someone to be in his maximum position, not to realize it, be disappointed, and change.[33]

Thus the maximization principle which postulates that agents want to and will be able to reach some sort of constrained maximum position is based on the wholly unrealistic assumption that expectations are perfect. The major problem encountered by agents in the real world is how to make rational decisions in the face of uncertainty; the neoclassical solution assumes away the crux of the problem by positing perfect expectations.

How might we improve on this state of affairs? Hutchison rejects the attempts of certain economists, who speak of approximately rational behavior or of 'tendencies towards equilibrium', as apologetic. He also rejects the 'optimistic approach', which attempts to search for more 'realistic' assumptions, for two reasons.

> First, if one is going to revise the former assumptions – whatever they were – in favor of assumptions more nearly decriptive of the economic life of a contemporary community, how is one to find out, without the most extensive statistical investigations, precisely what these assumptions are? . . . But then the second question arises: Given that the statisticians have furnished one with the answers, is there any reason at all for supposing that the assumptions will yield any significant chain of deductive conclusions? The postulates of the equilibrium system were specially chosen for their "tractability" . . . Why should the more realistic postulates continue to be tractable?[34]

The solution which Hutchison himself chooses is the empirical investigation, over a wide range of possible conditions, of individual economic behavior, to see exactly how people actually form their expectations.

> Whether and to what extent entrepreneurs behave "competitively" or "monopolistically", whether and to what extent people's decisions are dominated by present as against the whole expected future course of prices; to what extent people's economic actions are taken on the spur of the moment, or according to detailed plan; how far people come to any particular expectation at all or act unreflectingly according to habit; to what extent people learn from past economic mistakes and disappointments; how and to what extent people behave in any way one chooses to call rational – are questions which cannot be assured by any general "Fundamental Assumption" or "Principle". Although in some cases rough a priori reasoning may yield results which turn out fairly accurately when tested, ultimately all such questions as these can only be decided satisfactorily by extensive empirical investigation of each question individually.[35]

As the quotation above suggests, Hutchison believes that empirical investigations should be given a prominent role in economics; indeed, his work is permeated with the notions of empirical tests of hypotheses and of the generation of empirical laws. His invocation of the analytic–synthetic distinction for distinguishing the 'finished propositions of science' from pseudo-scientific speculation rests on his ability to conceivably test those propositions. While many economists believe that 'propositions of pure theory' constitute the laws of economics, Hutchison rejects that idea and offers a definition of scientific law which he feels is more consistent with definitions in other scientific disciplines.

> By apparently all other scientists apart from logicians, mathematicians, and many economists, scientific laws are regarded as inductive inferences *conceivably falsifiable*, though not *practically falsified*, empirically.
> . . .
> We suggest that the term "law" should be reserved only for those empirical generalizations such as Pareto's or Gresham's law or the law of diminishing returns, or diminishing marginal utility. *It is such laws as these that it is the central object of science to discover.* (emphasis added)[36]

As against Robbins's view that empirical studies should be primarily used to investigate when and where the postulates of economics are *applicable*, Hutchison argues that 'the applicability of pure theory to the facts of the world requires just those empirical regularities which are the basis for prognoses'.[37] Thus the search for empirical regularities which Robbins considered so useless is embraced by his positivist adversary.

The final topic mentioned here is Hutchison's treatment of the 'psychological method'. He notes first that no small confusion has been generated by the casual usage among economists of the terms psychological method of a priori facts, method of verstehen, and method of introspection. It is not clear what such phrases mean, nor is it evident how these methods are to be applied. Hutchison grants that such methods (however they are defined) may be useful for *suggesting* testable, scientific hypotheses, but they cannot be used to establish them, for two related reasons. First, introspection by definition deals with one person, so cannot be generalized. And second, if a scientist nevertheless attempts to generalize beyond one person (himself), he must at least try to confirm the generalization by asking others about their attitudes. But such reports may be suspect; psychologists after all 'warn against people's own too facile accounts and explanations of themselves as being infected with self-justifying "rationalizations"'.[38] Introspection then is not to be considered a rival of the empirical method; its usefulness lies on a totally different plane.

Philosophical Evaluation

How successful is Hutchison's assault on its predecessor? In order to assess its merits, we must place his position in relation to the philosophy of science that was contemporaneous with it. This is not difficult, for Hutchison all but explicitly embraces positivism in his monograph: his frequent references to the writings of members of the Vienna Circle; his advocacy of a demarcation principle for distinguishing between scientific and speculative propositions; his call for more empirical studies in economics – all of these indicate his support for a positivist approach to the dismal science. Indeed, his qualification that propositions need only be conceivably testable or reducible to such testable statements indicates that he is aware of and has done his best to avoid a mistake made by some of the Vienna Circle positivists, who insisted on the direct testing of non-analytic statements.

While it is easy to identify Hutchison's positivist leanings, the extent to which his stated position is an accurate account of positivism is another question, and one that requires a short review of the issues. Hutchison's view that nonanalytic propositions need only be conceivably testable or reducible to other testable propositions suggests that certain statements made in science are not directly testable. As Carnap and others realized by the mid-1930s, most sciences employ statements containing 'theoretical terms' which may not be explicitly definable in an empirical 'observation language'. There was no consensus on the status of such terms (in terms of the analytic–synthetic distinction) in the mid-1930s: though they are of obvious use to scientists (a point readily admitted by Hutchison), their failure to admit of explicit definition renders their status ambiguous. As was noted in Chapter 3, later positivists advanced a solution to this problem which allowed 'partial definition' of such statements in terms of 'interpretative systems' or 'dictionaries' such that 'a theoretical statement of a certain kind is true if and only if a corresponding empirical statement of a specified kind is true'.[39] By this solution, the problem of the status of theoretical terms (at least in terms of the analytic–synthetic distinction) is not only circumvented but is reduced to a non-problem. This was Hempel's point when he asserted that, 'the analytic–synthetic distinction . . . has lost its promise and fertility as an explicandum'.[40] But these ideas were not fully formulated until the 1940s and 1950s, so the question of how one was to regard the axioms and postulates of a theoretical science like economics was still an open one when Hutchison wrote in the late 1930s. His solution was to argue that the basic postulates of economics are, for a variety of reasons, necessarily analytic and devoid of empirical content. His argument requires further examination.

Hutchison first examines the formal structure of theories. He states that pure economic theory consists of a series of deductions from basic postulates, and that the deductive form of these arguments establishes their analyticity. Next, he argues that the terms used in such a deductive framework are only logical categories, and thus do not make reference to real objects. Neither argument establishes lack of empirical content. It is perfectly correct that the various components of neoclassical economic theory form a hypothetico-deductive system. It is also true that until some statements or terms within that system are given empirical counterparts, it is nothing more than an empty, mechanical calculus, and such words as, say, savings, capital, and cost (to use some of Hutchison's examples) have no empirical meaning. But clearly, the question of empirical content can only be raised once some of the terms of the theory are given empirical interpretation: an interpretation into the observation language, if one prefers. Note that every term need not have an explicit empirical definition, as long as certain terms (and these are usually contained in 'theorems' or 'derived sentences' rather than 'axioms' or 'postulates') are expressible empirically. These deductions are the predictions of the theory, and they can be tested against reality, which ensures that the theory *as a whole* meets the testability criterion, even if this is not true of all of its parts.

Hutchison's mistake is easier to perceive when we look at certain similar ideas in the field of logic. A major task of deductive logic is to inspect deductive arguments to determine whether they are valid or invalid. A deductive argument is a group of propositions of which one (the conclusion) is claimed to follow from the others (the premises) with absolute necessity. The sentences that comprise the premises and conclusion may be true or false, but it is important that this is wholly independent of the validity or invalidity of the arguments. Validity and invalidity are properties of arguments; truth and falsity are properties of statements. To illustrate, the following two arguments are of the same form, and both are valid, but one contains true propositions only, while the other contains false propositions only.

All men are mammals.	All flounders are mammals.
All mammals have hearts.	All mammals have wings.
Therefore all men have hearts.	Therefore all flounders have wings.

Thus, the validity of an argument does not guarantee the truth of the conclusion.

Neither does an invalid argument necessarily have a false conclusion. The following argument has a true conclusion, but it is invalid nonetheless.

> If I were the President then I would be famous.
> I am not the President.
> Therefore I am not famous.

(One can establish that the above argument is invalid by substituting 'Milton Friedman' for 'I'. If the premises are true and the conclusion is false, the argument is invalid.) Finally, false conclusions mean that either the argument is invalid or at least one of the premises is false, or both. If an argument is valid and all the premises are true, however, the conclusion *must* be true.[41]

While the distinctions made above are the beginning principles of logic, they are easily confused in more casual discourse. Hutchison seems to have made a mistake of this sort in maintaining that the deductive form of a theory establishes that it is analytic. Economic theory does form a hypothetico-deductive system whose 'form' is presumably 'valid', though scientists usually prefer to use the term 'logically consistent' in discussing that aspect of theories, since theories are often expressed in mathematical form. But the empirical content of a theory is quite independent of its logical consistency, depending instead on whether a theory is testable. Most important for this discussion, it is only after the testability of a hypothetico-deductive system has been established that it gains empirical content, and its statements become 'synthetic'. (Note that the *results* of testing, i.e. the confirmation or disconfirmation of theories, determines the *acceptability* of theories, but *not* their empirical content, which depends on testability.) All of this has been nicely put by Alexander Rosenberg, a philosopher who recently attempted an analysis of the terms of microeconomic theory.

> merely because one proposition is deducible from a second, the first is not thereby analytic, even if the second is assumed to be true. . . Of course, the conditional formed by the assumptions of microeconomics is analytic, but from this it does not at all follow that the implications themselves are analytic.[42]

Hutchison's third argument concerns the ceteris paribus clause: he claims that the irresponsible use of that clause renders the predictions of microeconomic theory effectively unfalsifiable. His point is well taken: if economists consistently respond that 'ceteris is not paribus' in order to save their theories from refuting instances, then those theories do become unfalsifiable. This does not imply that they are therefore necessarily analytic: while analyticity implies unfalsifiability, the converse is not necessarily implied. If Hutchison were to drop the accusation of analyticity and argue instead only unfalsifiability, perhaps his case could be made. He would then have to show that economists consistently 'save their theories' by invoking changes in the ceteris paribus conditions.

To summarize: Neither the deductive nature of microeconomic theory nor the existence of a ceteris paribus clause is sufficient to establish the analyticity of the statements of economic theory, though a misuse of the latter can immunize a theory from criticism. Part of the problem is little more than semantic. A more significant philosophical point here (and one which Hutchison did not directly address) is that there is no way to establish analyticity or syntheticity if we allow some terms to be only partially definable in terms of observables, which we certainly must do in science. Luckily, not long afterward it was shown in the philosophy of science that the analytic–synthetic distinction was problematical for analyzing theories in science, and few economists have employed it as an explanatory device since Hutchison. Given the general acceptance of that distinction at the time Hutchison first wrote, however, he should not be judged too harshly for his bold and innovative effort to prove the analyticity of 'the postulates of pure economic theory'.

We have shown that Hutchison's attempt to establish the analyticity of the fundamental generalizations of economic theory was unsuccessful. But what of some of his other proposals: for example, that economists should search for 'conceivably falsifiable, though not practically falsified' empirical generalizations or laws; that various aspects of economic behavior be empirically investigated; and that economists abandon the psychological method or method of introspection as means for evaluating or justifying their theories? These principles and practices advocated by Hutchison were to meet with nearly universal approval among economists in succeeding decades. Why were economists so eager to embrace the tenets of positivism?

The movement toward positivism was *not* the result of any expressly methodological treatises; Hutchison's book did not *cause* the mathematization and quantification of economic theory. Methodological works taken alone seldom change the minds of readers, their purpose instead is to *confirm* changes that are already in motion. Occasionally, a methodologist may even *anticipate* future alternative directions of scientific investigation. But of course, had the changes not taken place, the scribblings of men like Hutchison would seem as otiose and peculiar to us as those of a Veblen or Mises must seem to a convinced positivist.

What sorts of changes were taking place within the discipline? Some were purely technical: the collection of economic statistics, first by the NBER, and later by a growing number of private and governmental agencies; the development of linear programming and operations research during the Second World War, as well as the continuing progress in statistical and econometric techniques; the fruitful mathematization of consumer theory by Hicks and Allen, and its further development in Samuelson's revealed preference approach, both of which added rigor, generality, and apparently allowed the statement of 'operationally meaningful theorems'. Major conceptual innovations also took place, the most prominent among these being in the fields of monetary and macro-theory, welfare economics, and, later, in theories of economic growth. The new emphasis on hypothesis testing fit in well with the growth of applied fields in economics, where such testing was proligate. The apparent rigor and analytic clarity that was a hallmark of such developments seemed also to justify the belief that economics was becoming a more objective, scientific, and value-free discipline. In sharp contrast to such progress were the vague utterances of older, 'literary' economists, whose ignorance of more advanced techniques caused them often to appear simply as defensive apologists of an earlier time. Finally, the policies implied in the Keynesian revolution, and later investigations (both theoretical and empirical) of market failures and externalities, were far more interventionist than were earlier policies. The opposition (who at this point did not yet include any 'positivist' economists – Friedman was to change that in the 1950s), who disdained quantification and testing and who obstinately clung to such outdated notions as subjectivism, intro-spection, and a priori true synthetic statements, could only be viewed as dogmatic and anachronistic defenders of free markets. How could such ideologues be taken seriously when their funda-mental categories were supposed to be intuitively obvious, nontestable facts of nature: such constructs, after all, had been ruled out as metaphysical early on in the postivist program.

To go beyond the sketchy generalities outlined above would take us far afield – indeed, the exact nature and meaning of the transitions which took place in theory and technique in the 1930s is a matter on which discord rather than consensus currently seems to be growing.[43] Leaving this subject to the historians, we can mention in closing, however, one last point about the impact of Hutchison's essay. Robbins had differentiated between the 'fundamental generalizations' of economics (scarcity, more than one factor of production, scales of relative valuation, and uncertainty of future supplies) and the 'expository devices' of rational conduct and perfect expectation. Hutchison changed all this by placing the construct of the rational, maximizing economic agent who operates with full and perfect information on center stage: this construct, in his mind, is the 'fundamental assumption' of economic theory. The status and importance of this 'unrealistic' assumption, its role in economic theory, and the nature of its testing are questions that were to dominate economic methodological debate in the 1950s. That debate will be the subject of our next chapter.

The Austrian Revival

There has been a revival of interest in Austrian economics in the last ten years by a small but growing group of economists. The modern Austrian 'research program' is many-faceted. It is in part a doctrinal exegesis of the masters. Besides the obvious value of such work to historians of thought, some of it also sheds light on certain modern debates (e.g. in capital theory), as well as suggests that certain early Austrians (in particular, Hayek) were as aware of the problems of expectations, costly information, and knowledge dissemination as the revisionist Keynesians claim that Keynes was. Another aspect of their program is the reintroduction of a thoroughly subjectivist viewpoint into economics, and the tracing out of the implications of that reintroduction in such fields as consumer and demand theory and the theory of costs. Other work has focused on the crucial role of the entrepreneur in a market economy, and the development of the notion of market process to replace the idea of market equilibrium. (This latter has some affinity with the work of disequilibrium theorists, whose inability to rigorously model their ideas seems to have tarnished their credibility within the mainstream of macro-theorizing.) Some modern Austrian economists have even entered into such utterly non-Austrian research areas as macroeconomics – witness Roger Garrison's translation of Misesian business cycle theory into the IS-LM framework. Finally, and probably least accessible to the lay economist, are the forays of the Austrians into such areas as jurisprudence, ethics, history, and natural law philosophy, exercises that follow the lead provided by, in particular, Hayek, whose recently completed trilogy *Law, Legislation and Liberty* is considered seminal.[44]

The observation that it will take time to assess the impact of the Austrian revival is as true as it is banal. Their emphases on process, information, error, and subjectivism may appeal to those economists who are unsure that mathematical equilibrium models (be they static or dynamic, partial or general equilibria) are adequate to the many tasks that the profession faces. On the other hand, many economists will balk at certain of the Austrian claims, and perhaps one of the least palatable of these involves the peculiar methodological position that has come to be associated with Austrian economics in general. I refer, of course, to praxeology, the position that the categories of economics, as the science of human action, can be verbally deduced from a relatively few axioms of the human condition which are known to us a priori as true. This claim is painstakingly developed in Mises's lengthy 1949 treatise, *Human Action*; a briefer and more manageable presentation can be found in his *The Ultimate Foundations of Economic Science* (1962). Two implications of the praxeological approach that most economists would find noxious, if not laughable, are that empirical tests of hypotheses are irrelevant, since only a mistake in logic (and only 'verbal logic' is permissible) could yield false conclusions from a priori true premises, and that econometric studies contain nothing more than 'recent economic history'.

Many modern Austrians are lukewarm toward Mises's claims. Outside of the Austrian camp, however, praxeology is often attacked as *the* Austrian methodological position.[45] Mark Blaug considers the methodological claims of the Austrians 'a travesty', and finds 'Mises' statements of radical a priorism . . . so uncompromising that they have to be read to be believed'. He wonders aloud how anyone could take seriously Mises's 'cranky and idiosyncratic' writings on the foundations of economic science, and approvingly cites Samuelson, who once stated that he 'trembled for the reputation' of his subject when he read the 'exaggerated claims' made by the likes of, not only Mises, but Menger, Robbins, and the disciples of Knight, as well.[46]

Blaug presumably is engaged in rhetorical excess in these passages, but his unabashed abhorrence of the Misesian methodological position is not altogether uncommon. What are the reasons behind this almost anti-scientific response to praxeology? There is, of course, a practical concern: the human capital of most economists would be drastically reduced (or made obsolete) were praxeology operationalized throughout the discipline. But the principal reason for rejecting Misesian methodology is not so self-serving. Simply put, the preoccupation of praxeologists with the 'ultimate foundations' of economics must seem mindless, if not perverse, to economists who dutifully learned their methodology from Friedman and who therefore are confident that assumptions do not matter and that prediction is the key. When it is further mentioned that many modern Austrians are extremists in their faith in the beneficence of the market, it becomes easier to dismiss the entirety of Austrian thought as dogmatic and reactionary.

Regardless of its origins, such a reaction is itself dogmatic and, at its core, anti-scientific. In what remains of this chapter, this position will be defended by arguing that (1) many of the usual complaints against praxeology, so often considered to be conclusive, are anticipated and answered by Mises, and thus must be considered at this point inadequate, and (2) those that remain fail to take into account that the epistemological and methodological foundations of Austrian and neoclassical economics differ. The alleged basis of the standard approach, Popper's methodological falsificationism, is then critically examined. The chapter ends with an outline of how a nondogmatic critique of Misesian methodology might look. For ease of exposition, the terms 'praxeology' and 'Austrian methodology' will be used interchangeably. What follows applies only to Mises's position, however, so my loose usage of terms should not be taken to imply that all Austrians adhere to the praxeological position (see note 45).

The Inadequacy of the Usual Attacks on Austrian Methodology

1. Since few economists have studied the Austrian position, and even fewer have taken it seriously, it is not surprising that few serious critiques of it are to be found in the literature.[47] Future critics might begin by examining the first seven chapters of *Human Action*, in which the epistemological and methodological claims of praxeology are laid out. These chapters constitute a study in meticulous argumentation, and critics who have not thoroughly immersed themselves in the system are likely to miss the subtleties to be found there, with the result that they will at best only caricature the praxeological position. I list below some typical objections to Mises's system, with his responses to them.

Some may object that the praxeological postulate that 'all action is rational' is, at best, naively simplistic, and at worst, patently false. But we find that in Mises's system all action is rational because all action is *by definition* purposeful.[48] Simply put, rational and action define each other; the opposite of rational behavior is *not* irrational behavior but 'a reactive response to stimuli on the part of bodily organs and instincts which cannot be controlled by the volition of the person concerned.'[49] Now this definition of action and rational may appear strange to us, and perhaps not accord with common usage, but the same may be said of the neoclassical definition of rationality: all of us have argued with students who insist that rationality must mean more than transitivity in choice over a well-ordered preference function. In any case, the statement that 'all action is rational' is definitional within the praxeological system, and should be understood as such.

Some might object that habitual behavior must not be rational. But since habitual behavior still involves choice, it must again be rational by definition. What about an individual whose choices diverge from his scale of relative valuation, is not he irrational? The answer is no, because the *act* of choice *reveals* values, so that choices made cannot diverge from the chooser's preferences.[50]

One could go on and on. The point is that many of the methodological claims advanced by Mises that sound ludicrous and fantastic on first hearing become less controversial when they are placed in context. There are indeed certain substantial differences between the methodological views of the Austrians and other, more orthodox approaches; I take them up next. But it is simply poor scholarship to dismiss a position ex cathedra by citing certain apparently nonsensical statements out of context, then finding those who spoke them guilty of issuing incomprehensible pronouncements.

2. Perhaps the most significant disagreement between the Austrians and mainstream economists concerns the importance of hypothesis testing. We remember that positivists would not even consider a statement meaningful unless it was testable; and Popper embraced falsifiability as the criterion for distinguishing scientific from nonscientific statements. As is shown in succeeding chapters, there have been many disagreements among economists about just what it means for economics to be a positive science, but most agree that the testing of hypotheses must play some role. Neither the testing of the assumptions of a hypothesis, nor the comparison of its implications, or predictions, with the data, are considered useful by praxeologists. How are these strange notions justified?

It should be noted immediately that many economists do not consider the independent testing of the assumptions of a theory to be a useful exercise. But few of these would agree with the Austrian position that such testing is unnecessary because the postulates or axioms of the science of economics are known to be true with apodictic certainty, that is, they are a priori true. This assertion is defended by the claim that the axioms refer to the logical categories of the mind; to understand them, or even talk about their existence, presupposes their existence.

> If we qualify a concept or proposition as a priori, we want to say: first, that the negation of what it asserts is unthinkable for the human mind and appears to it as nonsense; secondly, that this a priori concept or proposition is necessarily implied in our mental approach to all the problems concerned. . .

The animals too are equipped with senses; some of them are even capable of sensing stimuli that do not affect man's senses. What prevents them from taking advantage of what their senses convey to them, in the way man does, is not an inferiority of their sense equipment, but the fact that they lack what is called the human mind with its logical structure, its a priori categories.[51]

Examples of praxeological axioms are causality and teleology; that action takes place through time and that knowledge of the future is uncertain are related theorems.

According to the analytic–synthetic distinction, a priori true statements (true, analytic statements) are considered cognitively significant but empirically empty. Mises rejects this approach, which he correctly attributes to the logical positivists, and takes a Kantian perspective in arguing that the axioms of praxeology, because they involve necessary categories of the mind, are both a priori true yet empirically meaningful.

Apriorist reasoning is purely conceptual and deductive. It cannot produce anything else but tautologies and analytic judgements. All its implications are logically derived from the premises and were already contained in them. Hence, according to a popular objection, it cannot add anything to our knowledge.

All geometrical theorems are already implied in the axioms. The concept of a rectangular triangle already implies the theorem of Pythagoras. This theorem is a tautology, its deduction results in an analytic judgement. Nonetheless nobody would contend that geometry in general and the theorem of Pythagoras in particular do not enlarge our knowledge.[52]

If, in the broad sense, the axioms of praxeology are radically empirical, they are far from the post-Humean empiricism that pervades the modern methodology of social science. In addition to the foregoing considerations, (1) they are so broadly based in common human experience that once enunciated they become self-evident and hence do not meet the fashionable criterion of "falsifiability"; (2) they rest, particularly the action axiom, on universal inner experience, as well as on external experience, that is, the evidence is reflective rather than purely physical; and (3) they are therefore a priori to the complex historical events to which modern empiricism confines the concept of "experience".[53]

The theorems attained by correct praxeological reasoning are not only perfectly certain and incontestable, like the correct mathematical theorems. They refer, moreover, with the full rigidity of their apodictic certainty and incontestability to the reality of action as it appears in life and history. Praxeology conveys exact and precise knowledge of real things.[54]

One source of the divisions between Mises and his critics should now be evident. Since the Vienna Circle, most approaches to the status of knowledge claims have asserted that the analytic–synthetic distinction has at least some merit; that even if the dividing line between the two was not clear, a distinction should be made between definitional and tautological statements, on the one hand, and synthetic, testable, and potentially falsifiable statements, on the other. Praxeology rejects this approach as wrong-headed. The discussion is raised above the methodological plane to the epistemological.

I will not attempt to discuss epistemological debates here, though it can be conjectured that the fact that Mises's system is based on epistemological claims which run contrary to positivism is one reason, and perhaps the most prominent one, why many economists find his position unintelligible. Even economists unschooled in methodology proper have inculcated, by nature of their training, the positivist notion of testing knowledge claims.

It is equally important to stress that the Austrian position is not damaged by arguments which simply point out that there is no such thing as a statement that is both true a priori and empirically meaningful. Of course there is no such thing, *if* one accepts the positivist analytic–synthetic distinction. But Mises not only rejects the distinction, he offers arguments against it. Whether one is convinced by those arguments is a separate matter. But clearly, the invocation of positivist tenets in the defense of that doctrine against the attacks of an expressly anti-positivist alternative is hardly convincing argumentation.

Hypotheses may also be tested by comparing their predictions with the data; indeed, this sort of testing enjoys more widespread support among economists than does the testing of assumptions. Do Austrians accept this second type of testing?

Before answering, it is worth emphasizing that the word 'prediction' is used by economists to denote many activities. Two of the most important of these are forecasting and hypothesis testing. Forecasting occurs when trends in a body of data are extrapolated into the future. While Austrians acknowledge that forecasts can have practical importance, they emphasize that such extrapolations are not based on universal economic laws. They are nothing more than summaries (with projections) of certain recent statistical regularities; this is why Austrians view econometric studies as little more than 'recent economic history'. While forecasting has some use, it is not the ultimate goal of economic science. (When

Austrians talk about the goals of economic science, they often claim that social science attempts to explain how purposeful human action can generate unintended consequences through social interaction, a notion first enunciated by Menger, and extended by Hayek.[55])

Prediction as a means of testing hypotheses is also rejected by the Austrians, on a number of grounds. First, it is argued that such testing is unnecessary, since the only way a false conclusion (prediction) can be generated in a system in which consequences are deduced from a priori true premises is if a mistake is made in the verbal chain of logic leading from premises to conclusions. Those interested in evaluating Austrian theories should focus on the verbal chain of logic rather than on the predictions of the theory.

This argument by itself is insufficient to establish the Austrian claim, since one way to discover whether the chain of logic requires checking is to see if it leads to predictions that are disconfirmed by evidence. Additional arguments offered indicate that the Austrians view the predictions of their theories in a unique way: they are admittedly unfalsifiable.

One reason that it is senseless to try to falsify economic theories is that there are no 'constants' in the social world equivalent to those encountered in the natural sciences. There are regularities, but they are not derivable from universal economic laws. In addition, 'there is an indeterminacy and unpredictability inherent in human preferences, human expectations, and human knowledge' which prohibit economists from predicting behaviour accurately in every instance.[56] Praxeologists thus reiterate the views expressed by Robbins and most of the nineteenth century writers on economic methodology, who believed that empirical studies should only be used to decide whether a particular theory is *applicable* to a given situation.[57]

> Our dissatisfaction with empirical work and our suspicion of measurement rest on the conviction that empirical observations of past human choices will not yield any regularities or any consistent pattern that may be safely extrapolated beyond the existing data at hand to yield scientific theorems of universal applicability.[58]

> Historical fact enters into these conclusions only by determining which branch of theory is applicable in any particular case.[59]

Once again we find that the methodological pronouncements of the Austrians seem to run counter to well-established views in the profession. But there is more to it than that. Whether you are a logical positivist, a logical empiricist, or a Popperian falsificationist in the philosophy of science, four defining characteristics of your methodological view are: that theories should be testable; that a useful means of testing is to compare the predictions of a theory with reality; that predictive adequacy is often the most important characteristic a theory can possess; and that the relative ordering of theories should be determined by the strength of confirmation, or corroboration, of those being compared. If the philosophy of science has had any impact on economic methodology, it is in this area, for most economists are trained to believe in the crucial importance of testing their hypotheses. Indeed, it may reasonably be conjectured that a majority of economists would consider the construction of theoretical models which are capable of generating testable predictions to be the hallmark of scientific activity. And it seems that the converse is also a widely-held sentiment: a proposed theory which is not expressed in testable (preferably, falsifiable) form is not scientific, and cannot be considered as a serious rival to well-established (and presumably) highly confirmed theories. Thus we find that the responses of many mainstream economists to alternative systems of thought follow their own predictable pattern: Austrians are derided because they try to insulate their theories from criticism by refusing to test their theories and by claiming that their assumptions are a priori true; Institutionalists, with their 'story-telling' or holistic 'pattern models' and an emphasis on explanation rather than prediction, similarly protect their theories by refusing to make risky predictions; and Marxists, who do at least make some predictions, spend most of their time concocting ad hoc additions to their theories to save them when their predictions are disconfirmed. Proponents of these alternative systems may believe that mainstream economists reject their programs on ideological grounds, and that is doubtless true in some cases. But I think that it is equally true that economists trained in a tradition that insists on the importance of hypothesis testing cannot help but view alternative systems that eschew testing with, at best, bemused curiosity, and at worst, utter disdain.

Even so, the fact remains that a methodological critique of one system (no matter how perverse that system's tenets may seem) based wholly on the precepts of its rival (no matter how familiar those precepts may be) establishes nothing.

Some Doubts about Falsificationism in Economics

But this may be only the tip of the iceberg. In the first half of this book, criticisms raised against both logical empiricism and Popper's falsificationism have been documented. If these criticisms are accepted, the philosophical foundations of standard economic methodology are suspect, and the Austrian case is strengthened even further.

The next three chapters will be spent in examining the impact that positivism has had on economic methodology. It should perhaps be noted, however, that few methodologists (as opposed to working economists who have learned the rhetoric of positive economics) today consider any of the variants of positivism to be viable. The same cannot be said for Popper's methodological falsificationism, however. Indeed, in two recent works by economists, Popper's prescriptions shine through unmistakeably. Yet there are strong reasons to suspect that falsificationism might not be the best methodology for economics to attempt to follow, either. We cannot try to establish such a controversial argument in this short section. We will examine it with some care, however, and return to it from time to time in later chapters.

In its simplest form, falsificationism can be stated as follows: Scientists should not only empirically test their hypotheses, they should construct hypotheses which make bold predictions, and they should try to refute those hypotheses in their tests. Equally important, scientists should tentatively accept only confirmed hypotheses, and reject those which have been disconfirmed. Testing, then, should make a difference.[60]

We may ask three distinct questions regarding the prospects for falsificationism in economics: *Should* it be used in economics? *Is* it being used in economics? and, *Can* it be used in economics?

Most working economists probably believe that the answer to all three questions is yes, while critics of the standard approach might be expected to answer no in each case. More interesting are the responses of those economic methodologists who explicitly endorse falsificationism in their writings: two examples are Terence Hutchison, who introduced the profession to falsificationism, and Mark Blaug. By their endorsements, it is clear that both think that economics *should* follow a falsificationist methodology. But significantly, neither think falsificationism *is* (or has been) given sufficient consideration by economists. While Hutchison's task in 1938 was to convince economists that theirs should be an empirical science, Blaug's complaint in 1980 is that, while economists have learned to mouth the rhetoric of falsificationism quite well, they have not learned to practice it.

But, surely, economists engage massively in empirical research? Clearly they do but, unfortunately, much of it is like playing tennis with the net down: instead of attempting to refute testable predictions, modern

economists all too frequently are satisfied to demonstrate that the real world conforms to their predictions.
. . .
Empirical work that fails utterly to discriminate between competing explanations quickly degenerates into a sort of mindless instrumentalism and it is not too much to say that the bulk of empirical work in modern economics is guilty on that score.
. . .
. . . the central weakness of modern economics is, indeed, the reluctance to produce theories that yield unambiguously refutable implications, followed by a general unwillingness to confront those implications with the facts.[61]

Blaug speaks of the 'reluctance' of economists to practice falsificationism. The key question, of course, is whether or not falsificationism *can* be applied successfully in economics. And it is here that a number of nagging doubts enter in. First is the fact reported on by Blaug that falsificationism has yet to be put into operation in economics.

Second, and more important, there are a number of obstacles that appear insurmountable, blocking the practice of falsificationism in economics. Hutchison himself mentions some of these in an engaging recent study, *Knowledge and Ignorance in Economics* (1977). Noting that a true test of a hypothesis (à la Popper) requires both a finite number of checkable initial conditions and well-established general laws, Hutchison finds that in many cases in economics neither criterion is met. Certain of the initial conditions are inherently uncheckable (tastes, information, expectations), and instead of general laws, economists must use 'trends, tendencies, patterns or temporary constancies'.[62] These and other sentiments expressed in his book, which was written nearly forty years after he introduced positivism into economics, are perhaps the most eloquent and effective pieces of evidence against the prospects for putting falsificationism to use in economics.

Neither Hutchison nor Blaug would throw falsificationism aside as a useless methodology, though each is well aware of its limitations in economics. Each has sections on the contributions of Kuhn and Lakatos in his volume, and each emphasizes that the sciences vary, that no simple mechanical algorithm for evaluating theories exists, that the sciences are not 'all of one piece'. Thus we find Hutchison approvingly citing J. R. Ravetz that 'the world of science is a very variegated one . . . and the "methods" of science are a very heterogeneous collection of things'.[63] Blaug is even more direct, and it is worthwhile to quote him at length.

We have now reached one of our central conclusions: just as there is no logic of discovery, so there is no demonstrative *logic* of justification either; there is no formal algorithm, no mechanical procedure of verification, falsification, confirmation, corroboration, or call it what you will. To the philosophical question "How can we acquire apodictic knowledge of the world when all we can rely on is our own unique experience?" Popper replies that there is no certain empirical knowledge, whether grounded in our own personal experience or in that of mankind in general. And more than that: there is no sure method of guaranteeing that the fallible knowledge of the real world is positively the best we can possess under the circumstances. A study of the philosophy of science can sharpen our appraisal of what constitutes acceptable empirical knowledge but it remains a provisional appraisal nevertheless. We can invite the most severe criticism of this appraisal, but what we cannot do is to pretend that there is on deposit somewhere a perfectly objective method, that is, an intersubjectively demonstrative method, that will positively compel agreement on what are or are not acceptable scientific theories.[64]

Neither Hutchison nor Blaug can be accused of being a naive falsificationist. Yet each still believes that falsificationism should be *tried* whenever possible, and more important for our theme, that to *fail* to try is bad faith, and leads to bad science. (Hutchison complains of a 'crisis of abstraction' in economics; Blaug complains generally of the failure of economists to produce falsifiable theories, but is most vehement in his discussion of the Austrians.)[65]

I think that few who have taken the time to study Popper fully can avoid being impressed by his noble vision of what constitutes legitimate scientific activity. Popper urges scientists to constantly follow procedures that are both psychologically grueling and, often, operationally infeasible: to state their theories in testable form, the more daringly testable the better; to submit them to such tests, not just once but over and over again; and finally, to take the results of such tests seriously, to toss aside the failed hypotheses. Even then, such rigorous procedure does nothing to guarantee the soundness of our tentative, provisional knowledge; all it does is help us to avoid falling overlong into gross error. There is a passionate idealism in Popper's message, but it is linked with an overriding sense of humility about man's capabilities. One is reminded of Reinhold Niebuhr's interpretation of Adam's fall from grace: for man to sin is inevitable, but it is not necessary; we know what sin is, and should always try to avoid it, even if avoidance is ultimately impossible. In the realm of science, error is inevitable, but we should also always try to avoid it.

There are, then, good reasons to try to put Popper's methodological falsificationism into effect in economics. But intellectual honesty, and indeed Popper's spirit of criticism itself, demands that we be cognizant of two rather disturbing facts: there is little evidence that it ever *has* been successfully applied, falsificationist rhetoric notwithstanding; and as to the crucial question of whether it *can* be applied, there are at least some serious obstacles to its implementation, given that the subject matter is a social science like economics.

These considerations lead us to conclusions which appear to be at odds with those of the proponents of methodological falsificationism in economics. We may agree that the invocation to *try* to implement methodological falsificationism should be retained. But it is a dangerous dogma, and one that is antithetical to scientific criticism in general, to dismiss as unscientific alternative routes to knowledge in the social sciences which do not conform to the ideals of methodological falsificationism. In a phrase, methodological falsificationism is not the last word in economics; but perhaps *methodological pluralism* is. Crucially, methodological pluralism need not and *must not* be equated with an *absence* of criticism. Rather, it must be coupled with the imperative that, just as there are many paths to knowledge, there are many forms of *criticism*, and the more that are heard, the better. Viewed in this way, methodological and critical pluralism may even come closer to the *spirit* of Popper's invocation to 'Be critical', given the obstacles to falsificationism in the social sciences. It would, in any case, save the proponents of methodological falsificationism in economics from the embarrassing dilemma of having to dismiss as unscientific the analyses of Austrians, Marxists, Institutionalists, and the like because they pay no heed to methodological falsificationism, while at the same time having to sheepishly admit that their ideal has not been tried within standard economic theory, either. Methodological falsificationism in the social sciences is an inspiring and noble critical ideal; it would be a tragic mistake if its name was invoked only as a dogmatic exclusionary device.

The Critique of Austrian Methodology

Though I have just argued that methodological falsificationism may not be the optimal methodology for economics, this should not be construed as an argument against criticism in general. My position is just the opposite: because there are many roads to criticism, an overemphasis on the specific Popperian directives artificially limits the types of critical discourse considered permissible. In addition, it was shown that neither positivism nor falsificationism are effective critical tools for evaluating these competing systems of thought whose proponents reject the epistemological and methodological frameworks of the more standard approaches.

To demonstrate that alternative systems can be criticized, *often from within their own frameworks*, what follows is a brief outline of how a nondogmatic methodological critique (i.e. one that does not originate from within the categories of a rival system) of praxeology might look.[66]

We begin by examining the Austrian methodological literature to see which avenues of criticism they would accept as legitimate. We discover that there are two: we may question the truth of the axioms and postulates from which their analysis begins; or, we may inspect the verbal chain of logic which leads from the postulates to the conclusions.

Taking the postulates of praxeology first, we begin by asking that all the primitives, or axioms, be carefully defined. Derived theorems must be clearly distinguishable from postulates, and the rationale behind the groupings should be evident. Particular attention should be given to whether all the postulates and definitions are consistent with one another. Next, terms that are used in *describing* how the Austrian system fits together must be separated out – terms in the metalanguage, if you will. Thus, the meaning and implications of, say, 'methodological individualism' or 'a priori' must be readily understood. Does a priori really mean prior to any experience, or is it to be used as synonomous with analytic, or definitional? What are the boundaries between a priori and the other categories? Does methodological individualism imply reductionism? If so, why stop at the level of the acting human agent; why not press on to chemical, biological, and physical levels? Is the use of social aggregates by definition unfruitful, or is that only a matter of methodological preference? The pursuit of these and other similar lines of questioning should insure that the Austrian position is outlined in sharp relief, that there are no hazy, vaguely defined areas in which refuge from criticism might successfully be sought.

Still focusing on the postulates: since the Austrian system is presumably founded on facts of human existence which are known to us a priori as true, the discovery of counterexamples should be costly for its survival. The primary postulate of praxeology is that all action is purposeful, hence rational. Can we think of any example of nonpurposeful action? Robert Nozick suggests that operant behavior may be a plausible candidate. If we were to accept operant behavior as a legitimate counterexample, would that necessarily imply that the Austrian program be abandoned? (Nozick notes that, at a minimum, empirical studies would again become necessary to investigate whether acting agents were really acting purposefully, or were simply following their conditioning.)[67]

Turning next to the verbal chain of logic, we find the Austrians willing to accept the inspection of that chain for errors as a legitimate form of criticism. We might first inquire just what sorts of mistakes in logic are to count: is it simply a matter of the validity of argument forms, or are other mistakes possible? How about the addition of hidden assumptions? For example, most Austrians claim that theirs is a scientific, value-free discipline, firmly within the Wertfreiheit tradition.[68] Yet it also seems undeniable that certain value judgments (regarding freedom of choice, freedom from coercion and the value of the individual, to list just a few) are present in the Austrian system. If such value judgments do exist, do they constitute mistakes in verbal logic? Would an inconsistency between an earlier, primitive statement and a later, derived one be considered an error in logic? As a possible example of this sort of mistake, Nozick cites Mises's position on preferences and choice, 'The notion of preference makes no sense apart from an actual choice made.' He then asks how it is possible to discuss concepts like indifference or opportunity cost without some notion of preference that is separate from choices actually made.[69]

We have not exhausted the questions that could be posed regarding the postulates of praxeology or the verbal chain of logic used in the Austrian system. It was not our intention to launch a comprehensive assault against the Austrians, nor is it clear that any of the issues raised above would be decisive in such a critique. The point of all of this is to suggest that a critique of Austrian methodology *which adheres to the categories and methods employed by the Austrians themselves* may be possible and should be attempted. This approach is preferable for at least two reasons: it is less dogmatic than the usual doctrinaire mouthing of the tenets of positivism or falsificationism; and because it meets the Austrians on their own ground, it would be far more costly for them if the critique was successful.

A different route for criticizing praxeology makes use of the notion of theory choice that is developed in greater detail in succeeding chapters. The principle question of theory choice is, simply enough: On what grounds do we choose among competing theories? Many criteria of theory choice have been identified: empirical ones, like predictive adequacy and explanatory power; structural ones, like logical consistency, elegance, and agreement with existent theoretical structures; and some which fit into neither category, like realism, generality, and fruitfulness. But we find in the Austrian literature no discussion of theory choice. The reason is not difficult to discover: since the Austrian system is presumably founded on a priori true postulates, it is either true or false. There is no *need* to compare it with other systems with the idea of ranking them: the Austrian system is either true, or it is false. All evaluation, then, must 'come from within'.

Though this may not accord with the common belief that the comparison of theories is generally fruitful, it is by no means an unacceptable stance. However, it does run into problems of its own, chiefly because a priori true postulates (and the systems that follow from them by deduction) at least *seem* capable of multiplication.

It may be true that there exists but one set of a priori true postulates from which may be deduced all true knowledge of the social sphere. But it is also true that through the years man has been able to come up with many alternative first postulates for such systems, and indeed, many of these on first appearance seem quite convincing. There would be no problem in adjudicating among such systems if, once a truth were properly stated, no reasonable man could deny it (or deductions from it). But this is not the case, and as such, the objective observer faces a dilemma when confronted with competing systems whose postulates are claimed to be a priori true, for no grounds are offered on which to base a choice. The dilemma can be illustrated by comparing the claims of praxeology with those of Martin Hollis and E. J. Nell in their book, *Rational Economic Man* (1975).

Like Mises, his two 'Classical–Marxian' counterparts assert that economic science must begin from certain fundamental axioms, postulates which have the status of necessary (though unproven) a priori truths about the human condition. For Mises, this 'ultimate given' is the fact of human action. Compare this with the 'fundamental concept' chosen by Hollis and Nell: an extended version of production, by which they mean 'reproduction of the economic system'. The authors note that there exist many candidates for the basic concept, such as choice, exchange, the market, money, labor, or capital. They further contend, in good rationalist style, that there can be only one set of fundamental axioms.

> necessary truths cannot conflict; alternative theories, that is, theories with incompatible implications, are not allowable, and even complementary theories must be fit together and made to cohere. We cannot allow the possibility of different fundamental concepts, for different concepts will give rise to different theories, as different as Robbins and Marx.[70]

What reasons do they offer for considering production as essential?

The general point is simple. Choice depends on choosers, exchange upon traders, labor upon workers, and so on. Choosers need reasons and abilities, traders must have goods and skills, workers jobs and skills. Hence the agents in question, and their replacements when they grow old or ill, when they die or retire, must be trained and supported, as must the context in which the agents characteristically operate. The reproduction of the system, in short, is primary.[71]

How can the objective observer adjudicate between these two positions? Surely Hollis and Nell are correct that the economic system must be capable of reproducing itself, for without that, no system would exist to analyze. But surely Mises is correct, that any analysis would be empty (and worse, impossible) if human action, as praxeology defines it, was not operative. Both seem quite essential for the study of any economic system.

Neither side will concede that empirical investigations or tests of assumptions or implications can yield worthwhile results; indeed, their complaints against 'positivism' and 'empiricism' are roughly similar. All we have are two weak suggestions, one from each camp: we can check the 'verbal chain of logic' from axioms to conclusions in Mises's world; whereas Hollis and Nell suggest that we simply make sure that they are using 'real' definitions. Of course, we might look at the conclusions of their analyses (markets efficiently provide information, maximize free choice, and force individuals to bear the costs and reap the rewards of their own decisions is the Austrian view, whereas Hollis and Nell present a Sraffian production model and emphasize that, when production yields a surplus, institutional factors and market power determine how it is split up) and decide according to our individual faith in, or distrust of, markets. Such a route is hardly scientific, though unfortunately it may be the path most traveled.

The dilemma of adjudicating between these two competing a priori systems is one that can be generalized. Even if all verbal or mathematical deductions are made correctly, the starting point of such systems (unprovable, necessary truths about reality) will always *seem* capable, psychologically if not actually, of multiplication. And as long as proponents of such systems eschew any resort to empirical testing or other forms of criticism, there appears to be no way to choose among a (possibly) ever growing number of such systems. Theories which do not claim to be derived from a priori true first postulates do not encounter this problem, since they may be compared with other theories according to the usual criteria of theory choice.

If proponents of theories which are purportedly founded on a priori true axioms are to convince the uninitiated of the worth of their systems, they must do more than just argue the merits of their chosen postulates. Otherwise, there is little to distinguish them from other proponents of systems based on self-evident postulates. Their choices, it seems, are twofold. They could attempt to criticize, and hopefully discredit, all rival systems. Such a task would not only be time-consuming, it would be literally never-ending. The second alternative, and one that appears more reasonable, is to propose certain criteria which could be used to critically evaluate their own and other such systems. This might involve a rethinking of the potential uses of empirical work for evaluation of postulates, or perhaps some entirely different forms of criticism not yet alluded to here.

We may close with a word of falsifiable, and possibly false, strategic advice. Very little in the neo-Austrian literature (nor, it seems, in the Cambridge, UK post-Keynesian–Marxian–Ricardian cluster of theorizing) depends crucially on the methodological views criticized here. If members of either group are intent on establishing a firm methodological foundation before pursuing other work, so be it. My personal view is that the primary task before such groups does not lie in the realm of methodological construction, nor even that of methodological criticism. Rather, their efforts are best directed at making positive and substantive contributions within their respective theoretical frameworks. If they succeed there, methodology will follow just like (as local wisdom has it) white on rice.

Much territory has been covered in this opening chapter on the methodology of economics. It began with an outline of Lord Robbins's methodology, which was taken as representative of the prevailing attitudes in twentieth century economic methodology prior to Terence Hutchison's introduction of positivism. Hutchison's case against Robbins was then detailed and evaluated. Although his treatment of the logical status of the 'basic propositions' of economic theory was reasonable, given the beliefs prevalent in philosophy in the late 1930s, we saw with the benefit of hindsight that Hutchison's analysis of the topic is flawed. If we look at later developments in economics, however, that error proves to be inconsequential: members of the discipline were soon to embrace many of the prescriptions propounded by Hutchison. His accolades for empirical research and the testing of theories did not fall on deaf ears; his invocations soon became the standard rhetoric of economic methodologists. Whether the rhetoric was ever translated accurately into action is, of course, a separate matter.

We turned next to the praxeologists. Members of this group share with Robbins a distrust of empirical work, but are unique in claiming that the axioms of human action are not just self-evident, but true a priori. This curious view is so alien to positivist philosophy of science (praxeological categories violate such basic assumptions as the analytic–synthetic distinction and the requirement that statements be testable to be cognitively significant) and to the beliefs and practices of most economists (who view the importance of testing as incontrovertible) that it is often dismissed out of hand. This is unfortunate, for the confrontation of opposing views can be fruitful. But worse, the attitude of certain economists that the claims of such groups are not even to be considered (since they are not scientific) is *itself* a dogmatic and anti-scientific stance that cannot be justified.

Those who refuse to take groups like the Austrians (and, for that matter, Institutionalists, post-Keynesians, and others) seriously fall into a number of errors. First, it becomes too easy to caricature a position. This has happened to the Austrians, a number of whose positions can be made to seem ludicrous if taken out of context, but which are quite straightforward when matters of linguistic usage are considered. Next, it may not be recognized that a rival epistemological and methodological system is being advocated. The Austrians do this, and offer arguments against positivism. But instead of either responding to such arguments or trying to show weaknesses in the Austrian framework, too many critics of the praxeology feel it is sufficient to respond that, because the Austrians do not follow the tenets of positivism, they are not to be taken seriously. Such a position completely misses the point. If we finally note that positivism and Popperian falsificationism have both been criticized within the philosophy of science, such a position becomes unforgiveably arrogant, as well.

In recent years, economic methodologists have given increasing recognition to the fact that positivism may no longer be a viable foundation for methodology. This development is welcome. Certain analysts have recently suggested that Popper's methodological falsificationism avoids the errors of positivism and provides a workable, though as yet mostly untried, alternative. Though not pursued in detail, arguments against that position were offered, and I suggested that methodological pluralism might work better than methodological falsificationism in economics, especially if it broadens the permissible channels of critical discourse in the discipline.

To illustrate that there are additional paths to criticism beyond those deemed most acceptable by positivists and falsificationists, the praxeological position was again examined and numerous criticisms of it were offered, none of which focused directly on the empirical testing of hypotheses. The section concluded with a challenge to the

Austrians to come up with some means by which their system could be compared to its rivals.

When discussing Hutchison's contribution, it was noted that he placed the 'fundamental assumption' of rational conduct at the center of the methodological arena, and insisted that economists henceforth be quite clear as to what empirical content it was meant to possess. That issue was to be much discussed in later decades. To this topic we may now turn.

Notes

1   I will not treat nineteenth century methodological thought in economics; for a competent survey with footnote citations of most of the secondary literature, see Mark Blaug, *The Methodology of Economics* (Cambridge, England: Cambridge University Press, 1980), Chapter 3. Hutchison was the first to introduce positivism into economics in an explicit methodological treatise; other economists, however, aired positivist ideas in their work. One example is Vilfredo Pareto; a detailed study of Pareto's methodological contribution is Vincent J. Tarascio, *Pareto's Methodological Approach to Economics: A Study in the History of Some Scientific Aspects of Economic Thought* (Chapel Hill, N.C.: University of North Carolina Press, 1966).

2   Lionel Robbins, *An Essay on the Nature and Significance of Economic Science*, 2nd edn (first published, 1932) (London: Macmillan, 1935), p. 16.

3   Ibid., p. 24.

4   Ibid., p. 1.

5   Ibid., p. 73.

6   Ibid., pp. 74–5.

7   Ibid., pp. 78–9.

8   Ibid., p. 79.

9   Ibid., pp. 80–3. A thorough and convincing critique of the claims of historicism is Ludwig von Mises, *Epistemological Problems of Economics*, trans. by George Reisman (first published, 1933) (Princeton, N.J.: Van Nostrand, 1960).

10   Robbins, op. cit., p. 89.

11   Ibid., pp. 91–6.

12   Ibid., p. 92.

13   Ibid., pp. 93–4, 96.

14   Ibid., pp. 112–18.

15   Ibid., pp. 121, 131.

16   Ibid., pp. xi, xvi, 54, 84, 106.

17   Ibid., p. 93.

18   Ibid., p. 81.

19   Frank Knight, ' "What Is Truth" in Economics?' *Journal of Political Economy*, vol. 47 (February–December, 1940), p. 17.

20   For example, Murray Rothbard finds an 'Aristotelean and neo-Thomist' approach to the epistemological status of the axioms of praxeology preferable to Mises's post-Kantian view. See his 'Praxeology: The Methodology of Austrian Economics,' in Edwin G. Dolan (ed.), *The Foundations of Modern Austrian Economics* (Kansas City: Sheed and Ward, 1976), pp. 19–39. Hayek's work on 'scientism' is contained in his *The Counter-Revolution of Science: Studies on the*

Abuse of Reason, 2nd edn (first published, 1952) Indianapolis, Ind.: Liberty Press, 1979).

21 Blaug, op. cit., p. 55.

22 Blaug uses the word verification and its several derivations in a variety of different contexts. He mentions the 'verifiability principle of meaning' (p. 11) used by members of the Vienna Circle to distinguish meaningful from meaningless statements. 'To verify' is also taken to mean 'to prove true', and is contrasted with 'to falsify' (pp. 12–13). In discussing economists, he notes that Machlup uses the term verification when he really means falsification (pp. 108–11, 114–15). Verification sometimes means the demonstration that the world conforms to one's predictions, which describes, according to Blaug, the usual practice of modern-day economists (p. 256). We find that many nineteenth century economists were verificationists, too – but here the term is used to describe those who would use empirical studies only to check the applicability of economic reasoning, and not to test theories (p. 55 and *passim*).

23 Terence W. Hutchison, *The Significance and Basic Postulates of Economic Theory* (first published, 1938), reprinted (New York: Augustus M. Kelley, 1960), pp. 9–10.

24 Ibid., p. 23.

25 Ibid., p. 24.

26 Ibid., p. 25.

27 Ibid., p. 27.

28 Ibid., p. 30.

29 Ibid., pp. 42, 46.

30 Ibid., pp. 24–5.

31 Ibid., p. 85.

32 Ibid., p. 87.

33 Ibid., pp. 101, 103.

34 Ibid., p. 74.

35 Ibid., pp. 113–14.

36 Ibid., pp. 62, 64.

37 Ibid., p. 69, cf. p. 164.

38 Ibid., p. 142.

39 Carl G. Hempel, 'The Theoretician's Dilemma,' in Herbert Feigl, Grover Maxwell, and Michael Scriven (eds), *Minnesota Studies in the Philosophy of Science*, Vol. II (Minneapolis: University of Minnesota Press, 1958), p. 72.

40 Carl G. Hempel, 'The Empiricist Criterion of Meaning,' in A. J. Ayer (ed.), *Logical Positivism* (Glencoe, Ill.: The Free Press, 1959), p. 129.

41 See any standard text on logic for a more complete discussion of these matters.

42 Alexander Rosenberg, *Microeconomic Laws: A Philosophical Analysis* (Pittsburgh: University of Pittsburgh Press, 1976), pp. 153–4.

43 Note the differences in emphasis in, for example, G. L. S. Shackle, *The Years of High Theory: Invention and Tradition in Economic Thought 1926–1939* (Cambridge, England: Cambridge University Press, 1967) and Phyllis Deane, *The Evolution of Economic Ideas* (Cambridge, England: Cambridge University Press, 1978). Cf. Terence Hutchison's *On Revolutions and Progress in Economic Knowledge* (Cambridge, England: Cambridge University Press, 1978), Chapter 9.

44 For Garrison's work on Misesean business cycle theory, see his 'Austrian macro-economics: A Diagrammatical Exposition,' in Louis M. Spadaro, *New Directions in Austrian Economics* (Kansas City: Sheed, Andrews and McMeel, 1978), pp. 167–204. In a conversation, Garrison noted that his attempt to translate Mises's business cycle theory into the IS-LM framework was not universally appreciated. Fellow Austrians were displeased that he was working with aggregates; and his professors at the University of Virginia disparaged his model as untestable.

References for other Austrian contributors are included in the Notes for Further Reading at the end of this volume.

45   The claim that many contemporary Austrians do not embrace the tenets of praxeology is based on conversations I had with a number of Austrian economists while on research leave at New York University in 1981–82. Murray Rothbard comes closest to being a true Misesian, though he differs in his interpretation of the logical status of the categories of human action: for him they are broadly empirical. In their forthcoming book on Austrian economics, Gerald O'Driscoll and Mario Rizzo offer a reconstruction of Austrian methodology which integrates Hayekian subjectivism, the concept of a mind-construct (a theoretical device usually associated with Alfred Schutz and Fritz Machlup), and an approach to institutional development which draws heavily from the works of Carl Menger, Ludwig Lachmann, and Hayek. Finally, Israel Kirzner views the Misesian approach, and methodology in general, rather pragmatically. In discussing praxeology, Kirzner notes that Mises's first and most fundamental insight was that by regarding human action as purposeful, yet based on an individual's subjective perception of particular knowledge, much could be derived in terms of understanding the workings of an economic system. It was only after having had this insight that Mises felt compelled to categorize in philosophical terms the logical status of the axioms and theorems of his system. It seemed to Mises that the Kantian notion of statements being both a priori true and synthetic best described the postulates, but because such a position was not in vogue (logical positivism and, later, logical empiricism both denied the possibility of such statements) Mises dedicated a great deal of effort to defending it. In Kirzner's mind, such a defense is far less important than the insights to be derived from viewing human action in individualistic, subjectivistic, and purposive terms.

46   Blaug, op. cit., pp. 91–3.

47   One candidate is Robert Nozick, 'On Austrian Methodology,' *Synthese*, vol. 36 (1977), pp. 353–92. Less recent and original is Alan Sweezy, 'The Interpretation Of Subjective Value Theory in the Writings of the Austrian Economists,' *Review of Economic Studies*, vol. 1 (June 1934), pp. 176–85.

48   Ludwig von Mises, *Human Action: A Treatise on Economics* (first published, 1949), 3rd revised edn (Chicago: Henry Regnery, 1968), pp. 19–20.

49   Ibid., p. 20.

50   Ibid., pp. 94–7.

51   Ludwig von Mises, *The Ultimate Foundation of Economic Science* (first published, 1962), 2nd edn (Kansas City: Sheed, Andrews and McMeel, 1978), pp. 18, 16.

52   von Mises, *Human Action*, p. 38.

53   Rothbard, 'Praxeology: The Methodology of Austrian Economics,' loc. cit., p. 25. But note that Rothbard differs from Mises in his interpretation of the logical status of the categories of human action.

54   von Mises, *Human Action*, p. 39.

55   For example, see Israel Kirzner, 'On the Method of Austrian Economics,' in Dolan (ed.), op. cit., p. 41.

56   Ibid., p. 42.

57   Blaug, op. cit., Chapter 3.

58   Kirzner, loc. cit., p. 43.

59   Rothbard, loc. cit., p. 21.

60   We have stated falsificationism in its simplist form on the presumption that most economists would claim that *that* was the methodology that they practiced. I agree with Blaug that none *actually* practice it, that most aim at confirming theories, and that disconfirmations are seldom treated seriously. I *disagree* that

economists can, if they just change their practice, become falsificationists some-day: their subject matter prohibits it.

61   Blaug, op. cit., pp. 256, 257, 254.
62   Terence Hutchison, *Knowledge and Ignorance in Economics* (Chicago: University of Chicago Press, 1977), p. 21.
63   Ibid., p. 36. The quote is from Jerome Ravetz, *Scientific Knowledge and its Social Problems* (Oxford: Clarendon Press, 1971), pp. 173, 410.
64   Blaug, op. cit., pp. 27-8. This passage describes the views of Lakatos, or even Feyerabend, better than those of Popper. To the extent that it *is* Popper, it is the *recent* Popper; the *early* Popper was not the Lakatosian sophisticated methodological falsificationist portrayed in this passage, nor is it clear that the *present* Popper is.

        Blaug has not always been clear in his survey which Popper he is talking about; he does not treat the *development* of the philosopher's ideas very well. One almost gets the feeling that Popper emerged as a full-blown sophisticated methodological falsificationist. Blaug's annoying habit of citing only the dates of reprinted editions and not giving original publication dates contributes to this confusion.

        To be fair to Blaug, however, there is a tension in Popper's work that makes its exposition difficult. Popper refuses to give up critical falsificationism, yet he is forced to admit that there is no perfect method, which suggests that *other* methods might reasonably be tried. His failure to apply falsificationism to his own method is also a drawback. Some of Popper's followers (e.g. Lakatos, Feyerabend) have been bolder in pursuing the results of methodological pluralism beyond falsificationism; their results are mixed.
65   Ibid., pp. 91-3, Chapter 15; Hutchison, *Knowledge and Ignorance*, Chapter 4.
66   Certain of the examples used in the following discussion are drawn from Robert Nozick's superlative essay, 'On Austrian Methodology'.
67   Ibid., pp. 365-9.
68   For example, see Israel Kirzner, 'Philosphical and Ethical Implications of Austrian Economics,' in Dolan (ed.), op. cit., pp. 75-88.
69   Nozick, loc. cit., pp. 369-73.
70   Martin Hollis and Edward J. Nell, *Rational Economic Man: A Philosophical Critique of Neo-Classical Economics* (Cambridge, England: Cambridge University Press, 1975), p. 243.
71   Ibid., p. 243.

7

Hutchison versus Machlup –
On Indirect Testing and the
Rationality Postulate

Though Milton Friedman's essay, which will be reviewed in the next chapter, was written three years before the exchanges between Hutchison and Fritz Machlup which occurred in the mid-1950s in the pages of the *Southern Economic Journal*, I will review that debate first for the simple reason that, while Friedman's work can easily stand as an independent contribution to the methodology of economics, Machlup's case is explicitly directed against the views outlined in Hutchison's book.

Machlup's Attack

In his 'The Problem of Verification in Economics', Machlup develops a sophisticated defense of the assumptions of economic theory from attacks such as those advanced by Hutchison, whom he labels an 'ultra-empiricist'. It is evident in his article that Machlup has a thorough grounding in contemporaneous philosophy of science, and he is able to use that knowledge successfully against Hutchison.

'The Problem of Verification in Economics' begins with some typically Machlupian 'defining of terms', the most important of which is 'verification' itself: verification is

> a procedure designed to find out whether a set of data of observation about a class of phenomena is obtainable and can be reconciled with a particular set of hypothetical generalizations about this class of phenomena.[1]

He notes that verifiability only has to do with whether a proposition can be *shown* to be true or false, not whether it actually is true or false: thus, a verifiable statement may in fact be false. Hypotheses can never be completely verified; rather, they can only fail to be disconfirmed by evidence. And, finally, while numerous confirming instances support the 'correctness' of a hypothesis, even stronger support is offered by 'the place it holds within a hierarchical system of inter-related hypotheses'.[2] The only shortcoming of this section is Machlup's unfortunate choice of the word verification to describe the topic under investigation; confirmation would have been less confusing. Machlup is fully aware of the problems involved with a literal interpretation of the terms 'verification' and 'falsification', and he avoids these problems by carefully defining his vocabulary in terms of confirmation and disconfirmation. Why he chooses to label his topic 'the verification problem' is therefore curious: perhaps he felt the word verification was more widely known among economists than the term confirmation. In any case, the reader should bear in mind that when Machlup uses the word verification he is not using it in the same way that most philosophers of science do, namely, to describe the criterion of cognitive significance first employed by the Vienna Circle positivists.

After the above attempt at terminological clarification, Machlup turns to the key questions which surround 'the verification problem': Should all propositions in economics be verifiable? Should we retain the ones which are not?

He asserts that there exist two general sorts of responses to these questions. One type of response is given by the a priorists, who believe that

> economic science is a system of a priori truths, a product of pure reason, an exact science reaching laws as universal as those of mathematics, a purely axiomatic discipline, a system of pure deductions from a series of postulates, not open to any verification or refutation on the grounds of experience.[3]

He cites Ludwig von Mises, Frank Knight, Max Weber, Lionel Robbins, and certain early economists like Cairnes and J. S. Mill as adherents of one form or another of a priorism, and claims that most of them base their belief on the fact that the assumptions of economic theory are not recordable by external objective observation but relate to subjective inner experience. These economists do not disparage empirical testing, but they would test only the predicted results which are *deduced* from the assumptions of economic theory, and not the assumptions 'in isolation'.[4]

In opposition to a priorism is ultra-empiricism, which is advocated by those who 'refuse to recognize the legitimacy of employing at any level of analysis propositions not independently verifiable'; this position is the basis for broadsides against the assumptions of theory as being 'unverified, unverifiable, imaginary, unrealistic'.[5] Taking Hutchison as an example of an ultra-empiricist par excellence, Machlup reviews his work and notes that the English economist believes that, if the discipline is to progress, all assumptions which are not independently verifiable should be replaced by postulates obtained through statistical investigations.

Machlup states that the error in the ultra-empiricist position lies in a failure to distinguish 'the difference between hypotheses on different levels of generality and, hence, of different degrees of testability'.[6] To use Braithwaite's terminology, whom he quotes along with Royce, only 'lower-level' hypotheses are testable, and the testing of a hypothetico-deductive system is effected by testing the lower level hypotheses. To make these ideas more accessible to economists, Machlup gives concrete examples of three types of assumptions and hypotheses used in economics: fundamental assumptions (that people act rationally and can arrange preferences in a consistent order; and that entrepreneurs prefer more to less profit with equal risk), specific assumptions (e.g. 'that the expenditures for table salt are a small portion of most households' annual budgets; that the member banks are holding very large excess reserves with the Federal Reserve Banks'), which are empirically testable, and 'deduced low-level hypotheses' (e.g. 'that a reduction in the price of table salt will not result in a proportionate increase in salt consumption; that a reduction in the discount rate of the Federal Reserve Banks will at such times not result in an increase in the member banks' lending activities'), which also are testable.[7] He next constructs an 'analytic apparatus' which describes how hypotheses are tested in economics: given a testable assumed change (a 'disequilibrating variation') taken together with certain testable conditions regarding the specifics of the 'case', 'setting', and 'economy' (though 'we need not be particularly strict' about their verification), and finally with the untestable 'Postulates of Motivation', we may derive a deduced change (an 'equilibrating variation') which may be compared to reality.[8]

The fundamental postulates which refer to the 'assumed type of action' need not be independently verified. He follows philosopher Felix Kaufmann in claiming that their logical status cannot be fit into the usual analytic–synthetic categories; rather, they are 'rules of procedure' which 'remain accepted as long as they have heuristic value, but will be rejected in favor of other rules (assumptions) which seem to serve their explanatory function more successfully'.[9] He also follows Alfred Schutz's reformulation of Max Weber's thesis that postulated motivational assumptions be 'understandable', 'in the sense that we could conceive of sensible men acting (sometimes at least) in the way postulated by the ideal type in question'.[10]

Hutchison's Ambiguous Response

It is clear from his responses in 'Professor Machlup on Verification in Economics' that T. W. Hutchison feels he has been grossly misrepresented. Scoring Machlup's a priorist–ultra-empiricist dichotomy as vague and unclear, Hutchison states that, in any case, he is no ultra-empiricist.[11] He defends this claim by citing his (by now familiar) quotation that propositions in science need only be conceivably testable or reducible to such propositions, which clearly allows for indirect tests of assumptions. Hutchison then moves to a discussion of fundamental hypotheses in economics, noting that the only one mentioned by Machlup is the maximization principle. The problem that arises with Machlup's formulation of that principle is that of discovering just what content it is meant to possess.[12] Is it meant to say something about actual behavior, or is it merely an empty statement to the effect that people maximize, whatever their behavior? A more preferable formulation of the maximization principle than 'consumers maximize utility' would be that 'preferences can be arranged by consumers in an order', since the latter has testable implications. Hutchison then approvingly cites the history of value theory from Fisher and Pareto through Slutsky and Hicks to Samuelson and Little as evidence of a trend toward more testable formulations of the theory. He neatly summarizes his differences with Machlup with the following words:

> In short, while admitting the principle of indirect verification, we cannot agree to the kind of loose and sweeping appeal to it which Professor Machlup seems to be making. Much more particularity and precision seems to be desirable.[13]

His piece concludes with a warning about the dangers of adhering too closely to a view that disdains the empirical testing of assumptions.

> brandishing this generalisation that all economic action was (or even must be) "rational" some economists – notably Professor Mises, whom Professor Machlup seems so concerned to defend – have proceeded to claim that wholesale political conclusions were logically deducible from it, and were thus to be regarded as established conclusions of economic science.[14]

In his reply, Machlup agrees that his opponent's quote on reducibility should refute the charge of ultra-empiricism, but argues that much of Hutchison's comment indicates that he still adheres to that position. And indeed, Hutchison is ambiguous in his comment. At one point he states, 'It can certainly be agreed that actual independent tests may not be "required".'[15] Yet his citation of the later history of utility theory as representing progress indicates he is an ultra-empiricist, for much of that work (especially that of Samuelson) is nothing more than an attempt to make the assumption of transitively ordered preferences empirically testable (or conceivably so).[16] The most valuable aspects of Hutchison's comment lie in his demands that Machlup clarify what is meant by indirect testing, and that he indicate exactly what content the fundamental assumption is meant to possess. Machlup provides fuller explanations in his rejoinder. An indirect test occurs when an untestable assumption A is combined with testable assumptions B to get a testable consequence C which must be derivable from A and B together but which cannot be derived from either A or B alone.[17] He contrasts this with a direct test of the profit maximization assumption, in which researchers would attempt to establish the relative frequency of decisions consistent with profit maximization. He concedes immediately that such tests would reveal that the assumption does not always conform to the facts, and admits that at times the deviations could be significant. But not to worry,

What then should be done? Just what is being done: to accept maximizing conduct as a heuristic postulate and to bear in mind that the deduced consequences may sometimes be considerably out of line with observed data. . . . the "indirect verification" or justification of the postulate lies in the fact that it gives fairly good results in many applications of the theory.[18]

Machlup concludes by noting that 'good judgement' must be employed in deciding just 'when, where, and how far' the assumption can be applied, and that its rejection entails finding another assumption to replace it that either covers a wider range of problems, is simpler, or is more accurate.[19]

Philosophical Evaluation

Before evaluating the two positions from a philosophical perspective, we must determine exactly what each economist is claiming. That is no simple task, for each has hedged his position with qualifying remarks. It has already been mentioned that Hutchison would not 'require' direct testing. And Machlup is not always clear about whether he thinks the fundamental assumption is *untestable*, or only that it is *unnecessary* to test it. To represent the two economists as holding diametrically opposed views on the issue of testing thus would involve a certain amount of caricaturing. Our more cautious interpretation is as follows.

Both economists agree that the testing of hypotheses is important in economics. Machlup believes that only deduced, 'lower level' hypotheses require 'verification', and he outlines how such testing could be carried out. While Hutchison does not require that every statement in a theory be tested, he does insist that each be *testable*: one should be able to conceive of how a test could be carried out. Moreoever, Hutchison prefers that the behavioral postulates of economics reflect the actual observed (and statistically recorded) behavior of economic agents. Machlup requires no such correspondence. The crucial behavioral postulate for both economists is the assumption of rational, maximizing behavior. Whose is the more sophisticated position, from a philosophical perspective? The answer is clear: the laurels belong to Machlup.

The major philosophical issues are threefold: the structure of scientific theories, the status of theoretical terms, and the nature of hypothesis testing. Hutchison advanced an early solution to these questions in his 1938 tract. Pure economic theory forms a deductive system. The fundamental postulates of economics, because they are part of a deductive system and beçause they are protected by a ceteris paribus clause, are unfalsifiable, thus analytic, and thus devoid of any empirical content. I argued in the last chapter that Hutchison was unable to establish these claims.

Machlup's approach is different from that of Hutchison, and derives directly from the philosophy of science dominant in the 1950s. Philosophers of that time argued that a scientific theory forms a hypothetico-deductive system. Such a system is an empty, mechanical calculus until some of its terms are given an empirical interpretation via correspondence rules. It is often impossible to give every term in such a structure an empirical counterpart; in particular, sentences containing theoretical terms which refer to unobservable entities are problematical empirically. To resolve this dilemma, the indirect testability hypothesis was formulated: instead of testing each sentence in a theory for cognitive significance, the theory as a whole should be the focus of testing. If the theory as a whole is confirmed, then sentences containing theoretical terms gain meaning indirectly. In many cases, the axioms, postulates, or primitive statements contain theoretical terms and are untestable, whereas the deduced sentences, derivative theorems, or predictions of a theory are statements that may be tested.[20] All of this, of course, is compatible with Machlup's methodological views. Indeed, he quotes philosopher Braithwaite and even uses the phrase 'hypothetico-deductive system' in his article.

Some parts of Machlup's presentation would not be well received by philosophers. For example, most would prefer the term confirmation to verification. Next, few would approve of his almost casual remark that initial conditions need not be meticulously checked in a test situation.[21] And finally, most would reject Machlup's claim that the rationality assumption is neither analytic nor synthetic but a 'rule of procedure'. This particular approach is based on early proposals by Moritz Schlick and Felix Kaufmann for solving the problem posed by untestable statements in science. Clearly, the indirect testability hypothesis eliminates the necessity of categorizing untestable statements as rules, making that somewhat peculiar approach superfluous.[22]

Having made these qualifications, it is still clear that Machlup had a better understanding of the philosophy of science that was contemporaneous with his efforts than did Hutchison. This is not surprising. While Hutchison spent a few years as a lecturer in Germany, Machlup received his education in Vienna. That environment assured a thorough methodological education, including exposure to the ideas of such diverse thinkers and groups as Max Weber, Alfred Schutz, the logical positivists, Karl Popper, and his teacher, Ludwig von Mises.

Machlup's methodological schooling allowed him to formulate a position consistent with the philosohpy of science of his time. The more important question, of course, is whether his methodological views are appropriate for the discipline of economics. Such a question by its very nature cannot be answered by the examination of related issues within the philosophy of science. To answer it, we must inspect the beliefs and practices of economists.

We will assert without supporting arguments that most economists would accept the characterization that economic theory forms a hypothetico-deductive system.[23] The area where disagreement centers is whether and to what extent the fundamental postulate of maximizing behavior need be testable and tested. In terms of the philosophical issues, the question may be posed as follows: Is the indirect testability hypothesis a universal methodological precept which is applicable to all the sciences, or is it only a specific and nongeneralizable methodological dictum which should only be applied to physics, the science for which it was developed? More generally, we must inquire about the content, status, testability, and importance of the 'fundamental axiom' of maximizing behaviour, as perceived by members of the economics profession.

The Rationality Postulate – An Overview

The rationality postulate as exposited in introductory and inter-mediate texts is of varying degrees of rigor. In its simplest formu-lation, it consists of the assertion that atomistic economic agents pursue their own self-interest: that consumers (or households) seek to maximize utility and that firms seek to maximize profits. Some recents texts also apply the model of maximizing behavior to political agents.[24] Goals are pursued subject to budget and cost constraints. More advanced treatments note that the ability to detect indifference between market baskets of goods and the ability to choose consistently given a well-ordered preference function defines rationality in consumer theory, while rational firms must operate on their production function, choose least-cost combi-nations of inputs for each possible level of output, and choose the level of output which maximizes profits. Second order conditions, if treated at all, are relegated to the footnotes. Parametric variations allow comparative static predictions; they also permit derivation of demand and supply curves for the individual and firm. After a few comments on Giffen goods, independence of utility functions, and output-invariant factor prices, aggregation produces market demand and supply curves with the usual slope. Finally, perfect information over present and future states is assumed throughout, except for brief discussions of the role of expectations, the market as infor-mation disseminator, or an occasional insertion of the modifier 'expected' before the words utility and profit.

Critics of these models have much with which to work. The pursuit of self-interest, it is claimed, is useless if defined too narrowly, for impulsive or habitual behavior is then ruled out, and empty if defined too broadly, for then all behavior becomes maximizing behavior. Lexiographical orderings, exploratory choice behavior, and growing, or changing, or ill-formed preferences all violate the assumption of a consistent and stable preference ordering for consumers, and such behavior can be encountered in situations in which information is costly and choice is based on (possibly volatile) expectations. Whenever variables other than profits enter an owner's or manager's utility function, profit maximization for the firm may not result. No consistent preference ordering may exist in firms with multiple decision-makers; in such cases, satisficing behavior may replace optimizing behavior. Satisficing may also occur in an uncertain environment, and uncertainty may be caused by oligopolistic interdependence or, in nonoligopolistic markets, incomplete information regarding the relevant cost and demand functions. Finally, certain attempts to rescue profit maximization (by positing decision-makers who possess a complete listing of the sets of all possible states of the world together with a probability distribution fully defined over that set) beg the question in situations of genuine uncertainty, when decision-makers are not even sure what the various states of the world are, much less have estimates of the related probability distributions.

Such criticisms have provided the impetus for a host of alternative investigations of decision-making in economics. To mention only some of the more prominent, the pioneering efforts of Herbert Simon in the area of decision theory, Cyert and March's work on the behavioral theory of the firm, the contributions of proponents of various managerial theories of the firm, Harvey Liebenstein's path-breaking study of x-efficiency, G. L. S. Shackle's numerous investigations of the importance of expectations in a kaliedic world: all have had an impact on the profession's understanding of the concept of rational decision-making.[25] We cannot hope to explore the methodological foundations of these myriad alternative formulations, though that might prove to be a fruitful area for further study.

We will examine some of the more standard approaches to the question of rational decision-making in economics, emphasizing those that attempt to establish the logical status of the rationality postulate. This investigation will be arbitrarily limited by looking at responses to the following questions; other ordering schemes are possible.[26] We will be particularly interested in seeing how alternative approaches handle the possible problem areas of imperfect information and changing tastes and preferences.

Some Questions Concerning the Rationality Postulate

If economists believe that the assumption of rationality is important, then the postulate must be clearly defined, we must know what it means. One way of doing this is to inquire about its logical status: is it analytic, synthetic, or something quite different?

1.   If we answer *analytic*, is the postulate empirically empty? If not, what meaning does the assumption possess?
2.   If we answer *synthetic*, which of the following best characterizes our approach to its testability?
   a.   It must be stated in testable form.
   b.   It must actually be tested.

(As was mentioned above, within the philosophy of science, only certain logical positivists would demand that 'assumptions' be testable. Both logical empiricists (who are confirmationists) and Popperian falsificationists would look only at the predictions of a theory when testing. More recently, in Imre Lakatos's MSRP, propositions contained in the 'hard core' of a research program are not subject to empirical testing, and among those the assumptions of a theory are usually listed. Within economics, however, numerous studies testing the rationality postulate have been undertaken, so a discussion of these issues seems warranted.)

3. Perhaps the question of logical status along analytic–synthetic lines obscures rather than illuminates the issues at hand. Are alternative approaches more insightful?

After examining each of these questions in turn, I will suggest in the conclusion that Machlup's formulation of the problem, after all is considered, may well be the most fruitful.

1. The rationality assumption as analytic – Many critics of the maximizing model claim that the rationality postulate is analytic, and thus empirically vacuous. This was Hutchison's claim in his 1938 tract; Alan Sweezy took the formulations of 'Austrian economists' to task on similar grounds.[27]

Ludwig von Mises and others who insist that the fundamental axioms of human action are known to us a priori reject the analytic–synthetic dichotomy propounded by positivists. As was shown in the last chapter, the positivist claim that analytic statements cannot possess empirical content is rejected by Austrian economists because it does not permit the possibility of statements which are both a priori true yet have empirical content.

Problems with the praxeological approach were noted in the last chapter and will not be repeated here. It may be mentioned, however, that the modern Austrian position recognizes and explicitly treats the possibilities of changing tastes and imperfect information. In the Austrian view, all action is purposive, and the act of choosing reveals preferences. What happens, we may ask, if choice reveals a pattern of preferences which are not ordered? May we conclude that the chooser is irrational? Not at all. In a world of less than perfect information, our preferences may change as we gain information. Each act of choice reveals preferences as they exist *at the time of choice*, and nothing more; our next choice may seem inconsistent with previous choices, but it, too, is consistent with our preferences at the time that next choice is made. Thus, no purposive behavior is ever irrational; all choice takes place in time; and inconsistent behavior over time is solely indicative of changes in either preferences or information. Indeed, the modern Austrians perhaps more than other groups place information, ignorance, and even error at the heart of their vision of how markets work. As one example, Israel Kirzner emphasizes how the existence of error makes the role of the entrepreneur crucial in a market economy, for it is the entrepreneur's efforts to pursue unperceived or unexploited profit opportunities (created by the ignorance and error of others) which directs the allocation of resources in a market process.[28] Though their methodological pronouncements may seem bizarre, the modern Austrians (to their credit) explicitly recognize the importance of the problem of information in their research program.

2a. The fundamental assumption as synthetic, to be stated in testable form – We showed earlier that Terence Hutchison believed that the propositions of economic theory must be stated in testable form; otherwise, they are nothing but tautologies and are empirically empty. Another effort at establishing the empirical content of economic theory was undertaken by Paul Samuelson in the late 1930s.

In his classic article of 1938, Samuelson states that all past attempts at formulating a theory of consumer choice, including Hicks and Allen's 1934 revision of Marshallian demand theory along ordinalist lines, 'shows vestigial traces of the utility concept', and this 'despite the fact that the notion of utility has been repudiated or ignored by modern theory'.[29] In his paper, he shows how the usual results of the theory of consumer behavior can be derived using only market data, without recourse to the notion of utility. The revealed preference approach which emerged was thus 'operational', making reference only to observable market phenomena to yield its results. In later papers, Samuelson identifies the empirical implications of his theory for individual and group price–quantity behavior, constructs what are equivalent to indifference curves for the two-good case, and finally, after Houthakker developed the strong axiom, was able to exclude nonintegrability as a problem for his approach.[30]

In his *Foundations of Economic Analysis* (1947, 1965), Samuelson presents his results again, and takes time to reflect on his efforts. What follows are two passages taken from that book; juxtaposed, they are little short of remarkable.

> The importance of this result [the revealed preference equation on price–quantity behavior] can hardly be overemphasized. In this simple formula are contained almost all the meaningful empirical implications of the whole pure theory of consumer's choice. Moreover, these are expressed in the form which is most suitable for empirical verification.[31]
> . . .

Many writers have held the utility analysis to be an integral and important part of economic theory. Some have even sought to employ its applicability as a test criterion by which economics might be separated from the other social sciences. Nevertheless, *I wonder how much economic theory would be changed if either of the two conditions above were found to be empirically untrue. I suspect, very little.*[32] (emphasis added)

What does Samuelson mean here? He has gone to great pains to state the theory of consumer behavior in operational terms, yet he doubts whether disconfirming test cases would cause economists to reformulate the theory. Does Samuelson repudiate, or acquiesce in, such behavior? If the latter, he must show what substantive difference exists between untestable statements and propositions which, though stated in testable form, are untouched by disconfirming test results. And if the former, why did he not attempt to test his proposition at some point?

A later chapter is devoted to an analysis of Samuelson's methodological position. For now, we will only note that certain ambiguities have already surfaced in our first look at Samuelson's methodological writings. The importance of disconfirming test results is a matter for close attention, to be taken up next.

2b. The rationality assumption as synthetic, to be tested – Though Paul Samuelson never tested his theory, other researchers employed the revealed preference framework for the empirical testing of consumer theory. I report here on five such tests, which were chosen for the variety of approaches to their subject.

(i) Arnold Weinstein asked subjects in various age groups to rank randomly offered pairs of ten commodity bundles. He then inspected the data, seeking for intransitivities among triads of offerings. As shown in the table below, provided by Jack Hirshleifer, he found consistent orderings over most triads and, further, that the proportion of transitive responses increased with age.[33]

Table 7.1 *Transitivity Experiment Results*[a]

Group	Proportion of Transitive Responses (%)
52 children aged 9–12	79.2
36 teenagers aged 14–16	83.3
46 high school seniors aged 17–18	88.0
18 mature adults (mostly teachers)	93.5

[a] Weinstein (1968) in Hirshleifer (1980), p. 64.

(ii) Using data collected by a consumer food panel set up in the 1950s at Michigan State University, two studies (Koo, 1963, and Koo and Hasenkamp, 1972) attempted to test the strong axiom of revealed preference. The data were gathered from exhaustive diaries turned in weekly by families in the test group. Data were collected on over 1000 items; in addition, the diaries included information on the cost of meals and number of meals eaten away from home, the income received each week, the number of guest meals served, the number of meals received as guests, and the number of people in the household each week. The first study looked at 215 families who turned in 52 weekly reports in 1958, the second at families turning in 52 reports in the years from 1955 to 1958, with 140 families reporting for 1955 and 1956, 158 for 1957, and 211 for 1958. The results of the weekly reports were grouped into 13 observations of 4 week periods. The data were placed in matrix form, transformed using Boolian matrices, and inspected to determine the number of consistent matrices, ranked by the size of consistent matrices and the percentage of families in each category.[34]

In the first study, less than 1 percent of the families had consistent 13 × 13 matrices, and less than 1 percent had consistent matrices of dimension 5 × 5 or less (see Table 7.2).[35]

Table 7.2   *Size of Consistent Matrix by Number and Percentage of Families*[a]

Size of Consistent Matrix (n × n)	Number of Families	Percent of Families
4	1	0.47
5	0	0.00
6	3	1.40
7	7	3.26
8	43	20.00
9	65	30.23
10	48	22.32
11	29	13.49
12	17	7.91
13	2	0.93
Total:	215	100.00%

[a] *Source:* Koo (1963), p. 658.

In the second study, 9 families, for one or more years, had matrices that were completely or acyclically ordered, and 74 families had 12

× 12 matrices. On the other end of the scale, 62 families had matrices of size 3 × 3 or less. Closer inspection of 64 families which participated in all four years also revealed seasonal stability within each year, and a nonvariability over time of the number of acyclically ordered bundles for each family. In a sense, the 'rationality level' of each household was time invariant and varied in a consistent way with the seasons.[36]

(iii) In a study published in 1973, six researchers utilized a token economy to test the fundamental equation of revealed preference theory. Experimental subjects consisted of thirty-eight patients on a female ward for chronic psychotics at the Central Islip State Hospital in New York. At the time the study began, the token economy had been in operation on the ward for a year; about half the patients had participated for over six months. The patients purchased commodities at a store on the ward, with tokens that were received for jobs performed on the ward. After observing purchases at 'given prices' for seven weeks, another seven-week period followed in which 'price changes' were announced and put into effect at the beginning of each week. Prices of various commodities were either halved, doubled, or remained the same during each weekly period.[37]

Exactly half of the thirty-eight subjects exhibited consistent behavior in terms of the predictions of the theory. For most of the rest of the subjects, the data contradict the theory only for a single pair of weeks. When the data were reinspected for the possibility of measurement error, in seventeen of the nineteen contradictory cases the observational errors were too large to allow the researchers to distinguish between observational errors and contradictions of the theory.[38] On the basis of previous independent studies, it was suggested that in the two remaining contradictory cases the consumption patterns in earlier time periods may have had systematic residual effects on consumer purchases in later periods.[39]

(iv) The final study reports on two experiments conducted with white male albino rats, two subjects per experiment. In the first experiment, the caged subjects were provided with both rat chow and water, and a constant level white masking noise was provided at all times to minimize the effect of extraneous noises. Each cage was equipped with two levers; depression of levers provided the subjects with .05 ml dipper cups filled with (on the left) root beer and (on the right) Collins mix. During the shaping and baseline experimental stages, each subject was allotted 300 lever presses per period. During the experiment, either income (number of presses per period) or relative prices (size of dipper cup) could be varied. The experiments showed that the rats changed consumption patterns in response to changes in the budget set, consuming more of the lower priced commodities and less of the higher priced commodities.[40] In a second experiment using food and water and involving large rotations in the budget line for these essential commodities, consumer behavior was disrupted (e.g. rats failed to expend all of their income, and weight loss resulted). The researchers concluded that such results may suggest that certain behavioral disorders may be linked to changes in 'socioeconomic factors such as poverty and unemployment'.[41]

The empirical studies reported on above seem to support the hypothesis that transitively ordered preferences are commonly encountered, be the subjects adolescents, households, female psychotics, or albino rats. Such tests would seem to provide unambiguously interpretable confirming instances of the rationality assumption, as applied to consumer behavior. Are we then justified in tentatively accepting, or, alternatively, not rejecting, the assumption of rationality? To answer this, we must examine more closely just what such tests imply.

1. The importance of confirming test instances – All of the researchers followed proper scientific procedures in reporting the results of their tests. In particular, all were extremely careful not to jump to unjustified conclusions; indeed, most pointed out possible sources of error or bias in their experimental designs.[42]

Turning next to the test results, what do we find? We know that test results can never establish a hypothesis as true, but only prevent its rejection. In the extreme case in which data are known to be perfect and every test instance yields a perfect confirmation, Hume's riddle of induction still prevents us from asserting on inductive grounds a hypothesis as proven. But we need not worry about this, for there were no cases of perfect confirmation in any of the studies cited. The strongest result we can claim is that in *some* of the studies *most* of the subjects chose consistently. Should we accept the rationality postulate if confirmation is less than perfect? Should some formula be invoked to weigh the strength of confirmation of the hypothesis? What formula should be used? And how can the choice of formulas be defended; in other words, must not all such formulas be chosen arbitrarily? All of these questions indicate the difficulties involved in interpreting confirming test results in any test of a hypothesis, and, more generally, the difficulty of using strength of confirmation as a criterion for judging hypotheses.

Some of the tests are plagued with additional interpretational problems. In particular, the importance of the confirming instances in the last two studies can be debated. Does the finding that mental patients in a token economy choose (for the most part) consistently have any relevance to the outside world? And which of the following conclusions follows most naturally from the results of the experiments with rats?

a. Consumer theory is so general, it applies even to nonhuman populations.

b. Consumer theory is so restrictive, it works only in extremely simple two-good cases in which all outside disturbances are held constant.

c. For consumer theory to work, a subject must be rat-like, something like Veblen's 'lightening calculator of pleasures and pains, who oscillates like a homogeneous globule of desire of happiness under the impulse of stimuli that shifts him about the area. . .'.[43]

Again, to point all of this out is not to accuse the researchers of proceeding improperly. Our goal is simply to emphasize the difficulties involved in interpreting confirming test results.

2. The importance of disconfirming test instances – Each study had some disconfirming test instances, cases in which transitively ordered preferences were to some degree absent. How were such instances handled in the studies?

a. In some cases, they simply were not mentioned. For example, in the studies utilizing food panel data, the data are presented with very little interpretation.

b. In others, it was shown that certain apparently disconfirming instances may have been due to errors in measurement: to correct for this was one of the stated goals of the study which used a token economy.

c. Finally, attempts at explaining disconfirming instances led some researchers to hypothesize violations of assumed initial conditions. Thus, Hirshleifer proposed that intransitivities were greater among younger children because their choices are often exploratory. As such, we cannot assume their preference functions to be well ordered.[44] In a like manner, the researchers studying the token economy hypothesized that earlier consumption patterns affected choices in later periods for the two subjects whose choices clearly involved intransitivities.

Which of the above are appropriate responses to disconfirming test instances? Clearly, the failure to mention disconfirming instances violates proper scientific procedure. Disconfirming instances are crucial because they force the scientist to inspect the hyposthesis under test, any auxiliary hypotheses (which may include assumed initial conditions), the test design, and the data, to see what went wrong. In the cases mentioned, disconfirming instances led researchers to try to control for measurement error, and to hypothesize changes in the ceteris paribus conditions. Both of these are scientifically acceptable responses to disconfirming test instances, though they could be improved by attempts to independently test for the hypothesized changes.

A Popperian would state that qualification even more strongly. He would insist that the data be clean, the test design, straightforward, and initial conditions, checked, all prior to the test. Such procedures guarantee that the test is a test of the rationality hypothesis only, and not a test of the other components. A Popperian would further insist that the hypothesis be either rejected or modified in the face of disconfirming instances. And finally, he would not accept any ad hoc modifications of the hypothesis, only substantive ones. Clearly, Popper's dictums were not followed in any of the studies reviewed above. Those who insist that Popper's methodology be followed in economics should be cognizant that it is a strict code of rules that they are advocating.

3. For the last line of inquiry, we may propose a counterfactual: What would happen if there were more disconfirming instances? Would it then be necessary to reject the rationality assumption?

The answer is no. Simply put, the rationality assumption need never be rejected, even in the face of thousands of disconfirming test instances; it can always be saved.

Of course, there is a sense in which every hypothesis can be saved, but the methods of preservation that would have to be employed would strike even the most convinced advocate as ad hoc. Thus, to insist that all disconfirming instances are due to measurement error, without ever specifying the source of the error, is unconvincing.

We are not talking about such weak defensive strategems here. The rationality assumption need never be rejected because *it can never be straightforwardly tested*; disconfirming test results can always be attributed to changes in initial conditions *which are not themselves susceptible to testing*. More specifically, in the face of disconfirming results, one can assert that the consumer still chose rationally in each case, but that his preferences had changed.

One need not assume schizophrenic behavior on the part of the consumer to argue that changing preferences can explain observed intransitivities in choice. Hirshleifer argued convincingly that children's preferences may change as they grow and gain experience, but why should we assume that such a growth process comes to an end at the age of majority? Certainly there are other periods in our lives when changing circumstances might bring even drastic changes in our tastes – leaving school, changing jobs, changing marital status, having children, 'finding' God, or discovering the joys of gardening are but a few of these. Changing perceptions of the future may cause abrupt changes in preference patterns; so might the recognition that past beliefs were founded on faulty or incomplete information. Changes in expectations about any of a number of things (income, prices of goods, size of family, health, a rich uncle's health, the possibility of a nuclear war) may change present preference patterns. Finally, in tests in which household data are collected, the replacement of an individual preference function with a group preference function is by itself sufficient grounds for expecting some disconfirming results, given Arrow's impossibility theorem.

It is crucial for us to understand the point being made. *The possibility of changes in tastes and preferences, which are not themselves susceptible to empirical test, vitiates* any *test of the rationality postulate, whether the result is a confirming or a disconfirming instance.* Data that reveal transitive preference orderings are usually taken to mean the consumer is rational. *If* the consumer's tastes were changing, however, revealed transitivities might indicate *irrational* behavior. Similarly, intransitivities can be interpreted as due to changing tastes or due to irrationality on the part of the consumer. Neither a confirming nor a disconfirming test result, then, is unambiguously interpretable.

Some would rejoin that this line of reasoning is faulty. After all, they would argue, we all admit that tastes may change in the course of a lifetime. But surely it is reasonable to assume a *short run* stability in preference orderings, surely we may posit that tastes are stable in, say, an afternoon's time. If so, then a legitimate test of the rationality postulate would search for intransitivities in choice in the short run – a subject would be confronted with a variety of market baskets in a single afternoon, and his choices could then be evaluated for intransitivities.

But even in such experiments, revealed intransitivities need not cause us to reject the rationality postulate. For if the goods over which a subject has to choose were at all numerous, one could reasonably argue that observed intransitivities reveal only the consumer's rational decision not to keep all the necessary information required for perfectly consistent choice in his head. Robbins noted the 'marginal utility of not bothering about marginal utility' and J. M. Clark warned against 'the irrational passion for dispassionate rationality'; either could be invoked to preserve the assumption of rationality.[45]

Thus, we find that any disconfirming instance can be judged undamaging to the rationality assumption by claiming that ceteris was not paribus; that in this case, either the assumption of stable preferences or that of perfect information is at fault, rather than the hypothesis of rational behavior. If disconfirming instances were common, it might cause us to question the *usefulness*, or *applicability*, of a theory which assumed perfect information or stable preferences. But it need not lead us to reject the assumption of rationality itself.

For those bent on rejecting the usefulness of the hypothesis, the world is a kaleidic place, people change and grow, and information is not perfect. For those who urge its retention, the hypothesis works reasonably well in most instances, and violations are fruitful areas for further investigation, that is, analyses of rationally changing tastes or decision-making under uncertainty.[46] But there are no empirical grounds for the acceptance or rejection of the postulate of rational action itself.

Even if this point is conceded, the consistent empiricist still might argue that additional tests could establish the *usefulness* of the hypothesis. However, even here he may encounter difficulties. Suppose that a perceived increase in the volatility of the inflation rate by consumers causes their expectations to become more important in their spending decisions, and leads to greater intransitivities in their choice patterns. Studies of consumer data in the 1950s and 1960s in the United States might lead us to believe that consumer theory is useful, since few intransitivities would be observed. That conclusion might be reversed if the data were collected in the late 1960s and 1970s. Most important, what would be our expectations about its usefulness for the 1980s? Must we boldly conclude that the hypothesis works when it works, but does not work when it fails? Empirical studies may reveal conditions when we may expect with some confidence that the hypothesis can or cannot fruitfully be applied, but that subordinate role for empirical studies was granted fifty years ago by Robbins, and involves a substantial concession on the part of positivists who promise a far more substantial place for empirical tests in their methodological program.

The dilemmas discussed above are more general than the topic at hand, and may be summarized in a sentence – acceptance *or* rejection of any hypothesis on strictly empirical grounds is problematical whenever initial conditions cannot be independently checked and underlying relationships among variables are subject to unpredictable change. This observation is central to later discussions of theory choice.[47]

It seems, then, that there is at least some evidence that the indirect testability hypothesis has applications outside of the natural sciences, for the direct testing of the rationality assumption in economics appears problematical. Of course, we have investigated only consumer theory, and should not generalize too quickly from those results. On the other hand, the information problem seems capable of vitiating most tests of the postulate, and that problem is presumably present in many economic decision-making situations.

We may close with the conclusion that those who would insist on testing the rationality postulate can be characterized accurately as ultra-empiricists. That position finds little support in the philosophy of science (only certain logical positivists would support it); more important, it does not seem that a straightforward test of the assumption is possible. Other conclusions are possible, of course. Some may wish to reject the assumption, since it is untestable. Others may try to develop a test. Neither route seems particularly fruitful to this reviewer, but they most assuredly are options.

Perhaps the best conclusion is to simply point out that certain positions are no longer tenable. In particular, economists cannot now claim that the assumption is testable, or worse, that it is highly confirmed. It is, rather, a (currently) untestable hypothesis, and if that does not sit well with empirically-minded economists, they should either denounce their ultra-empiricist methodology, or reject the rationality assumption as metaphysical.

3. Many alternative investigations of the rationality postulate which do not directly employ the analytic–synthetic distinction exist, but few deal with the problems mentioned above better than the two formulations reviewed below. These are Alchian and Becker's demonstrations that the major theorems of economic theory do not depend on the assumption of rational behavior, and Machlup's assertion that rational economic man is an ideal type.

3a. In the introduction to his 1950 article, 'Uncertainty, Evolution, and Economic Theory', Armen Alchian readily concedes that in the absence of complete information and perfect foresight, the assumption of profit maximization is '*meaningless* as a guide to specifiable action'.[48] He then analyzes what effects this concession has on the theory of the firm. He notes that in the real world relative realized profit, rather than maximum profit, is the criterion of success for firms. He further notes that surviving firms may have attempted to maximize profits, but that that is surely neither necessary nor sufficient for their survival. Fortuitous circumstance, luck, or chance may far outweigh 'proper motivation' as determinants of positive profits.

> Positive profits accrue to those who are better than their actual competitors, even if the participants are ignorant, intelligent, skillful, etc.

The crucial element is one's aggregate position relative to actual competitors, not some hypothetically perfect competitors.[49]

As long as there is a sufficient number of participants in a market, even *random* behavior yields predictions that apply to the *group* as a whole; namely, that those firms which *for whatever reason* choose actions that permit survival are successful and will be 'selected' for survival by the economic system. The assumption of random behavior is an extreme case and is used only to establish the point. In an uncertain world, however, even seemingly nonoptimal behavior (e.g. trial and error or imitative behavior) may be viable with success-producing results.[50] Alchian summarizes his contribution as follows:

> The existence of uncertainty and incomplete information is the foundation of the suggested type of analysis; the importance of the concept of a class of "chance" decisions rests upon it; it permits of various conflicting objectives; it motivates and rationalizes a type of adaptive imitative behavior; yet it does not destroy the basis of prediction, explanation, or diagnosis. It does not base its aggregate description on individual optimal action; yet it is capable of incorporating such activity where justified.[51]

Alchian and Friedman are acknowledged by Becker as having provided initial insights in his 1962 essay, 'Irrational Behavior and Economic Theory'. Becker faces head on in his introduction the criticisms of the standard theory mentioned above. Noting that rational behavior 'simply implies consistent maximization of a well-ordered function', he lists some possible objections to that formulation: 'that households and firms do not maximize, at least not consistently, that preferences are not well ordered, and that the theory is not useful in explaining behavior'.[52] His purpose is not to defend the rationality assumption against such charges. Rather, it is to shift the focus from the individual decision-maker to the market as a whole, from assumptions about rationality to derived theorems about market demand curves. Such curves will be negatively inclined even if the behavior of a majority of individual households is irrational; his study implies that the predictions of economic theory are compatible with many types of assumed decision rules.[53]

Becker walks the reader through a compensated price change using the traditional rational consumer and indifference curve analysis, showing that a substitution effect occurs in response to compensated relative price changes. He then investigates two types of 'irrational' behavior – that of 'impulsive, erratic' households and that of 'inert, habitual' households. The behavior of the former can be duplicated by some random selection process (say, throwing a die); in the latter case, households will always try to achieve past consumption bundles.[54]

The key to Becker's analysis is to focus on the effects of changing *opportunity sets* for the expected *market* outcome. For both cases, assume *AB* is the original budget line, *p* is the original consumer equilibrium, and *CD* is the new income compensated budget line, whose position reflects a decrease in the price of *Y* relative to *X*. Traditional theory predicts the new equilibrium *p'* will lie on *CD* somewhere between *C* and *p*. Impulsive households would act as if they consulted some probability mechanism, and the average consumption of a large number of independent households would lie at the middle of the opportunity set; hence consumption of *Y* would increase and that of *X* decrease. The opposite extreme from impulsive is habitual behavior, in which case households attempt to consume exactly what they did in the past. Households initially in

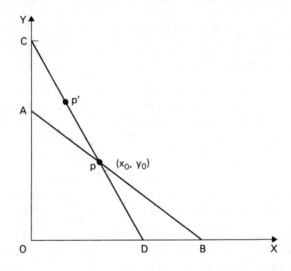

the *Ap* region could remain there after the price change, but households in the *pB* region would be forced to adjust their consumption. In particular, any household that consumed more than *OD* amount of *X* before would have to reduce its consumption of *X* to at most a level of *OD*. Again, for the market as a whole, the average consumption of *X* would decline and *Y* would rise in response to a relative increase in the price of *X*.[55] The major result of consumer theory, downsloping market demand curves, is thus consistent with many forms of individual behavior. In a later section, the theory of the firm is inspected with similar results. The methodological implications of his demonstrations are not lost on Becker, as is seen in the following quotation:

> Patterning the theory of households after market responses (i.e., assuming rational consumers) was not only unnecessary, but also responsible for much bitter and rather sterile controversy. Confidence in market rationality misled some into stout defenses of rationality at all levels, while confidence in household irrationality misled others into equally stout attacks on all rationality. What has apparently been over-looked is that both views may be partly right and partly wrong: households may be irrational and yet markets quite rational.[56]

Though Becker's ingenious use of opportunity sets (which consists primarily in pointing out the effects of changing scarcity of resources) and emphasis on the market rather than the individual is exceptionally well-presented, neither his nor Alchian's analysis has gone unchallenged.[57] But let us grant their points that a distinction must be made between individual decision-makers and markets, and that by shifting attention to the market level, the question of individual rationality becomes far less important. Such an approach still opens the door for studies of the actual decision-making processes of consumers and firms, that is, the more 'realistic' studies of such researchers as Simon, Cyert and March, Liebenstein, and others. Indeed, the fact that negatively inclined demand curves are consistent with many types of decision rules gives impetus to investigations of the wide variety of such rules that may exist. Let those concerned only with market level responses continue to expend their resources proving that 'water runs downhill'; those concerned with new areas of investigation will try to discover how decision-making actually takes place.

This implication has not gone unnoticed by certain economists who wish to preserve the maximizing model in economics. Milton Friedman is perhaps most famous. If we believe with Friedman that theories with more realistic assumptions are no advance, that agents need only act 'as if' they were maximizing, that theories should be judged by their predictive adequacy rather than their explanatory power, and that the major prediction of consumer theory is a down-ward sloping market demand curve, then it is hard to conceive of any alternative model of decision-making that could be justified. Friedman's sometimes elusive, always bedeviling methodological stance will be analyzed in the next chapter. Another approach is exemplified by Becker's later work. In *The Economic Approach to Human Behavior* (1976), he applies economic analysis to such diverse areas as crime, fertility behavior, time allocation by households, marriage, and other traditionally noneconomic topics. He consistently assumes stable preferences, and in a later article with George Stigler asserts that changes in preferences can be attributed to changes in income and relative prices, and thus are themselves susceptible to economic analysis.[58] I will not attempt to evaluate this rapidly growing research tradition here. If detractors insist that an approach to social phenomena which claims to be capable of explaining everything in effect explains nothing,[59] it still must be conceded that this novel attempt to bridge interdisciplinary gaps at least promotes potentially rewarding argumentation and debate.

3b. This chapter began with a review of Fritz Machlup's 'The Problem of Verification in Economics'. Probably no other economist has devoted more pages to the investigation of methodological issues than Machlup, as is evidenced by a recent collection of his work in that area.[60] Because he is so prolific, I will draw on a number of Machlup's articles in an effort to accurately represent his position regarding the rationality assumption.

The reader of this chapter should have no trouble accepting Machlup's initial observation that little consensus exists regarding the logical nature of *homo oeconomicus*; that 'going from a priori statements and axioms, via rules of procedure, useful fictions and ideal types all the way to empirical data, the spectrum of logical possibilities seems to be complete'.[61] Since choice of approach seems mostly a matter of 'methodological taste', he refrains from attempts at arbitration. His own solution, he hopes to show, has certain advantages, and 'may stand a good chance of being acceptable to the representatives of the most divergent views'.[62]

That solution is to claim that *homo oeconomicus* is an ideal type. The term 'ideal type' has had a myriad of interpretations, especially among philosophically-oriented German social scientists of the late nineteenth century, and Machlup devotes two essays to a review of the debates surrounding the meaning of the term.[63] An etymological perfectionist, he laments that in the normal senses of the words, 'the ideal type is neither ideal nor a type'.[64] For Machlup, the ideal type known as *homo oeconomicus* is a mental (as opposed to an operational) construct, an 'artificial device for use in economic theorizing', a man-made artifact whose name should be changed to *homunculus oeconomicus* to indicate its origins in the human mind.[65] All ideal types must be distinguished from operational, or real, types.

Operational (empirical, epistemic) concepts, defined by observational, experimental or statistical operations, are needed for empirical propositions (correlational laws). *Exact* (abstract, pure) constructs, formed by idealization, invention, and construction, are needed for nomological – theoretical propositions (theoretical laws).[66]

. . .

As soon as one passes from observation, classification, comparison and calculation (correlation, regression, etc.) to reflection and theorizing about causal relationships among phenomena, one consciously or unconsciously replaces the real types with ideal types. . . the real type is a category of observation, classification, description, and measurement, while the ideal type is a category of reflection and argumentation.[67]

. . .

Homo oeconomicus is the metaphoric or figurative expression for a proposition used as a premise in the hypothetico-deductive system of economic theory.[68]

This view of the rationality postulate has implications for the proper uses of economic theory. The consumers and firms referred to in our theories are mental constructs, they do not refer to real individuals or business enterprises, they are not *operational*. Theory is primarily an aid to thinking, a heuristic device in which we trace out the predicted responses of imagined agents to imagined changes in the environment they face.

the economist's chief task is not to explain or predict human action of every sort, or even all human action related to business, finance, or production, but instead only certain kinds of people's reactions (response) to specified changes in the conditions facing them. For this task a *homunculus oeconomicus*, that is, a postulated (constructed, ideal) universal type of human reactor to stated stimuli, is an indispensable device for a necessary purpose.[69]

In applying economic theory to the real world, Machlup emphasizes that one must assume preferences and information as given. He provides examples of situations in which such assumptions are unwarranted, and concedes that 'if the bulk of all cases were of this kind, the usefulness of our theoretical system would be much reduced'.[70] Because the theory is only capable of yielding qualitative predictions about the reactions of hypothetical agents, Machlup is disdainful of attempts at quantitative prediction. Indeed, much confusion in contemporary methodological thought is caused by attempts to either 'operationalize' or test what are only ideal types, or useful heuristic fictions.[71]

Finally, we must ask Machlup on what grounds he would favor the rejection of the assumption of rational economic man. One necessary condition is the existence of a suitable replacement:

These assumptions may well be rejected, but only together with the theoretical system of which they are a part, and only when a more satisfactory system is put into its place; in Conant's words, "a theory is only overthrown by a better theory, never merely by contradictory facts."[72]

As is evident in his AEA presidential address, Machlup does not believe that any suitable replacements for the theory of the firm have yet been proposed. He readily admits that alternative theories of the firm are useful for explicating *other* aspects of a firm's behavior or structure, and lists ten of the 'at least twenty-one concepts of the firm employed in the literature of business and economics'.[73]

Summary and Conclusion

Machlup was right: the various approaches to the rationality postulate reported on here lead to a wide range of methodological prescriptions. All approaches have at least one thing in common: the recognition that, to be plausible, an explanation of the logical status and nature of the rationality assumption must come to terms with the questions of changing preferences and information. While final adjudication may well be a matter of methodological taste, to again invoke Machlup, we can examine the diverse positions reviewed above for relative strengths and weaknesses.

1. The modern Austrian program has many merits – the Austrians know how markets work, and their understanding of that process is more subtle than many of their colleagues; they explicitly address the problem of information in their analysis; and their system is coherent and consistent. This last may also be the greatest weakness of the modern Austrian approach, for in their quest for consistency they have constructed a system which, in the eyes of many of their critics, is tautological, hence empirically empty, hence meaningless.

The Austrians are unimpressed by such criticisms since, in their view, they have developed a system based on an alternative epistemology. Within that system, the goal of internal consistency is achieved if all purposive action is defined as rational and all preferences are revealed at the moment of choice, for then no state of the world can result in behavior that is not rational. External criticism is swept aside by asserting that the above postulates are known a priori, that the theorems which are correctly derived follow with apodictic certainty, and that no other science of human behavior has such characteristics. The analytic–synthetic distinction, the acceptance of which implies that the Austrian program is hopelessly confused, is rejected as wrong-headed, as is the work of any economist with an empirical bent. Finally, the only acknowledged grounds for criticizing the modern Austrian system is to challenge its assumptions or to question the validity of the 'verbal chains of logic' that lead from the postulates to the theorems.

As was mentioned in the last chapter, the Austrians are at least partially justified in their self-confidence: since most criticisms of their program have been based on alternative epistemological and methodological systems, the criticisms have not been established. The Austrians should not be *complacent*, however, since unsuccessful arguments against them have nevertheless *persuaded* most economists who have considered those criticisms. Both Austrians and their critics have their work laid out for them: the former must show how their system may be compared to rivals, and the latter must try to criticize the Austrians from within the Austrian system itself. Criticism is enhanced and both camps gain credibility when those on the outside of a system try to get inside, and those on the inside try to see it from without.

2. Given the above remarks concerning a priori true systems, the positivist insistence on empirical tests of hypotheses seems profoundly sensible. By testing assumptions, hypotheses, and theories against incontrovertible data, the disconfirmed may be discarded, the confirmed (with appropriate circumspection) may be tentatively accepted, or at least fail to be rejected, and scientific knowledge by this process will slowly but surely expand.

But in the case of the rationality postulate, a dilemma is encountered. The empirical definition of rationality put forth by economists is transitivity in observed choice, given that two initial conditions (themselves untestable) hold: preferences are well-ordered and stable, and information is complete. But if those initial conditions cannot themselves be tested, the results of tests of the rationality assumption cannot be unambiguously interpreted. While confirming instances go unexamined, disconfirming instances can be met with the claim, ceteris was not paribus. Seldom is it mentioned that, *if* ceteris was not paribus and consistency in choice was nevertheless observed, it would indicate irrational behavior on the part of the consumer. Our delight at the promise of empirical techniques for the unambiguous evaluation of theories is transformed suddenly to despair, at least in this case – the absence of independent tests of initial conditions renders tests of the rationality postulate vacuous.

3. Given the apparent failure of both a priorism and positivism to adequately solve the question of the exact nature of the rationality postulate, alternatives that do not emphasize logical status were

examined. One of these disregards the individual decision-maker and redirects focus to the market: why concern ourselves with individuals if markets are rational? This approach may be viable, but it seems to imply that alternative investigations of decision-making processes should be undertaken, since such areas constitute voids which beg to be filled. Some analysts, however, try to prevent that step.

a. Friedman warns that attempts to make assumptions more 'realistic' are not only unnecessary but methodologically unsound – simplicity, not realism, is a methodological virtue; realism in assumptions is a methodological vice.

b. Since complications involve the initial conditions, the standard analysis can be revitalized by showing that decision-making under uncertainty can be reduced in most important cases to decision-making under risk, and that changes in preferences can be attributed to changes in relative prices and incomes, in the broadest senses of those words.

Of these two countermoves, the latter is the more appealing, in that it has seemingly generated some novel findings, and certainly sparked some debate. Since it is a new 'research program', it will not be evaluated here. Friedman's more famous (perhaps the adjective notorious could also be used) methodological stance is investigated in the next chapter.

4. We come at last to Machlup, perhaps the most methodologically astute of the analysts. As he claimed in 'The Verification Problem', his position lies somewhere between those of the 'a priorists' and the 'ultra-empiricists'. He does not attempt to test the rationality assumption, for as an 'ideal type', it cannot be tested. Though his notion of an 'ideal type' is an unfamiliar one, Machlup's position is otherwise consistent both with the H-D model of theory structure, and with the Lakatosian concept of a research program's 'hard core' of untestable, metaphysical assumptions. On the other hand, Machlup is no a priorist; he does not insist that neoclassical theory is true by definition, nor does he maintain that it is everywhere applicable. Rather, he agrees with Friedman that the best 'test' of a theory is its usefulness, as measured by its applicability. And indeed, his position regarding the role of empirical studies in economics (to see if a particular theory is applicable in a particular situation, rather than to test it, with the idea of rejecting it if it is disconfirmed) accords well with the positions of economists on the subject throughout the nineteenth century and into the third decade of the present one.[74] If one takes the long view, Machlup is a contemporary representative of the dominant view on the role of empirical studies, whereas both Austrians and positivists must be

viewed as relatively recent challengers.

It was mentioned that Machlup shares some similarities with Friedman; are there differences between them? The answer hinges on the definition of 'realism'. Friedman does not feel that the realism of a theory's assumptions is important. In the next chapter, Friedman is described as an instrumentalist. If that is an accurate characterization, realism refers to truth value. Machlup believes that assumptions should be 'realistic', but he uses the term to mean 'understandable' or 'plausible'. Clearly, the various meanings of the word realism as it is used by economists constitute a subject that warrants further study.

Though admittedly a matter of methodological taste, Machlup's position seems to this reviewer to be the most methodologically sound, probably because he grasped the fundamental methodological issues so early on and with such clarity. (Becker would no doubt insist that my preference for Machlup's approach is determined by the nature of my prior investment in human capital, namely, investigation of the links between philosophy of science and methodological inquiry in economics.) My impatience with a priorism and positivism is due to their claiming too much – Austrians assert wrongly that their analysis applies everywhere and cannot be overthrown, positivists believe wrongly that empirical techniques are sufficient for adjudicating among alternative theoretical formulations. Machlup avoids these errors, and makes some positive contributions, as well.

His notion of an ideal type, though initially unfamiliar and strange-sounding, has both historical precedence and a certain intuitive appeal. The term emphasizes that 'rational economic man' is a theoretical construct; that is, it does not refer directly to 'the real world'. Its usage would protect us from the dilemmas we often encounter as teachers, of trying to defend our models as applicable while simultaneously emphasizing (admitting?) that no consumers or firms 'really' act that way. Machlup's insistence that empirical studies can never establish nor falsify a theory, but can be used to judge its applicability, also strikes me as wise counsel. This approach emphasizes that our theories *will not* always be applicable, thereby avoiding the corner that the Austrians seem (on some readings) to have painted themselves into. The ultra-empiricist dilemma is also avoided: we are not forced to reconcile the rhetoric of disconfirmation with the fact that the assumption is untestable. Machlup's dictum that the assumption be 'realistic' is too ambiguous to evaluate, but at least it is a plausible restriction. And finally, his observation that even a disconfirmed theory will not be rejected unless a suitable replacement exists not only agrees with the findings of Kuhn and Lakatos regarding theory change, it anticipates them by a decade!

For all of his careful analysis, Machlup might still be accused of waffling on certain points. In particular, he really has not told us very much about how a theory might be overthrown. His suggestions whet the appetite, but do not satisfy the hunger. At this point, I might only suggest, in his defense, that he is not unique, and that perhaps the beginning of wisdom when dealing with the issue of theory choice lies in realizing the limitations of any scientific methodology.

Notes

1 Fritz Machlup, 'The Problem of Verification in Economics,' in Fritz Machlup, *Methodology of Economics and Other Social Sciences* (New York: Academic Press, 1978), p. 138. For further examples of Machlup's penchant for definitions, see Fritz Machlup, *Essays on Economic Semantics* (Englewood Cliffs, N.J.: Prentice-Hall, 1963).

2 Machlup, 'Verification. . .,' op. cit., pp. 138–41, quote on p. 141. Machlup's claim that the place a hypothesis holds within a hierarchical system is even more important than its degree of confirmation is clear evidence that he is no positivist. The similarity of his *conclusions* with those of Friedman regarding the testing of assumptions has led some to believe that both are positivists. Machlup is not; nor is Friedman, who is an instrumentalist.

3 Ibid., p. 141.

4 Ibid., pp. 142–3. Machlup's interpretation is different from Blaug's, who claims that the nineteenth century 'verificationists' used empirical studies only to 'verify' rather than 'test' their theories; that disconfirming test results were always dismissed with the phrase, 'ceteris was not paribus'. See Mark Blaug, *The Methodology of Economics* (Cambridge, England: Cambridge University Press, 1980), pp. 66–81.

5 Machlup, 'Verification. . .,' op. cit., p. 143.

6 Ibid., p. 145.

7 Ibid., p. 147.

8 Ibid., pp. 148–50.

9 Ibid., p. 152.

10 Ibid., p. 153.

11 T. W. Hutchison, 'Professor Machlup on Verification in Economics,' *Southern Economic Journal*, vol. 22 (April 1956), pp. 478–9.

12 Ibid., p. 480.

13 Ibid., p. 482.

14 Ibid., pp. 482–3.

15 Ibid., p. 481.

16 This is discussed in greater detail in a later section of this chapter. The early work by Pareto and its refinement by Hicks and Allen seems to represent a movement toward less *restrictive*, more *understandable*, but not necessarily more *testable* assumptions. This interpretation agrees with that of G.L.S. Shackle, *The*

Years of High Theory (Cambridge, England: Cambridge University Press, 1967), Chapter 8, who argues that while Hicks's indifference curve approach is no more *operational* than Marshall's formulation, it does have other advantages. Shackle confuses the topic somewhat when he states that Hicks's apparatus has one advantage over Marshall, then lists five (not *all* of which are independent, but some are): economy of assumptions, simplicity, generalness, efficiency, and that the indifference curve is 'one of those notational inventions that can nearly think for itself'.

17   Fritz Machlup, 'Rejoinder to a Reluctant Ultra-Empiricist,' in Machlup, *Methodology of Economics*, p. 494.
18   Ibid., p. 494.
19   Ibid., p. 494–5.
20   See Chapter 3, this volume.
21   I can make no sense of this remark by Machlup, unless it is meant as a descriptive rather than prescriptive comment.
22   The discussion in Alexander Rosenberg, *Microeconomic Laws: A Philosophical Analysis* (Pittsburgh: University of Pittsburgh Press, 1976), pp. 24–28 is helpful.
23   Exceptions would lie outside of the mainstream, in any case. For example, Institutionalists following the pattern model of scientific explanation would reject the idea that all legitimate theory must be expressible in the form of a hypothetico-deductive system. See Charles Wilber and Robert Harrison, 'The Methodological Basis of Institutional Economics: Pattern Model, Storytelling, and Holism,' *Journal of Economic Issues*, vol. 12 (March 1978), pp. 61–89.
24   An example is Richard McKenzie and Gordon Tullock, *Modern Political Economy: An Introduction to Economics* (New York: McGraw, Hill, 1978).
25   Citations can be found in the Notes for Further Reading.
26   James Buchanan divides economic theory into four categories, the logic of economic choice, the abstract science of human behavior, the predictive science of economic behavior, and the behavioristic science of the economy; Clem Tisdale looks at the concept of rationality in models where information is perfect and in others where information is limited. See James Buchanan 'Is Economics the Science of Choice?' in his *What Should Economists Do?* (Indianapolis, Ind.: Liberty Press, 1979); Clem Tisdale, 'Concepts of Rationality in Economics,' *Philosophy of Social Science*, vol. 5 (1975), pp. 259–72.
27   Alan R. Sweezy, 'The Interpretation of Subjective Value Theory in the Writings of the Austrian Economists,' *Review of Economic Studies*, vol. 1 (1934), pp. 176–85.
28   Israel Kirzner, 'Economics and Error,' in Louis Spadaro (ed.), *New Directions in Austrian Economics* (Kansas City: Sheed, Andrews and McMeel, 1978), pp. 57–76. For an earlier and more comprehensive treatment, see his *Competition and Entrepreneurship* (Chicago: University of Chicago Press, 1973). A recently published collection of his essays on the subject is *Perception, Opportunity and Profit: Studies in the Theory of Entrepreneurship* (Chicago: University of Chicago Press, 1979).
29   Paul Samuelson, 'A Note on the Pure Theory of Consumer's Behavior,' *Economica*, vol. 5 (February 1938), p. 61.
30   Paul Samuelson, 'The Empirical Implications of Utility Analysis,' *Econometrica*, vol. 6 (October 1938), pp. 344–56; 'Consumption Theory in Terms of Revealed Preference,' *Economica*, vol. 15 (November 1948), pp. 243–53; 'The Problem of Integrability in Utility Theory,' *Economica*, vol. 17 (November 1950), pp. 355–85. All of Samuelson's early articles on consumer theory can be found in Joseph Stiglitz (ed.), *The Collected Scientific Papers of Paul A. Samuelson*, Vol. I (Cambridge, Mass.: MIT Press, 1966). See also Hendrick Houthakker,

'Revealed Preferences and the Utility Function,' *Economica*, vol. 17 (May 1950), pp. 159–74.

31 Paul Samuelson, *Foundations of Economic Analysis* (first published, 1947) (New York: Atheneum, 1974), p. 111.

32 Ibid., p. 117.

33 Arnold Weinstein, 'Transitivity of Preference: A Comparison Among Age Groups,' *Journal of Political Economy*, vol. 76 (March–April 1968), pp. 307–11; Jack Hirshleifer, *Price Theory and Applications* (first published, 1976), 2nd edn (Englewood Cliffs, N.J.: Prentice-Hall, 1980), p. 64.

34 Anthony Y.C. Koo, 'An Empirical Test of Revealed Preference Theory,' *Econometrica*, vol. 31 (October 1963), pp. 646–58; Anthony Y.C. Koo and Georg Hasenkamp, 'Structure of Revealed Preference: Some Preliminary Evidence,' *Journal of Political Economy*, vol. 80 (July–August 1972), pp. 724–9.

35 Koo, 'An Empirical Test. . . .,' loc. cit., pp. 658–63.

36 Koo and Hasenkamp, 'Structure. . .,' loc. cit., pp. 729–40.

37 Raymond Battalio, John Kagel, et al. 'A Test of Consumer Demand Theory Using Observations of Individual Consumer Purchases,' *Western Economic Journal*, vol. 11 (December 1973), pp. 415–21.

38 Ibid., pp. 422–7.

39 Ibid., pp. 423–7.

40 John Kagel, Raymond Battalio, et al. 'Experimental Studies of Consumer Demand Behavior Using Laboratory Animals,' *Economic Inquiry*, vol. 13 (March 1975), pp. 22–31.

41 Ibid., p. 37.

42 For example, Koo notes that families who would take the time to fill out and turn in 52 weekly food diaries may be more careful than the normal family in its food purchases; the sample may not be representative of the population. See Koo, 'An Empirical Test. . .,' loc. cit., p. 663. Other qualifications were offered in his and other studies.

43 Thorstein Veblen, 'Why Is Economics Not an Evolutionary Science?,' in Max Lerner (ed.), *The Portable Veblen* (New York: The Viking Press, 1948), p. 232. Hopefully it is clear that I am having some fun with the 'experimental economics' research program in the text. It must be emphasized that the researchers working in this program have without exception been extremely judicious and cautious in interpreting their results: disconfirmations are viewed as helpful for suggesting new areas of study rather than as grounds for rejecting the underlying theory. In addition, the researchers offer a wide range of arguments supporting the use of nonhuman populations for examining economic hypotheses: such studies allow for greater control and more accuracy regarding measurement error; they are less costly and avoid risks to humans; they have pure scientific interest and allow workers in psychology, biology, and economics to learn from one another; they allow man to learn how his actions affect the nonhuman animal environment. A methodological study of the 'experimental economics' research program should be undertaken; it would yield some interesting (and no doubt provocative) results.

44 Hirshleifer, op. cit., p. 64.

45 Clark's statement was noted in George Stigler and Gary Becker, 'De Gustibus Non Est Disputandum,' *American Economic Review*, vol. 67 (March 1977), p. 82.

46 The former approach is exemplified in Stigler and Becker, *Ibid.*; a review of some of the literature dealing with uncertainty is Jack Hirshleifer and John Riley, 'The Analytics of Uncertainty and Information: An Expository Survey,' *Journal of Economic Literature*, vol. 17 (December 1979), pp. 1375–421.

47 As is mentioned in the last chapter, I feel that these problems are responsible for the failure of economists to issue falsifiable hypotheses, as documented in Blaug, *The Methodology of Economics*, pp. 127–8, 159–264. Cf. J. Agassi, 'Tautology and Testability in Economics,' *Philosophy of Social Sciences*, vol. 1 (1971), pp. 49–63, for the view that many statements in economics are neither tautological nor synthetic, but simply untestable. More on this in the final chapters.

48 Armen Alchian, 'Uncertainty, Evolution and Economic Theory,' in his *Economic Forces at Work* (Indianapolis, Ind.: Liberty Press, 1977), p. 18.

49 Ibid., p. 20.

50 Ibid., pp. 27–32.

51 Ibid., p. 33.

52 Gary Becker, 'Irrational Behavior and Economic Theory,' *Journal of Political Economy*, vol. 70 (February 1962), p. 1.

53 Ibid., p. 2.

54 Ibid., p. 5.

55 Ibid., pp. 4–9.

56 Ibid., p. 8.

57 Critics include Israel Kirzner, 'Rational Action and Economic Theory,' *Journal of Political Economy*, vol. 70 (August 1962), pp. 380–5; and Sidney Winter, 'Economic "Natural Selection" and the Theory of the Firm,' *Yale Economic Essays*, vol. 4 (Spring 1964), pp. 224–72.

58 Gary Becker, *The Economic Approach to Human Behavior* (Chicago: University of Chicago Press, 1976); and Stigler and Becker, 'De Gustibus. . .,' loc. cit., pp. 76–90.

59 This argument is advanced in Alexander Rosenberg, 'Can Economic Theory Explain Everything?,' *Philosophy of Social Science*, vol. 9 (1979), pp. 509–29.

60 Fritz Machlup, *Methodology of Economics and Other Social Sciences* (New York: Academic Press, 1978). Page references will refer to pagination in this collection rather than to that in the original articles.

61 Fritz Machlup, 'The Universal Bogey: Economic Man,' in Machlup, *Methodology of Economics*, p. 297.

62 Ibid., p. 298. Cf. p. 270.

63 Machlup, 'The Ideal Type: A Bad Name for a Good Construct,' and 'Ideal Types, Reality, and Construction,' both in Machlup, *Methodology of Economics*, pp. 211–65.

64 Machlup, 'The Ideal Type. . .,' op. cit., p. 213.

65 Machlup, 'The Universal Bogey. . .,' op. cit., p. 298.

66 Machlup, 'The Ideal Type. . .,' op. cit., p. 214.

67 Machlup, 'Ideal Types, Reality and Construction,' op. cit., p. 258.

68 Machlup, 'The Universal Bogey. . .,' op. cit., p. 297.

69 Ibid., p. 300.

70 Ibid., p. 301. His argument that *changes* in information are more important than the *store* of information is no doubt meant as a palliative to analyses like Sidney Winter's op. cit., in which firms operating with less than full information might take actions which contradict the theory's predictions, for example, decrease prices in 'response' to a wage increase. See Machlup, 'Theories of the Firm: Marginalist, Behavioral, Managerial,' op. cit., p. 414.

71 Machlup, 'The Universal Bogey. . .,' op. cit., p. 301. This was, of course, his point in his argument with Hutchison reviewed at the beginning of this chapter; for more on the dangers of operationalism, see 'Operational Concepts and Mental Constructs in Model and Theory Formation,' and 'Operationalism and Pure Theory in Economics,' op. cit., pp. 159–203.

72 Machlup, 'Verification. . ., 'op. cit., p. 147. The reference is to educator James

B. Conant, *On Understanding Science* (New Haven: Yale University Press, 1947), p. 36. If this idea sounds Kuhnian, it should come as no surprise that Kuhn was influenced by Conant.

73 Machlup, 'Theories of the Firm. . .,' op. cit., pp. 416–18.
74 See Blaug, op. cit., Chapter 3, for a survey of the ideas of nineteenth century economic methodologists.

8

Friedman's Methodological Instrumentalism

Friedman's Marketing Masterpiece

Milton Friedman's 'The Methodology of Positive Economics', which is the lead article in that economist's 1953 book *Essays in Positive Economics*, is probably the best known piece of methodological writing in economics. It is also a marketing masterpiece. Never before has one short article on methodology been able to generate so much controversy. It has been reviewed often, usually negatively. Yet ironically, the methodological prescriptions advanced in his essay have become widely accepted among many working economists. And this has happened without Friedman ever having directly responded to his critics! What follows is still another attempt at an analysis of Friedman's classic. A brief summary of the article reveals it to be a statement of prescriptivist methodological principles that reflects, in many respects, what we have called the mature positivist view of economic science. In at least one respect, however, Friedman's position is unique: his belief that the 'realism' of assumptions of theories does not matter. This position, when coupled with his emphasis on prediction in science, allows us to interpret Friedman not as a positivist, but as a 'methodological instrumentalist'.

Friedman begins with the assertion that many disagreements in economics, and especially those which concern policy decisions, arise from confusion over the distinction between positive and normative economics. He feels that more agreement on the positive effects of a certain policy action would lead to more clarity (and perhaps even more agreement) on normative issues. The stated goal of his article, then, is to provide our discipline with a more solid foundation and understanding of what properly constitutes positive economics. Friedman then turns to an analysis of the purpose of theory in a positive discipline.[1]

The ultimate goal of a positive science, he claims, 'is the development of a "theory" or "hypothesis" that yields valid and meaningful (i.e., not truistic) predictions about phenomena'.[2] Criteria for the acceptability of hypotheses follow. Theories should be logically consistent and contain categories which have meaningful empirical counterparts. Given this, theories must also advance 'substantive hypotheses' which are capable of testing; further, 'the only relevant test of the *validity* of a hypothesis is comparison of its predictions with experience'[3] (emphasis in the original). Finally, since an infinite number of hypotheses which are consistent with an observed set of facts generally exist, other criteria (such as simplicity and fruitfulness) must usually be invoked to choose among competing hypotheses.[4]

Testing a theory by its predictions is often a difficult task in the social sciences: data are not always readily available; controlled experiments are generally impossible; and even when data exist there are few 'crucial experiments' which can categorically decide between hypotheses. Such difficulties have led some economists to undertake procedures which Friedman finds to be methodologically unsound: while some have turned to 'purely formal or tautological analysis', which no longer makes reference to empirical fact, others have begun evaluating theories according to the 'realism of their assumptions'.[5] Friedman feels this latter approach is especially dangerous. To disparage a theory for having 'unrealistic assumptions' is ludicrous, since most significant theories are actually *characterized* by descriptively inaccurate assumptions.

> the relation between the significance of a theory and the "realism" of its "assumptions" is almost the opposite of that suggested by the view under criticism. Truly important and significant hypotheses will be found to have "assumptions" that are wildly inaccurate descriptive representations of reality and, in general, the more significant the theory, the more unrealistic the assumptions.[6]

Friedman defends his position with examples from physics, botany, and economics. By the end of the paper, it is clear that Friedman has certain specific debates in economics in mind when he discusses methodology. He is opposed to attacks directed against certain 'unrealistic assumptions' in neoclassical theory (e.g. the perfectly competitive model; the utility and profit maximization assumptions) and the concomitant acceptance of new, alternative theories which make more realistic assumptions about the structure of markets and the behavior of economic agents (e.g. the theory of monopolistic competition; managerial and behavioral theories of the firm).

Philosophical Evaluation

In many areas, Friedman's views are in line with the logical empiricism of such philosophers as Hempel, Braithwaite, and Nagel. He asserts almost immediately that differences between the natural and social sciences in terms of subject matter are not fundamental, that 'positive economics is, or can be, an "objective" science, in precisely the same sense as any of the physical sciences'.[7] The assertion of the methodological unity of science is well-hedged with qualifying remarks, though I think this reflects less on the nature of positivist thought in the 1950s (which was not cautious regarding the unity-of-method thesis) than it does on that econo- mist's cognizance of past methodological controversies within economics. When we reach his section on the purpose of science it becomes obvious that Friedman is not just playing at positivism: he holds a view which is even more strict than those held by the logical empiricists of his time. On his interpretation, the goal of science is the development of theories which are capable of yielding 'valid and meaningful' predictions, with no mention of any explanatory function for science.[8] This position would cause discomfort among the logical empiricists of the 1940s and early 1950s. For while the covering-law theorists defined scientific explanation as the deduction of an explanandum-statement (i.e. a prediction) from a set of statements that includes a list of antecedent conditions and at least one general law; and though Hempel equated the temporal symmetry of explan- ation and prediction; it was, after all, *explanation* and not prediction that these philosophers emphasized when they discussed the goal of science. To do otherwise brings one dangerously close to the nineteenth century positivist view that explanation is impossible in science (i.e. the goal of science is to discover correlations among phenomena and make predictions from them), a position that was categorically denied by the logical empiricists.

Friedman gets back on the track when he defines the structure and function of scientific theories. He claims that a theory is 'a complex intermixture' of two elements: it is at once a 'language' and 'a body of substantive hypotheses'.[9] Viewed as a language, it is a set of tautologies, a filing system, a formal structure devoid of content: he could easily have included 'a hypothetico-deductive system' to complete his characterization. He further asserts that the structure has no meaning until certain empirical counterparts are designated:

this is the step which Hutchison failed to take, and translated into the language of the philosophy of science it simply states that, for a system to be empirically meaningful, some of the axioms or theorems must correspond to observables. This view of theory as a partially interpreted hypothetico-deductive system accords well with the precepts of logical empiricism, as does his further requirement that a theory be a 'body of substantive hypotheses'.

Here Friedman is stating his formulation of the 'verification problem': that hypotheses are either confirmed or disconfirmed according to their ability to predict.

> Viewed as a body of substantive hypotheses, theory is to be judged by its predictive power for the class of phenomena it is intended to "explain." Only factual evidence can show whether it is "right" or "wrong" or, better, tentatively "accepted" as valid or "rejected" . . . the only relevant test of the *validity* of a hypothesis is comparison of its predictions with experience. [10]

His choice of the word validity is unfortunate, since in logic that word refers to argument *forms* rather than the acceptability of an argument on the basis of evidence. Thus, a deductive argument can be invalid while its conclusions are nonetheless true. This terminological point aside, Friedman is saying that a hypothesis must to some extent be confirmable or disconfirmable if it is to be considered a hypothesis at all; if it meets this criterion we can test it against the evidence; and finally, the way to test the hypothesis is to compare its predictions against experience. Numerous qualifications follow this assertion (e.g. evidence can never prove the correctness of a theory, only fail to disprove it; predictions from past events to less distant past events are permissible) which indicate that Friedman has a good understanding of the confirmability issue, as does his further (and wholly positivistic) remark that choice between competing hypotheses which meet the prediction criterion must be based on the often arbitrary criteria of simplicity and fruitfulness. [11] This accordance with contemporaneous positivist thought is all the more remarkable given that Friedman cites no philosophers in his essay.

Friedman's next few arguments are the source of his article's notoriety. He states that a theory cannot be tested by the realism of its assumptions, that therefore the realism of the assumptions of a theory is unimportant, that unrealistic assumptions are usually a characteristic of the most significant scientific hypotheses, [12] and finally that instead of looking at the assumptions of a theory, we should concentrate on the predictions of a theory. This may seem like just another formulation of the indirect testability hypothesis, since it states that a theory should be tested by its predictions rather than by its assumptions. But it is not: the indirect testability hypothesis asserts that assumptions need not be directly *testable*. It does *not* assert that the 'realism' of a theory's assumptions is immaterial. A conflation of arguments has occurred: Friedman has combined the indirect testability thesis with his own unique contribution concerning the realism of assumptions. Only the former finds any support in the philosophy of science.

Friedman is to be commended for offering the first (albeit crude) statement of the indirect testability hypothesis in economics. (Remember, Friedman's article antedates Machlup's by two years.) But what are we to make of the other half of his argument: that the 'realism of assumptions' is not of concern when judging among theories? A problem appears at the outset: it is not at all clear what Friedman means when he uses the term 'realistic'. If a theory's assumptions are realistic, does this mean that they are 'descriptively accurate'; or 'intuitively plausible'; or perhaps 'testable'; or, more strongly, 'testable and confirmed'; or, as some have read (and even stronger), 'true'?

Another ambiguity in Friedman's article arises when his curious view about the realism of assumptions is coupled with his remark that prediction, and not explanation, is the goal of science. In a review of Friedman's essay, philosopher Ernest Nagel criticizes the economist for not adequately defining realism, and accurately pinpoints Friedman's failure to distinguish between theories which are only instruments for prediction and theories which provide explanations as well as predictions about economic phenomena.

the essay is marked by an ambiguity that perhaps reflects an unresolved tension in his views on the status of economic theory. Is he defending the legitimacy of unrealistic theoretical assumptions because he thinks that theories are at best only useful instruments, valuable for predicting observable events but not to be viewed as genuine statements whose truth and falsity may be significantly investigated? But if this is the way he conceives theories (and much in his argument suggests that it is), the distinction between realistic and unrealistic theoretical assumptions is at best irrelevant, and no defense of theories lacking in realism is needed. Or is he undertaking that defense in order to show that unrealistic theories cannot only be invaluable tools for making predictions but that they may also be reasonably satisfactory explanations of various phenomena in terms of the mechanisms involved in their occurrence? But if this is his aim (and parts of his discussion are compatible with the supposition that it is), a theory cannot be viewed, as he repeatedly suggests that it can, as a "simple summary" of some vaguely delimited set of empirical generalizations with distinctly specified ranges of applications.[13]

These ambiguities have continued within the secondary literature, which is now enormous.[14] Depending on the author, the term realistic has been interpreted as meaning testable, highly confirmed, or true.[15] In addition, many criticisms of Friedman's position dissolve if he is read as saying that theories are only instruments for prediction, as is shown presently. What is needed is a clarification of Friedman's position which resolves these ambiguities while still remaining true to the views expressed in his 1953 article.

A Restatement – Friedman as a Methodological Instrumentalist

Such a restatement was never offered by Friedman, but the task was attempted recently by Lawrence Boland, who characterizes him as an instrumentalist. Significantly, in private correspondence with Boland, Friedman stated that Boland's characterization of his views as instrumentalist is 'entirely correct'.[16] To understand what follows, a brief review may be helpful.

Instrumentalists claim that theories are best viewed as *nothing more* than instruments. Viewed thus, theories are neither true nor false (instruments are not true or false), but only more or less adequate, given a particular problem. Just as a hammer is an adequate instrument for certain tasks, and not for others, theories are evaluated for their adequacy, which is usually measured by predictive power. As Boland points out, Friedman's methodology includes elements of instrumentalism, conventionalism, and inductivism.[17] However, Friedman's most controversial statements, that the purpose of science is prediction and that the 'realism' of assumptions does not matter, are instrumentalist. Critically, if Friedman is an instrumentalist, 'realism' must refer to truth value. Realism is then unimportant because theories are not true or false, but only instruments.

Boland correctly asserts that instrumentalism is a methodological response to the problem of induction.[18] In addition, it is one side in the debate over the existence of the entities referred to by theories and theoretical terms. In that debate, instrumentalism is contrasted with realism: realists claim that theories and theoretical terms should make real references, instrumentalists deny it. Where one stands in such a debate determines one's perception of the role, status, and function of theories and theoretical terms in science. Philosophers Joseph Agassi and Imre Lakatos claim that one's position on such issues even affects the way the history of science is written.[19]

In his attacks against 'realistic assumptions' Friedman was not advancing an argument concerning the non-existence of theoretical entities: he was concerned with methodology, not epistemology. For this reason, I have labeled Friedman a 'methodological instrumentalist' to emphasize that though his analysis is consistent with the methodological implications of instrumentalism, he never dealt with the epistemological issues associated with the philosophical position.

If Friedman was unaware that he was an instrumentalist, that same failure in cognition apparently plagued his critics as well. The widespread failure to understand Friedman's position prompted Boland to proclaim,

> *Every* critic of Friedman's essay has been wrong. The fundamental reason why all of the critics are wrong is that their criticisms are not based on a clear, correct, or even fair understanding of his essay.[20] (emphasis in the original)

Though his phrasing is melodramatic, Boland's point is well taken: his essay carefully documents the absence of understanding among Friedman's critics of the Chicago economist's instrumentalism. Boland concludes his essay with the less justifiable sentence, 'no one has been able to criticize or refute instrumentalism'.[21] Such a statement leaves the reader with the impression that Friedman's position is not only untouched, but perhaps vindicated. In the remainder of this chapter, I attempt to challenge such a conclusion by criticizing Friedman's methodological instrumentalism from both philosophical and methodological perspectives.

The Philosophical Rejection of Instrumentalism

The philosophical rejection of instrumentalism has two foundations: one is an argument about the proper goal of science, and the other a requirement on the truth value of theories.

1. The goal of science: Philosophers of science since the 1940s have been unanimous in their rejection of the notion that the only goal of science is prediction. Even such positivist philosophers as Carl Hempel have claimed that explanation, not prediction, is the goal of science; it was Hempel who with Paul Oppenheim developed the covering-law models of scientific explanation. More recent models of the structure and nature of explanation in science admit to even broader definitions of the concept than did the covering-law models.[22] Once one takes the position that explanation is the goal of science, the instrumentalist view of theories and theoretical terms is

considerably weakened. If science seeks theories that have explanatory as well as predictive powers, then theories that merely predict well may not be satisfactory, and the view that theories are nothing more than instruments for prediction must be rejected.

2. The truth value of theories: Even if it is admitted that science seeks theories that explain as well as predict, the instrumentalist has a second line of defense. It is well known that for any set of empirical data, an infinite number of mutually incompatible theories exist that can explain the evidence at hand. Even a moderate skeptic must therefore despair over the possibilities of ever finding the 'true' theory. Instrumentalism allows one to circumvent the entire issue by claiming that theories are only instruments and that as such it is meaningless to speak of them as being either true or false; as Boland puts it, instrumentalists 'think they have solved the problem of induction by ignoring truth'.[23]

But indeed, such an approach does *not* solve the problem. Instrumentalists fail to comprehend that though we may not know whether a theory is true or false, it in fact is true or false. An analogy from probability theory illustrates this point: when an estimate of a probability distribution is made, the estimate may be wrong, but the actual distribution exists if the population is finite. Even if we never know what the actual distribution is, we should still try to make the best estimate using all of the available information. In regard to theories, the philosophical realist (who is, in all such discussions, the opposite of the instrumentalist) recognizes at all times that his theory may be wrong, but is still willing to accept that risk and seek the true theory. The realist will support only those theories he believes may actually be true, and he will posit such theories for a time as being 'true by convention'. Realism thus contains elements of conventionalism. Instrumentalists refuse to take such a step, and philosopher Imre Lakatos views this as a gross error on their part.

> some conventionalists did not have sufficient logical education to realize that some propositions may be true whilst being unproven; and others false whilst having true consequences, and also some which are both false and approximately true. These people opted for 'instrumentalism': they came to regard theories as neither true nor false but merely as 'instruments' for predictions. Conventionalism, as here defined, is a philosophically sound position; instrumentalism is a degenerate version of it, based on a mere philosophical muddle caused by a lack of elementary logical competence.[24]

Whether instrumentalism arose due to 'a lack of elementary logical competence' on the part of its supporters is doubtless an arguable point; however, most contemporary philosophers of science share with Lakatos misgivings about the adequacy of instrumentalism. Philosophers who reject instrumentalism include most contemporary positivists – Karl Popper, Peter Achinstein, Grover Maxwell, and P. K. Feyerabend; the notable exception is Stephen Toulmin.[25]

Boland's defense of Friedman rests on the claim that his critics did not deal with that economist's instrumentalism. The arguments above indicate that instrumentalism finds few supporters in contemporary philosophy of science. Does this destroy Friedman's position? Not necessarily. I have repeatedly argued that well-established positions within the philosophy of science do not necessarily 'translate' when applied to the methodology of economics. To make a case against Friedman, one must also show that his methodological views are inadequate within his own discipline, which is a much more difficult task.

The Methodological Critique of Friedman's Position

There are at least three routes which, if taken, might help to vindicate Friedman's methodological instrumentalism, given the attacks on instrumentalism within the philosophy of science.

1. Prediction, not explanation, is the goal of economic science. If the only goal of economic science is the discovery of predictively adequate theories, instrumentalism is a viable methodological stance. Whether this represents the view of the majority of economists is, of course, one of the more lively areas of debate in contemporary economic methodology.

In Friedman's defense, it is unquestionable that an emphasis on predictive adequacy has dominated professional discussion of theory appraisal. Indeed, no criterion of theory evaluation has more widespread support than predictive adequacy. Perhaps not coincidentally, it is in fields in which Friedman did pioneering work that one finds economists today who are the most adamant in their insistence that predictive adequacy is the sole determinant of the value of a theory.[26]

Opponents of this view implicitly assume that the quest for true, explanatory theories is (or should be) more important than the discovery of predictively adequate theories. If one accepts this goal, instrumentalism fails for a number of reasons. First, the instrumentalist preoccupation with predictive adequacy forces scientists to prefer statistical correlation over causal explanation if the former provides better predictions. This violates the popular adage which prohibits 'measurement without theory'.[27] Next, as Bear and Orr show, false antecedents can generate true consequences; if we wish our theories to be true as well as predictively adequate, we cannot rely solely on predictive adequacy for evaluating them. Bear and Orr also demonstrate that the acceptance of instrumentalism rules out disconfirmation in science: a theory that is neither true nor false can be found inadequate, but not disconfirmed.[28] Finally, due to the subject matter of economics, it may be difficult to discover *any* predictively adequate theories.[29]

As Boland notes, none of these arguments damages Friedman's position if one believes the goal of economic science is the discovery of predictively adequate theories. Similarly, if one denies that as the goal of economics and replaces it with the search for true, explanatory theories, Friedman's methodological instrumentalism fails. An intermediate view, which would at least partially restore Friedman's position, states that in certain cases, when all that economists seek is an instrument for prediction, theories need not be required to explain the phenomena with which they are concerned. This considerably weakens Friedman's initial view, for it posits his methodological instrumentalism as *one* rather than as *the* 'methodology of positive economics'. Whether such a watering down of his position would be acceptable to Friedman is left unanswered.

2. Friedman is not an instrumentalist since he adds simplicity as a criterion of theory choice. One could admit the force of the philosophical arguments against instrumentalism and still support Friedman by arguing that that economist's methodology goes beyond simple instrumentalism. Specifically, Friedman adds additional criteria of theory choice (the most important of which is simplicity) to predictive adequacy for the appraisal of theories. Such a defense would claim that Friedman's position must be evaluated as a totality, and not for its purely instrumentalist aspects.

I will argue later that the necessarily arbitrary selection of only certain criteria of theory choice to supplement predictive adequacy is suspect, since the selection of such criteria is not always independent of the characteristics of one's favored theory. This does not, of course, damage Friedman's position if it can be shown that most economists value predictive adequacy and simplicity, even though the addition of simplicity cannot be objectively justified. Rather than hypothesize about what 'most economists' think, another approach to this problem is to see if Friedman *himself* has consistently practiced what he preached. We find that is not the case.

To be sure, in certain of his earlier works Friedman repeatedly stresses that simplicity and predictive adequacy should be used together in evaluating theories.[30] But in an important later piece, his Nobel Lecture, the virtues of simplicity are not extolled. Indeed, it almost seems that Friedman favors theories that are (Can it be true?) more *realistic!*

In his address, Friedman reviews some of the changes in thinking that have occurred in the profession in the last several decades on the relationship between inflation and unemployment. He views those changes as an illustration of 'the classical process for the revision of a scientific hypothesis' since they were occasioned 'primarily by the scientific response to experience that contradicted a tentatively accepted hypothesis'.[31] There have been three stages in the profession's analysis of the unemployment–inflation relationship. The first consisted of the simple acceptance of a stable, downward-sloping Phillips curve; the second involved the introduction of a long run, vertical Phillips curve (whose position corresponds to the natural rate of unemployment) together with a body of short run downward-sloping curves whose levels correspond to different sets of inflationary expectations. In the third stage, which we are now entering, economists concern themselves with explaining the apparent positive relationship between inflation and unemployment. Friedman believes that analytic progress in the second stage leaned heavily on pioneering work done in the areas of expectation formation and information and contract theory; he expects that similar progress in the third stage will rely on the investigations by Arrow, Buchanan, Tullock, and others who have applied economic analysis to questions of public policy formation.[32]

It is Friedman's conviction that the changes described above were brought about by the failure of earlier hypotheses to offer predictions that were consistent with the empirical evidence. That is undoubtedly true and indicates the important role of predictive adequacy in this branch of economics; but in not one place does he state that the most significant theories 'explain much by little'. Instead, he praises the newer theories for their 'richness', and for their ability to 'rationalize a far broader range of experience'.[33] But does not the concept of costly information, the inclusion of stochastically changing inflationary expectations, and the existence of long-term implicit or explicit contracts in goods and labor markets, does not all of that fly in the face of Friedman's earlier methodological dictums? And what about the holistic attempt (which characterizes the third stage) to include political variables in an economic analysis; is there any way to defend that addition as simpler, more economical, or less concerned with realism? Clearly, Friedman's invocation of simplicity is much more useful if one is defending the quantity theory of money or the profit maximization assumption than if one is discussing recent developments in Phillips curve analysis.

3. Friedman is not an instrumentalist; 'realism' should not be read

as 'truth value'. A final defense of Friedman claims again that he has been misread, that his real message is that the discipline must avoid accepting new theories if their only positive contribution is 'greater realism'.

There is nothing objectionable here; few economists argue that realism should be the *exclusive* criterion for choosing among theories, and those who have come close to this are generally ignored by the majority of the profession.[34] Friedman's own examples are managerial and organizational alternatives to the profit maximization assumption, and monopolistic competition as a replacement for the perfect competition model. Neither one has replaced its predecessor, though each is generally viewed as a useful supplement to existent approaches. Significantly, neither one became accepted solely for its greater 'realism'. Alternative theories of the firm generally attempt to investigate *different* areas of firm behavior than that covered by the standard analysis, which is the formation of relative prices and the allocation of resources in a market economy.[35] And monopolistic competition has many positive attributes which go beyond the nebulous 'greater realism': it is logically complete (or at least suffers from no defects that surpass those encountered in the theory of perfect competition); it has testable consequences, which generally fail to disconfirm the theory (the existence of low profits and an excess number of firms producing a product, the magnitude of the latter condition being dependent upon the extent of nonprice competition and the possibilities for product differentiation that exist in a given market); it is fruitful and suggestive, isolating and emphasizing phenomena that are neglected in the formal structure of the older theory (nonprice competition and advertising).[36] These are the reasons why monopolistic competition is taught today, not because that theory has the sole advantage of more realistic assumptions. If Friedman's only message is that 'greater realism' should not be used as the sole criterion of theory appraisal, then his advice has been followed.

Summary and Conclusion

Though many parts of Friedman's essay are consistent with the logical empiricism of his time, his preoccupation with prediction and his insistence that the 'realism of assumptions' is immaterial are not, which hinders attempts at a straightforward explication of his views. There are also ambiguities in the critical literature; perhaps most noticeable is the continuation of Friedman's practice of leaving the term 'realism' only loosely defined. Lawrence Boland's recent interpretation of Friedman as (primarily) an instrumentalist serves two purposes: it resolves the ambiguities in the original paper, and it shows that critics who have not explicitly addressed instrumentalism fail in their attacks. That Friedman concurs with Boland's characterization lends further support to his interpretation.

While accepting Boland's characterization, I do not believe instrumentalism to be an unimpeachable methodological stance. Indeed, a number of philosophers consider the criticisms of instrumentalism cited above to provide sufficient grounds for its rejection. The philosophical rejection of instrumentalism does not imply that Friedman's position must be rejected, though it does raise questions about the adequacy of his views.

This controversy might be avoided if it could be shown that Friedman is not *really* an instrumentalist. Two such interpretations were attempted (there may be others). One of these stresses Friedman's pronouncements concerning realism, and reduces his methodology to the prescription that 'realism' should not serve as the only, or penultimate, criterion of theory appraisal. Though few economists would object to such a bland prescription, it seems probable that Friedman means something more than this, else why would he allow the controversy to continue so long? The other more plausible interpretation is that prediction should be supplemented with additional criteria for judging among theories, and that among these, simplicity is the best, while realism is unacceptable. Since Friedman offers no justification for his particular choice of supplemental criteria, and since some of his later work contradicts his methodological pronouncements, this attempt at rehabilitation may similarly be considered (at least at present) unsuccessful.

While other attempts at reinterpretation may be forthcoming, the most plausible current reading is to state that Friedman is indeed an instrumentalist, and that though certain philosophers have rejected instrumentalism, it is still an acceptable methodological position for economics. If consensus among practitioners is any measure of the adequacy of a methodological approach, the value that economists place on predictive adequacy (in their rhetoric, if not always in practice) lends clear support to Friedman's views. The crucial question is whether predictive adequacy dominates explanatory power as the primary scientific goal of the discipline. On this question, no consensus exists. In some fields, predictive adequacy dominates; in others, explanatory power is dominant. Nor do these two exhaust the possibilities: for example, would general equilibrium theorists claim that their models satisfy either criteria?

I have argued that instrumentalism remains viable in those instances when the ability to make accurate predictions is the prime concern of the practicing economist. Those instances may either increase or decrease in significance with the passage of time. Instrumentalism is inadequate when economists claim to explain economic phenomena; as such, economists should not fall into the trap of believing that they have explained things when all that they have done is predict accurately.

Notes

Parts of this chapter are taken from my paper, 'A Critique of Friedman's Methodological Instrumentalism,' *Southern Economic Journal*, vol. 47 (October 1980), pp. 336–74.

1 Milton Friedman, 'The Methodology of Positive Economics,' in his *Essays in Positive Economics* (Chicago: University of Chicago Press, 1953), pp. 4–6.
2 Ibid., p. 7.
3 Ibid., p. 9.
4 Ibid., p. 10.
5 Ibid., pp. 11–14.
6 Ibid., p. 14.
7 Ibid., p. 4.
8 Ibid., p. 7.
9 Ibid., pp. 7–8.
10 Ibid., pp. 8–9.
11 Ibid., p. 10.
12 Ibid., p. 14. This is not to say that unrealistic assumptions should be viewed as a positive attribute of a theory, as some critics of Friedman have claimed. A close reading of Friedman indicates that, though the text reads, 'in general, the more significant the theory, the more unrealistic the assumptions', that passage is footnoted as follows: 'The converse of this proposition of course does not hold: assumptions that are unrealistic (in this sense) do not guarantee a significant theory.'
13 Ernest Nagel, 'Assumptions in Economic Theory,' *American Economic Review Papers and Proceedings*, vol. 53 (May 1963), p. 218.
14 A partial listing can be found in Lawrence Boland, 'A Critique of Friedman's Critics,' *Journal of Economic Literature*, vol. 17 (June 1979), p. 522.
15 In his 'Reply to Robert Piron,' *Quarterly Journal of Economics*, vol. 76 (November 1972), pp. 666–8, Eugene Rotwein states that if assumptions are to have explanatory power, they should be realistic or true. Jack Melitz uses the terms 'realistic', 'highly confirmed', and 'true' interchangeably in his paper, 'Friedman and Machlup on the Significance of Testing Economic Assumptions,' *Journal of Political Economy*, vol. 73 (February 1965), pp. 37–60. Finally, D. V. T. Bear and Daniel Orr state that Friedman's position comes down to the proposition that 'the truth of the assumptions is largely irrelevant' in their 'Logic and Expediency in Economic Theorizing,' *Journal of Political Economy*, vol. 75 (April 1967), p. 188.
16 I would like to thank Professor Boland for sharing this information with me. Stanley Wong, who studied under Boland, characterized Friedman as an instrumentalist in his 'The F-Twist and the Methodology of Paul Samuelson,' *American Economic Review*, vol. 63 (June 1973), pp. 312–25.
17 Boland, 'A Critique. . .,' loc. cit. pp. 509–16.

18 Ibid., pp. 506–9.
19 Joseph Agassi, *Towards an Historiography of Science* (The Hague: Mouton, 1963); Imre Lakatos, 'History of Science and Its Rational Reconstruction,' in R. Buck and R. Cohen (eds), *P.S.A. 1970: In Memory of Rudolf Carnap. Boston Studies in the Philosophy of Science*, Vol. VIII (Dordrecht, Holland: D. Reidel, 1971), pp. 91–136.
20 Boland, 'A Critique. . .,' loc. cit., p. 503.
21 Ibid., p. 521.
22 See the sections on scientific explanation in Chapters 3 and 4 for a more detailed account.
23 Boland, 'A Critique. . .,' loc. cit., p. 509.
24 Lakatos, 'History of Science. . .,' loc. cit., p. 95.
25 See the section on the realist – instrumentalist debate in Chapter 4 for a more detailed account of the arguments brought against instrumentalism.
26 The debate in macroeconomics over whether econometric models should explicitly capture all the channels of monetary influence (the nonmonetarist view) or leave such channels unspecified and stress only the ultimate impact (the monetarist view) is one example. The question of how to test the rational expectations approach to the modeling of expectation formation is another. For a review of the first issue, see Joseph M. Crews, 'Econometric Models: The Monetarist and Non-Monetarist Views Compared,' in Thomas Havrilesky and John Boorman, *Current Issues in Monetary Theory and Policy* (Arlington Heights, Ill.: AHM Publishing Corporation, 1976), pp. 179–90; the supplement to the *Journal of Money, Credit and Banking*, vol. 12 (November 1980) is devoted to rational expectations, and includes assessments of various issues by most of the major protagonists.
27 See Tjalling Koopmans, 'Measurement without Theory,' *Review of Economic Statistics*, vol. 29 (August 1947), pp. 161–72. An example of how statistical data can be used to generate adequate predictions is provided in Charles R. Nelson, 'The Predictive Performance of the FRB-MIT-PENN Model of the U.S. Economy,' *American Economic Review*, vol. 62 (December 1972), pp. 902–17.
28 Bear and Orr, 'Logic and Expediency. . .,' loc. cit., pp. 188–92.
29 The problem of predictive adequacy as a criterion of theory choice in economics will be one of the topics discussed in the last chapters of this book.
30 See in particular the exchanges prompted by his article with David Meiselman, 'The Relative Stability of Monetary Velocity and the Investment Multiplier in the United States 1897–1958,' in Commission on Money and Credit, *Stabilization Policies* (Englewood Cliffs, N.J.: Prentice Hall, 1963), pp. 165–268. For some reviews of the issues, see the articles in the section '25 Years After the Rediscovery of Money: What Have We Learned?,' *American Economic Review Papers and Proceedings*, vol. 65 (May 1975), pp. 157–81.
31 Milton Friedman, 'Nobel Lecture: Inflation and Unemployment,' *Journal of Political Economy*, vol. 85 (June 1977), p. 453.
32 Ibid., pp. 454–60.
33 Ibid., p. 470.
34 One example is Martin Hollis and Edward Nell, *Rational Economic Man* (Cambridge, England: Cambridge University Press, 1975).
35 This view is shared by (at least certain) members of both camps. See Fritz Machlup, 'Theories of the Firm: Marginalist, Behavioral, Managerial,' in *Methodology of Economics and Other Social Sciences* (New York: Academic Press, 1978), pp. 391–423; Richard Cyert and James March, *A Behavioral Theory of the Firm* (Englewood Cliffs, N. J.: Prentice-Hall, 1963).
36 The analysis in the text may seem to suggest too much consensus among economists on debates that are still alive in economics. I plead guilty to that

charge. Even so, my major point remains untouched: few economists today would argue successfully for a new theory *solely* on the grounds that it is more 'realistic'. Friedman's prescriptions have been followed, but his opponents are men of straw.

9

Samuelson – Operationalism, Descriptivism, and Explanation in Economics

Introduction

Paul Samuelson expounds two major theses in his writings on methodology: the first is that economists should seek to discover 'operationally meaningful theorems'; the second is that there is no explanation in science, only description.[1] Though his first thesis sounds like a statement of Percy Bridgman's operationalism applied to economics, we will see that in its intent it more closely resembles Terence Hutchison's methodology. In his second thesis, Samuelson does little more than mouth an anachronistic view of scientific explanation. Though his occasional forays into methodology are inconsequential when compared with Samuelson's substantive work in economic theory, they have elicited a variety of critical responses, some of which stand as important contributions in their own right. In this chapter, I review both Samuelson's work and critical essays by Fritz Machlup and Stanley Wong, and conclude with some comments on the variety of explanation in economics, with an emphasis on Institutionalist explanation, as described in a recent paper by Charles Wilber and Robert Harrison.

Samuelson's Operationalism and Machlup's Critique

It was noted earlier that Percy Bridgman, the founder of operationalism, insisted that concepts which are to be permitted into the domain of scientific discourse must be definable by a specifiable set of operations, that, in fact, 'we mean by any concept nothing more than a set of operations'.[2] Bridgman's operationalism was soon found to be intractable by philosophers of science. Its lingering influence in the social sciences is exemplified by Paul Samuelson's modified version of operationalism, first advanced in his early work on revealed preference in consumer theory, and later generalized to all of economic theory in his *Foundations of Economic Analysis* (1947, 1974).[3]

In that work, Samuelson notes that 'only the smallest fraction of economic writing . . . has been concerned with the derivation of *operationally meaningful* theorems'. Such a theorem can be defined as 'a hypothesis about empirical data which could conceivably be refuted if only under ideal conditions'.[4] The purpose of his study is to derive such theorems from 'two very general hypotheses', namely, that in the case of comparative statics, 'the conditions of equilibrium are equivalent to the maximization (minimization) of some magnitude', and that for dynamic systems, specification of the dynamic properties of a given system, with the aid of the correspondence principle, can permit the derivation of dynamic operationally meaningful theorems.[5]

Samuelson's operationalism is thus little more than the prescriptive statement that economists should proceed by deriving conceivably falsifiable hypotheses, which compares favorably with Hutchison's methodological invocations. The differences between them are twofold: Samuelson never advocates testing assumptions directly, but he does insist that dynamic stability be inspected before asserting comparative static results. In any case, his operationalism bears no resemblance to Bridgman's thesis, and cannot be dismissed with the physicist's position.

It is therefore not surprising that Samuelson's advocacy of 'operationalism' caused little consternation among economists. Perhaps the increasing usage of the term was the impetus for Fritz Machlup's critique of *Bridgman's* operationalism in the mid-1960s, for that article is *not* a response to the Samuelsonian variety. In any case, it is instructive to review Machlup's argument, since it speaks to a dilemma that any strictly empiricist program in economics must encounter: the difficulty of operationally defining many (of even the simplest of) economic terms.

He begins with a thorough review of Bridgman's operationalism, noting its defects. Machlup then makes his (by now) familiar distinction between operational concepts (based on operations with data, records, sensory observations, experiences, and the like – with all their impurities) and theoretical, or pure, constructs (which are hypothetical, idealized, based on analytic convenience, and exact).[6]

The demarcation between the operational and the theoretical is never as starkly drawn in science as it is in the above definition, he admits. However, an operational definition for even the most straightforward of concepts drawn from the theoretical domain may be difficult to pin down, if only because there may be many from which to choose. Take, for example, the seemingly unambiguous concept 'price', and take as its counterpart 'the price of steel'. To define it operationally,

> A large variety of operations could be used: One could procure the price lists of all steel producers and compute some sort of average, weighted or unweighted; one could ascertain their sales proceeds – gross or net of discounts, commissions, transport costs – and divide them by the total tonnage shipped; one could secure reports from steel buyers and arrange, weight, or otherwise manipulate their figures in various ways; one could rely on reports from the largest middlemen; one could propose as many as fifty different sets of operations, all sensible and reasonable, but yielding different findings.
> . . .
> None of these operational concepts of "steel price" corresponds completely to the simple construct "price," because the latter abstracts from the score of complications presented by "reality,". . .[7]

Machlup then moves to a more general discussion of theoretical systems and their structure. He asserts that all of the elements of a theoretical system are pure constructs, that to try to replace such constructs with empirical counterparts is often very difficult (as illustrated above), and finally that progress in science occurs by taking exactly the opposite route from that which operationalists advocate.

> The opposite position, argued in the present essay, also has numerous supporters. They see progress in science when empirical concepts are replaced by theoretical concepts, for only by redefinitions, transforming all terms into pure constructs, can a logico-deductive system be developed. . . The impurities and inaccuracies inherent in most or all practicable operations with sensory observations and recorded data destroy the logical links between different concepts. But without logical interrelations the propositions containing these concepts do not afford logically necessary conclusions. In the possibility of deducing such conclusions lie the sole purpose and value of any theoretical system.[8]

Machlup offers another illustration which is nothing short of masterful – he cites a hypothetical argument which might be made by an economist regarding the effects that a fifteen percent tax on imports might be expected to have on the British economy. He breaks that analysis down into eleven parts, and shows that for *some* of the concepts used in the theoretical argument operational counterparts are available; for *others* they could be obtained if it were really necessary; for a *third group* they could not be obtained even with the greatest expense and ingenuity; but that in the theoretical argument itself *all* concepts were pure constructs not operationally but nominalistically defined.[9]

On his own admission, Machlup's position is really an argument against proponents of empirical or operational *theories*. However, he has dramatically pointed out how difficult it can be to obtain operational definitions for any term in a theoretical system. The consequences for theory choice are significant and startling. Simply put, theory choice on empirical grounds is problematical if either *no* empirical counterparts exist for certain theoretical terms, or if a *variety* exist, and the use of different empirical proxies lead to different predictive results in the theory.

In his earlier articles on the 'verification problem', Machlup argued that the indirect testability hypothesis regarding the assumptions or basic postulates of theories was applicable in economics: the assumptions of economic theory need not be empirically falsifiable independent of their deduced consequences. That thesis was developed within the philosophy of (natural) science because some theoretical terms could not be given an empirical interpretation in the so-called protocol language. I argued that the indirect testability hypothesis was necessary in economics because the assumption of rationality cannot be tested without assuming that information is perfect and tastes and preferences do not change, neither of which is itself independently testable.

On the question of the indirect testability hypothesis, then, I concur with Machlup's findings, though having arrived at the conclusion by following a different path. In this article, however, Machlup takes a further step: he argues that *all* of the terms in a hypothetico-deductive argument are theoretical, and that attempts to give such terms empirical counterparts will often be frustrated. His conclusion is that economists should concentrate on improving their 'logico-deductive systems'.[10] Clearly, such a conclusion is not a necessary consequence of his argument; other conclusions are possible.

An Anachronistic View of Scientific Explanation

Samuelson's second contribution to economic methodology begins as a brief comment on Friedman's position on 'the realism of assumptions'. He gives the label the 'F-Twist' to Friedman's assertion that 'the (empirical) unrealism of the theory "itself" or of its "assumptions," is quite irrelevant to its validity and worth'.[11] To demonstrate the intractability of the F-Twist, Samuelson undertakes an exercise in symbolic manipulation in which he asserts that theories are merely equivalent restatements of assumptions and conclusions, that is, $A \equiv B \equiv C$, where A is defined as 'assumptions', B as 'a theory', and C as 'consequences or predictions'. By this view, if either the assumptions or the theory itself are unrealistic, then the deduced consequences about reality are bound to be false, and even if some of them are true (e.g. if some subset C^- of C hold true), it is not a relevant test of the theory B or of its assumptions A.[12]

Samuelson's position drew fire from Fritz Machlup a year later. Machlup concentrates on Samuelson's evaluation of the role of theory in science, claiming that a strict adherence to Samuelson's stated view is equivalent to 'a rejection of theory'.

> A theory, by definition, is much wider than any of the consequences deduced. If the consequences were to imply the "theory" just as the theory implies the consequences, that theory would be nothing but another form of the empirical evidence (named "consequence") and could never "explain" the observed empirical facts.[13]

Further,

> We never deduce a consequence from a theory alone. We always combine the postulated relationships (which constitute the theory) with the assumption of some change or event and then we deduce the consequence of the *conjunction* of the theoretical relationships and the assumed occurrence.[14]

Machlup then reviews Samuelson's justly famous work on international factor price equalization to show that that economist did not follow his own prescriptions regarding the importance of deriving 'operationally meaningful theorems' from empirical hypotheses, since his model is shot through with such unrealistic assumptions as diminishing marginal productivity, constant returns to scale, and two countries that produce two goods (food and clothing) with two qualitatively identical inputs (land and labor).[15]

Instead of denying Machlup's claim that his position rejects an explanatory role for theory in science, Samuelson embraces it in his reply.

> Scientists never "explain" any behavior, by theory or any other hook.
> Every description that is superseded by an "deeper explanation" turns out

upon careful examination to have been replaced by still another description, albeit possibly a more useful description that covers and illuminates a wider area.[16]

In this statement, Samuelson has blundered his way into defending a descriptivist view of the nature of scientific explanation. While it is evident that he has a firm grasp of the view that rejects as metaphysical the search for 'ultimate explanations', a view which dominated scientific thought at the end of the last century and which was no doubt transmitted to Samuelson via Bridgman,[17] it is just as clear that he has no knowledge of the prescribed but significant role attached to scientific explanation by logical empiricists since the 1940s, of whose ranks he would presumably consider himself a member. Samuelson fails to deal with this latter position, one that has nothing in common with the search for ultimate explanations, and casts himself in the role of advocate of a view long considered untenable, even within recent positivist philosophy of science.

Samuelson's methodological naiveté is even more evident in still another reply to critics, this one in the December, 1965 issue of the *American Economic Review*. One reviewer of his work was philosopher Gerald Massey, who provided him with some representative readings by Hempel and Nagel: this was apparently the first time that Samuelson had been exposed to the ideas of two of the most famous contemporary philosophers of science. Coming at this late date, however, it seems that Samuelson gained little from the readings, for he states in a footnote, 'I benefited from this course of study, which I believe deepened my understanding of my own position'.[18] This is indeed a curious comment, for the opening paragraph of one of the Hempel papers reads,

> Scientific research in its various branches seeks not merely to record particular occurrences in the world of our experience: it tries to discover regularities in the flux of events and thus to establish general laws which may be used for prediction, postdiction, and explanation.[19]

Samuelson's arguments against Hempel need not detain us: he claims to see little difference in Hempel's articles between explanation or prediction, on the one hand, and description, on the other, Hempel's disclaimers notwithstanding.[20] Massey should have referred him to Hempel's 'Explanation and Prediction by Covering Laws', in which that philosopher expounds a model of scientific explanation that few could mistake for a model of Samuelsonian description.[21] As was mentioned in Chapter 4, Hempel's view of the structure of scientific explanation has not gone unchallenged in the philosophy of science; however, alternative formulations have not returned to the descriptivist thesis, but have gone in the other direction by giving an even broader scope to explanation in science than did Hempel and other logical empiricists.

Our assessment of Samuelson's methodological contributions to this point has been from the perspective of the philosophy of science. Neither of his theses is very accessible from that vantage point. Though he praises operationalism, it has little in common with Bridgman's approach, probably to Samuelson's credit. And though he adamantly defends descriptivism, his defense is at best incomplete, since he fails to deal with the massive literature on scientific explanation developed in the twentieth century.

Of course, one need not mouth results from twentieth century philosophy of science to make a contribution to economic methodology. In particular, if one's methodological prescriptions accord well with specific research agendas within the discipline, then one has a legitimate claim on the attention of economists.

The viability of Samuelson's descriptivist thesis is difficult to assess, simply because few economists argue the merit of their theories from a descriptivist standpoint. Nor do many seem to seek descriptive theories, if 'descriptive' is interpreted as 'correlational'. (A more precise definition of 'descriptive' would be a necessary step if one wished to reconstruct the descriptivist thesis for its use in this century.) Samuelson's operationalism is another matter. In at least one significant research area, and one in which Samuelson was a pathbreaker, the effort to 'operationalize' a particular body of theory was claimed as an advance. I refer here to the development of the revealed preference approach in consumer theory. A comprehensive methodological critique of that famous development is contained in a recently published tract by Stanley Wong, *The Foundations of Paul Samuelson's Revealed Preference Theory* (1978), which carries the intriguing subtitle, *A Study by the Method of Rational Reconstruction*. Because this book is the first of its kind in the field, and because it speaks so directly and so forcefully to the topic at hand, I will take some time examining its claims. Though from its title it may appear to be only a contribution to the secondary literature, its approach guarantees it a position in the primary literature.

Wong's Critique of Revealed Preference Theory

Stanley Wong's short but persuasive study of Samuelson's revealed preference theory is a valuable contribution for at least three reasons.

First, he elucidates Popper's method of rational reconstruction, and applies it to a specific theoretical program in economics. That method has a number of distinguishing characteristics. The analyst must first separate the question of understanding a theory from the question of assessing the merits of a theory. To understand a theory, one reconstructs a hypothetical problem situation that the theory is meant to address. As part of that reconstruction, one should also attempt to explain why the theorist believes his own proposed theory solves the problem situation in question. In so doing, both the *theoretical aims* (or primary objectives) of the theorist and the *situational constraints* (this broad category includes prior theoretical approaches, as well as metaphysical, epistemological, and methodological beliefs) perceived by the theorist are documented. The goal of this first stage of reconstruction, then, is to thoroughly understand a proposed theory as a response to a given problem. The most difficult part of this process is to determine the situational constraints as perceived by the theorist, since few theorists do us the favor of explicitly stating their epistemological and metaphysical views. To his credit, Wong provides some illustrative examples from economics, as well as admits that his list of situational constraints is nonexhaustive.[22]

The next step is to assess a theory's merits, which again can be divided into two parts. Assessment involves criticism, both internal and external. Internal criticism is concerned with the question: Does the theorist reach his goals? Internal criticism normally involves consideration of the logical or mathematical consistency of theories and goals, and the solubility of problems; as such, it is often easier to establish and, when successful, more devastating in its results than external criticism. External criticism is a far broader category: the theorist's perceptions of the problem-situation, aims, and constraints are all open to question. It is criticism from outside the reconstructed problem situation, and includes disputes over the importance of the problem; the accuracy of the theorist's perceptions of the problem-situation, theoretical aims, and situational constraints; the interpretation of supporting and conflicting data; moral considerations; and so forth. Clearly, this sort of criticism is rarely conclusive, since it consists of questions over which 'reasonable men can disagree'. As such, it is crucial to stress the independence of internal and external criticism, which occupy different levels and play different roles in critical discourse.[23]

Wong's excellent discussion of the method of rational reconstruction is contained in the second chapter of his book, and is worthwhile reading for every economic methodologist.

Wong's second contribution is also pathbreaking – to my

knowledge, his is the first in-depth assessment of a current research program in economics from a methodological perspective. Of course, the works of philosophers (in particular Kuhn and Lakatos) have been used as frameworks to analyze past episodes in the history of economic thought. But those studies have little in common with Wong's: usually their topics are grandiose (Is the Keynesian Revolution a Kuhnian one? How should the emergence of marginalism be viewed, as a paradigm-switch or as the gradual emergence of a new research program? How many Kuhnian revolutions occurred in economics? and so forth); because the areas examined are vast and the articles are short, the conclusions drawn are more sketchy and suggestive than substantial; and often, the models of historical change receive far more attention than do specifically methodological issues.[24] (The final chapters of Blaug's *The Methodology of Economics* provide an intermediate case: though admittedly abbreviated, they contain a number of competent overviews of current research areas from a methodological perspective.) Wong's analysis is exemplary. His command of the philosophy of science is impressive: he is as comfortable with the analyses of logical empiricists and operationalists as he is with those of Popper, Agassi, and Lakatos. He is also conversant with the writings of methodologically-oriented economists. Finally, he has immersed himself in the revealed preference program as a research area in economics. An economic methodologist should be competent in at least two of the three areas mentioned: the philosophical issues, the writings of economic methodologists, and particular research traditions in economics. It is gratifying to discover an analysis in which all three are interwoven; it is an ideal toward which economic methodologists can aspire.

Finally, there is Wong's substantive contribution: a thorough critique of the methodological foundations of revealed preference theory, as it is represented in three of Samuelson's seminal articles on the subject. Well organized and carefully argued, Wong's criticisms center on two major themes. First, Samuelson's theoretical aims as contained in his three articles are mutually inconsistent. Samuelson first claimed to be constructing a new theory of consumer behavior which dispenses with the need to refer to utility (ordinal or cardinal) and preferences. He later switches to the claim that revealed preference theory provides an operational method for the construction of an indifference map for an individual. In his final commentary on the subject, Samuelson asserts that his theory is the observational equivalent of ordinal utility theory. As Wong easily shows, these goals are inconsistent. While Wong's first thesis is a form of internal criticism, his second is external: Samuelson's program depends for its validity on the plausibility of his own operationalist–descriptivist methodology, which cannot be sustained. The variety of criticisms brought against Samuelson's methodology primarily emphasize the limitations of a naively empirical approach to the problems of consumer theory.[25]

Wong's argumentation is not always impeccable. He accuses Samuelson of adhering to the verifiability doctrine of meaning, which states that hypotheses must be empirically verifiable to be considered acceptable (or cognitively significant). Wong then repeats the familiar objection to verifiability: complete verification is impossible whenever one cannot check every relevant case.[26] Admittedly, Samuelson and other economists often use the term verification. But the concept of falsification is also widely used: for example, Samuelson uses it in his introduction to his *Foundations*, which was cited earlier in this chapter. Most important, few economists who do use the term verification are referring to the verifiability approach to the question of cognitive significance. That approach was embraced by a few members of the Vienna Circle, but was uniformly rejected by later logical empiricists, who preferred the notion of confirmation. And though many economists speak the language of verification, their meaning, I think, is usually confirmation: that empirical evidence should to some extent (the more, the better, of course) support the hypothesis under question. There are problems with the confirmation approach, as was mentioned earlier, and these need to be discussed by economic methodologists. Verifiability, on the other hand, is a straw man: its refutation establishes little. In a like manner, Wong's critique of Bridgman's operationalism does little damage to Samuelson's peculiar formulation of that doctrine.

Neither is Wong totally on solid ground when he demonstrates that inconsistencies exist in Samuelson's program. It is hardly fair to demand that a theory's perceived purpose, place, and value remain unchanged as it moves from its inception to a more finished form. Wong is correct, however, to insist that Samuelson be cognizant of changes that have been made; indeed, such changes should be emphasized by the theorist. The desire to present one's position as a gradual evolution that contains no inconsistencies is a powerful one among scientists; internal criticism of the type that Wong suggests is an often-needed antidote to such temptations.

Finally, I disagree with Wong's assessment of the Hicks–Allen program. When first proposed, the indifference curve approach was heralded by its originators as achieving two goals: it linked consumer theory more closely to observable behavior, and it dispensed with the notion of measureable, cardinal utility. In *Value and Capital* (1939), however, Hicks views their contribution as simply the provision of a more general analysis that is free from utilitarian assumptions. Wong responds that this new 'tolerant' attitude 'undermines the significance of the Hicks–Allen problem'.[27]

If Wong is right, and the indifference curve apparatus accomplishes so little, why has it been retained for all of these years in the profession? It is, after all, one of the three most used pedagogic devices in economics, comparable with the Marshallian and Keynesian crosses. Must it really be dismissed because it did not accomplish the goals that were first envisioned for it by its creators? I think not. A far saner analysis is that of G. L. S. Shackle, who writes,

> The vast use that has been made of the indifference-curve in Anglo-Saxon work since 1934 is tribute enough to what Hicks and Allen achieved. They gave an incomparable tool of exact thought and assured insight to economists to whom algebra is uncongenial and verbal argument intractable . . . They began that demonstration, which has since advanced by giant strides, of the indifference-curve as one of those remarkable notational inventions that can nearly think for itself.[28]

These critical remarks are minor if we look at Wong's writing from a broader perspective; they reduce to the claim that, on occasion, he overstates his case. His study of Samuelson's revealed preference theory stands as the most comprehensive methodological rebuttal of a well-established research program in the methodological literature.

Does Explanation Exist in Economics?

As was shown in Chapters 3 and 4, the nature of scientific explanation has been much discussed in the philosophy of science. Philosophers seem agreed that explanation is an important goal (and some believe, the most important goal) of the scientific enterprise, and many accept the covering-law models as adequate depictions of legitimate scientific explanation. Recently, however, a significant and vocal minority has questioned the adequacy of the covering-law models, and a number of alternative interpretations of the nature of explanation in science has been advanced.

If anything, there is even more disarray in economics. Some economists reject the idea that explanation is an important goal of economic science. Friedman does not discuss explanation, but asserts that 'the ultimate goal' of a positive science is to develop predictively adequate theories. As we have just seen, Samuelson denies that scientists explain, unless explanation is defined as equivalent to description.

Other economic methodologists embrace the covering-law models as developed by Hempel and Popper. Terence Hutchison cites Popper's model in his discussion of the role of prediction in economics in his recent book, *Knowledge and Ignorance in Economics* (1977). Barbara Redman asserts that the D-N covering-law model can be fruitfully applied in economics, but that nonetheless many economic theories must be considered 'ideal types' because so many potentially relevant variables are of necessity impounded in ceteris paribus. She distinguishes between 'explanations in principle', in which the idealized models are used, and 'explanations in detail', in which 'real world' events are explained and for which much more institutional detail is necessary.[29]

Some economists have turned to alternative models of scientific explanation. Philosopher Rom Harré's work has been cited in articles by R. W. Pfouts and Steven Rosefielde. According to that philosopher, an explanation occurs when one can discover analogs to a phenomenon already understood, or when one reveals hidden mechanisms whose working explains a given phenomenon. Pfouts argues that 'explanation is, at least in part, a psychological phenomenon', and that that aspect is absent in Popper's model. Rosefielde draws on Harré and Secord's 'realist' theory of science, and proposes various 'relational' criteria of theory appraisal that can be added to the empirical and the 'hypothetico-deductive'.[30]

Two other economists who apply alternative models of explanation to economics are Charles Wilber and Robert Harrison. They claim that 'pattern models' have been employed by Institutionalists as their method of explaining economic phenomena. We have not heard from the Institutionalists yet, so we will examine the claims of Wilber and Harrison in some detail.

In the first half of their article, the authors depict Hempel and Oppenheim's D-N model of scientific explanation as 'the classic modern version of logical positivism', and claim that Friedman is the most highly visible positivist in economics. The link between Friedman and logical positivism is based on two considerations: his claim that prediction is the ultimate goal of a positive science, and the symmetry thesis, which asserts the logical equivalence of explanation and prediction. Next, they claim that positivism has failed in economics, primarily because economic theories are 'perfectly insulated from refutation'. Economists insulate their theories in a number of ways: changes in ceteris paribus are invoked, tests of hypotheses are rejected as insufficiently clear-cut, data are blamed for being unreliable. Their conclusion is that economic science is a 'grand parable' rather than a positive science.[31]

Wilber and Harrison thus agree with Blaug that falsificationism has been insufficiently practiced in economics. (Indeed, they would probably go further and claim that it is unworkable in our discipline.) Their arguments about the D-N covering-law model being the modern version of logical positivism, and about Friedman being a positivist, are both incorrect. The logical positivists never discussed explanation; only the logical empiricists of the 1940s and 1950s did. Moreover, there is much more to logical empiricism ('modern positivism') then the covering-law models: for example, the unity of science thesis, the indirect testability hypothesis, the H-D model of theory structure, strength of confirmation as the primary criterion of theory selection, and so on.

And, as was shown in the last chapter, Friedman is an instrumentalist, not a positivist, and instrumentalism should not be considered equivalent to positivism. It is true that both stress that theories must be capable of providing adequate predictions. But for an instrumentalist, theories are neither true nor false, but only instruments whose worth is to be measured by how well they predict. It is for this reason that the 'realism' of assumptions is irrelevant for Friedman; it also explains why he believes prediction, and not explanation, to be the goal of a positive science.

Logical empiricists, on the other hand, insist that explanation is an important goal of science: thus Nagel, himself a logical empiricist, criticizes Friedman for overemphasizing prediction and neglecting explanation. In addition, logical empiricists are concerned about the truth value of assumptions: one of the four 'conditions of adequacy' that all sound explanations must satisfy is that the components of the explanans must be true, or thought to be true. (This does not conflict with the indirect testability thesis, which simply recognizes the fact that it will not always be possible to give every component of a theoretical system an empirical counterpart.) Friedman is neither a 'positivist' nor a 'logical empiricist', and Wilber and Harrison's discussion is weakened by their claims to the contrary.

The second half of their article is more convincing and more original. In it, they claim that pattern models constitute the implicit mode of explanation that has been used over the years by various Institutionalists. Pattern models of explanation were developed by philosophers Abraham Kaplan and Paul Deising, and have the following characteristics:

1. Use of the participant–observer method, which is favored since it allows the investigator 'to remain close to the concrete form of the system'.

2. The task of the analyst is first to observe 'recurrent themes, such as forms of accepted practices, cultural norms, modes of production, and recognized social objectives'. The aim is not to find general laws or universal categories, but to find themes which emphasize and illuminate the wholeness and individuality of the system under study. As a result, 'holists find general laws (law of demand) and universal categories (utility) especially unsuited to the task of describing the unity of the particular system'.

3. The analyst next tries to make such information explicit by formulating tentative hypotheses about the system. This is, at first, an admittedly haphazard process. Checks are provided by consulting a wide variety of data, such as case studies, survey data, and personal observations.

4. The final step, which has been taken by only a few Institutionalists and which has met with success for still fewer, is to construct a model of the system. Such a model is quite different from the hierarchical, formal models employed by positivist philosophers and economists. The structure is 'concatenated', that is, 'it is constructed by linking validated hypotheses or themes in a network or pattern'. Such a model must constantly be revised since new data are always coming in and because the system is also undergoing evolution. 'Verification' of the pattern model occurs as it expands and more details of the system are seen to be consistent with it. No specific part of the explanation is given too much weight; falsification of the entire system takes place only if a revised pattern can incorporate an even greater variety of data.

5. Finally, the function of the pattern model is to provide understanding, while the function of hierarchical models is to allow prediction.[32]

Wilber and Harrison admit that holistic explanations have certain disadvantages. Explanations in that mode must constantly be checked against observations, cases, and examples, since 'holism separated from its empirical base easily becomes loose, uncontrolled speculation'. In addition, the generality and imprecision of such explanations rules out the usual 'verification' procedures. Such lack of rigor should hopefully be balanced by the greater creativity which is made possible by the pattern mode of explanation.

The authors conclude their piece by showing when each type of model is best employed.

Use of the pattern model appears appropriate when an explanation involves many diverse factors, each of which is important; when the patterns or connections among these factors are important; and when these patterns can be observed in the particular case under study. Use of the covering law model appears more appropriate when one or two factors or laws determine what is to be explained and when these factors or laws are better known and understood than the specific instance.[33]

Few could fail to be impressed by the Institutionalist methodological research agenda as it is portrayed in this article. It is a grand and ambitious vision. Indeed, by comparison standard economic analysis seems terribly restrictive, static, narrow, even pedestrian. Institutionalist analysis, if successful, is *social* science in the fullest sense of the word. That their program has independent support from a growing research tradition within the philosophy of science also counts favorably, though it should be emphasized that the pattern model approach is not the dominant model of the nature of scientific explanation.

It is also to Wilber and Harrison's credit that they are not naively optimistic about the possibilities of success regarding the construction of 'concatenated' models of the economic system. Their criticism of modern Institutionalists who prefer to rehash the analyses of more illustrious predecessors rather than to develop new models or extend existing ones is eminently fair-minded.[34] Whether their program has any hope of success depends crucially on how well future pattern model adherents can combat the formidable obstacles that confront them in their attempts to construct and defend particular models of social and economic phenomena.

This is the crux of the matter, for it appears that their program faces far more difficulties in its application than any we have yet examined. Unlike the neoclassicals (whether confirmationist or falsificationist), Austrians, post-Keynesians, or neo-Marxists, the Institutionalists have no explicit theoretical base. On the contrary, they reject the notion that a general theoretical structure is useful for understanding social and economic phenomena. This obviously rules out theory choice on nonempirical grounds, that is, criteria like theoretical-connectedness, logical consistency, elegance, and the like cannot be fruitfully applied. Yet, on their own admission, empirical criteria are not well-suited for deciding among competing programs: the usual 'verification' procedures are also ruled out. With so many of the usual criteria of theory appraisal eliminated at the outset, the Institutionalists must tell us in more detail just how competing pattern models are to be evaluated.

There is another problem, and it is perhaps more fundamental: in proposing a new methodological program for economics, Wilber and Harrison have put the cart before the horse. Few non-Institutionalists will be persuaded by a new methodological program without an existing pattern model which can be used as an example. Methodological criticism of a particular research tradition is rarely convincing without the provision of an alternative model. In a like manner, the provision of an alternative *methodological* research program is unlikely to persuade outsiders without a substantive example of how that program works.

To be fair, we cannot criticize Wilber and Harrison for failing to provide a substantive pattern model: their goal, after all, was to develop a methodological research agenda for Institutionalist economics, and they have succeeded admirably. Their claims for their new program are bold ones, and as such, their hardest work lies ahead. As Kuhn and Lakatos emphasize, struggling research programs should not be judged as harshly as their well-established rivals. But unless some well-argued examples of pattern models are forthcoming, in which their distinctive methodological claims are clearly exhibited, few economists will be convinced of the viability of the pattern model approach.[35]

A final comment: some Institutionalists view their particular contribution as complementary to the standard approach, rather than as a substitute.[36] That view certainly has some merit; additionally, it is probably more palatable to members of 'the mainstream'. If the complementarity of Institutionalist analysis becomes widely accepted among Institutionalists, however, some new questions emerge with which they must deal. They would need to show, first, which parts of neoclassical analysis should be rejected, and which should be retained, and why. And second, they must show how their investigations can be distinguished from the work of economic historians, who also often take a more holistic approach to their subject (cliometricians aside).

We began this section with a question: Does explanation exist in economics? The answer depends on who is asked. Some economists eschew explanation; others accept the covering law models; still others see explanation as the penultimate goal of economic science, but would redefine it, usually along lines that would broaden the scope of economic inquiry.

I will not venture an answer to this question, primarily because the question of explanation is inextricably interwoven with the question of theory appraisal. If we can demonstrate what constitutes an acceptable theory in economics we simultaneously define what constitutes an acceptable explanation of economic phenomena. If we cannot show how theories are chosen, on the other hand, it makes little sense to argue about what should count as a legitimate explanation, or whether explanation can exist. In many ways, theory appraisal is the penultimate question of methodology; it is what methodology is about, as it were. Whether rational theory choice is possible in economics is one of the subjects I take up next.

Notes

1 Three minor theses can be mentioned but are not treated in the text. The first is that mathematical training will become increasingly important for economic theorists. Though that may have been a debatable claim when he made it in the early 1950s, the past thirty years certainly offer ample evidence in support of his position. Second, Samuelson seemed relatively confident that successful macro-economic forecasting was a reasonable and reachable goal for economists in the mid-1960s. The number of firms and agencies issuing forecasts has grown; it is another matter entirely to inquire into relative success rates. In any case, he seems more circumspect in later articles on the subject. Finally, there is his state-ment of the correspondence principle (comparative static results cannot be trusted unless a corresponding stable dynamic system can be specified) and his related claims concerning the qualitative calculus. These last issues have been commented upon by numerous economists, and Blaug sums up the discussion nicely. See Paul Samuelson, 'Economic Theory and Mathematics: An Appraisal,' *American Economic Review*, vol. 42 (May 1952), pp. 56–66; 'Economic Forecasting and Science,' *Michigan Quarterly Review*, vol. 4 (October 1965), pp. 274–80; 'Lessons from the Current Economic Expansion,' *American Economic Review Papers and Proceedings*, vol. 64 (May 1974), pp. 75–7; *Foundations of Economic Analysis* (first published, 1947) (New York: Atheneum, 1975), pp. 5–7, 262, 284; D. F. Gordon, 'Operational Propositions in Economic Theory,' *Journal of Political Economy*, vol. 63 (April 1955), pp. 150–62; Mark Blaug, *The Methodology of Economics*, (Cambridge, England: Cambridge University Press, 1980), pp. 99–103 and bibliographical citations listed there.
2 Percy Bridgman, *The Logic of Modern Physics* (New York: Macmillan, 1927), p. 5, italics deleted. See Chapter 3 for a fuller discussion and criticism of operationalism. Certain extreme forms of behaviorism in psychology still bear the mark of Bridgman's influence.
3 Samuelson's work on consumer theory can be found in Joseph Stiglitz (ed.), *The Collected Scientific Papers of Paul A. Samuelson*, Vol. I (Cambridge, Mass.: MIT Press, 1966). Though not published until 1947, the *Foundations* was Samuelson's dissertation and was completed in the late 1930s.
4 Samuelson, *Foundations*, pp. 3–4.
5 Ibid., p. 5.
6 Fritz Machlup, 'Operationalism and Pure Theory in Economics,' in *Methodology of Economics and Other Social Sciences* (New York: Academic Press, 1978), pp. 192–4.
7 Ibid., p. 194.
8 Ibid., p. 197.
9 Ibid., p 201.
10 Ironically, Hutchison made the first point (that economic theory is nothing more than an empty, mechanical calculus) in his 1938 book. Furthermore, both economists agree that the existence of a ceteris paribus clause and the possi-bilities for its misuse (particularly if its components are uncheckable) make

falsification a thorny affair. Their disagreement is over the conclusions that should be drawn. Whereas Hutchison demanded (in his early works) that as many terms as possible, including assumptions, be given empirical interpretation, Machlup insists that operational definitions for many theoretical terms (postulates *and* theorems) are not easily discoverable. While the former view leads to increased empiricism and, if it is responsible empiricism, falsificationism, the latter implies severe limitations for both the possibility of forecasting in economics, and for positing an empirical basis for theory choice. Machlup's is clearly the less optimistic methodological stance.

11 Paul Samuelson, 'Discussion,' *American Economic Review Papers and Proceedings*, vol. 53 (May, 1963), p. 232.

12 Ibid., pp. 233–35.

13 Fritz Machlup, 'Professor Samuelson on Theory and Realism,' in *The Methodology of Economics and Other Social Sciences*, p. 481.

14 Ibid., p. 481. A similar argument is advanced in Stanley Wong, 'The F-Twist and the Methodology of Paul Samuelson,' *American Economic Review*, vol. 63 (June 1973), pp. 312–25.

15 Ibid., pp. 482–3. The reference is to Paul Samuelson, 'International Trade and the Equalization of Factor Prices,' *Economic Journal*, vol. 57 (June 1948), pp. 163–84.

16 Paul Samuelson, 'Theory and Realism: A Reply,' *American Economic Review*, vol. 54 (September 1964), p. 737.

17 See, for example, Bridgman, *Logic*, pp. 37–52.

18 Paul Samuelson, 'Professor Samuelson on Theory and Realism: Reply,' *American Economic Review*, vol. 55 (December 1965), p. 1166.

19 Carl Hempel, 'The Theoretician's Dilemma,' in Herbert Feigl, Grover Maxwell, and Michael Scriven (eds), *Minnesota Studies in the Philosophy of Science*, Vol. II (Minneapolis: University of Minnesota Press, 1958), p. 37.

20 Samuelson, 'Professor Samuelson. . .,' *loc. cit.*, pp. 1167–72.

21 Carl Hempel, 'Explanation and Prediction by Covering Laws,' in Bernard Baumrin (ed.), *Philosophy of Science: The Delaware Seminar*, Vol. I (New York: Wiley, 1963), pp. 107–33.

22 Stanley Wong, *The Foundations of Paul Samuelson's Revealed Preference Theory: A Study by the Method of Rational Reconstruction* (London: Routledge and Kegan Paul, 1978), pp. 9–21. The method of rational reconstruction was developed by Popper in two works, *The Open Society and Its Enemies* (Princeton, N.J.: Princeton University Press, 1950) and *The Poverty of Historicism* (London: Routledge and Kegan Paul, 1957). Others who have applied or extended the method are listed by Wong on p. 130, fn. 3.

23 Wong, *Foundations*, pp. 22–4.

24 Economists who have sought to enumerate how many (if any) Kuhnian revolutions occurred in the history of economics include D. F. Gordon, 'The Role of History of Thought in the Understanding of Modern Economic Theory,' *American Economic Review*, vol. 55 (May 1965), pp. 119–27; A. W. Coats, 'Is There a "Structure of Scientific Revolutions" in Economics?' *Kyklos*, vol. 22 (1969), pp. 289–96; Ron Stanfield, 'Kuhnian Scientific Revolutions and the Keynesian Revolution,' *Journal of Economic Issues*, vol. 8 (March 1974), pp. 97–109; Michael Devroey, 'The Transition from Classical to Neoclassical Economics: A Scientific Revolution,' *Journal of Economic Issues*, vol. 9 (September 1975), pp. 415–39; Dudley Dillard, 'Revolutions in Economic Theory,' *Southern Economic Journal*, vol. 44 (April 1978), pp. 705–24. Others compare Kuhn's model of scientific change with that of Lakatos to see which, if either, better mirrors the intellectual development of economics: see the papers by Blaug, Hutchison, and Leijonhufvud in Spiro Latsis (ed.), *Method and*

Appraisal in Economics (Cambridge, England: Cambridge University Press, 1976). The articles by Latsis, Coats, and deMarchi in the same volume examine particular research traditions in economics, though in less detail than in Wong's study. There have even been two histories of economic thought which employ the models of Kuhn and Lakatos: see Phyllis Deane, *The Evolution of Economic Ideas* (Cambridge: Cambridge University Press, 1978) and Terence Hutchison, *On Revolutions and Progress in Economic Knowledge* (Cambridge, England: Cambridge University Press, 1978). It is ironic that the rise in popularity in other disciplines of the works of these philosophers was contemporaneous with an apparent decline of their influence among at least some philosophers of science. See Frederick Suppe, (ed.), *The Structure of Scientific Theories* (first published, 1973), 2nd edn (Urbana, Illinois: University of Illinois Press, 1977), pp. 643–9. This supports Machlup's view that methodological work in economics often lags behind related developments in philosophy; that a methodological 'culture lag' exists between the two disciplines. See Machlup, 'Operationalism and Pure Theory in Economics,' op. cit., p. 189.

25 Wong, *Foundations*, Chapters 4–7.

26 Ibid., p. 57.

27 Ibid., p. 35.

28 G. L. S. Shackle, *The Years of High Theory* (Cambridge, England: Cambridge University Press, 1967), pp. 87–8.

29 Terence Hutchison, *Knowledge and Ignorance in Economics* (Chicago: University of Chicago Press, 1977), Chapter 2; Barbara Redman, 'On Economic Theory and Explanation,' *Journal of Behavioral Economics*, vol. 5 (Summer 1976), pp. 161–76.

30 R. W. Pfouts, 'Some Proposals for a New Methodology for Economics,' *Atlantic Economic Journal*, vol. 1 (November 1973), pp. 13–22; Steven Rosefielde, 'Post-Positivist Scientific Method and the Appraisal of Non-Market Economic Behavior,' *Quarterly Journal of Ideology*, vol. 3 (Spring 1980), pp. 23–33.

31 Charles Wilber and Robert Harrison, 'The Methodological Basis of Institutional Economics: Pattern Model, Storytelling, and Holism,' *Journal of Economic Issues*, vol. 12 (March 1978), pp. 64–9. Cf. William Dugger, 'Methodological Differences between Institutional and Neoclassical Economics,' *Journal of Economic Issues*, vol. 13 (December 1979), pp. 899–909, for a comparison of the Institutionalist approach with the neoclassical.

32 Wilber and Harrison, 'Methodological Basis. . .,' loc. cit., pp. 75–7, 80.

33 Ibid., p. 85.

34 Ibid., p. 79.

35 The pages of the *Journal of Economic Issues* contain Institutionalist analyses of a myriad of economic topics: technological change, the impact of multinational corporations, law and economics, labor markets, and so on. None so far have highlighted the specifics of the pattern model approach, however, and that is the sort of work that I see as necessary.

36 For example, see Irvin M. Grossack and Samuel M. Loescher, 'Institutional and Mainstream Economics: Choice and Power as a Basis for a Synthesis,' *Journal of Economic Issues*, vol. 14 (December 1980), pp. 925–36.

PART THREE

PROVISIONAL ANSWERS TO SOME UNSETTLED QUESTIONS

10

Is Philosophy of Science Useful for Understanding Methodology?

In this and the next three chapters, a few of what may be called the 'Big Questions' are addressed and some answers to them proposed. Not everyone will agree with the solutions recommended here. Indeed, little consensus should be expected regarding solutions to these problems.

But significantly, disagreement on such questions is eminently healthy. The critical discussion of such fundamental issues yields a variety of distinct solutions, and as these potentially fruitful research agendas are revealed and explored, extended and polished by advocates, scrutinized and criticized by antagonists, the frontiers of the discipline will expand.

The question under examination in this chapter is: Is the philosophy of science a useful tool for understanding economic methodology?

The Benefits of Understanding the Philosophical Issues

The last four chapters may be viewed as an attempt to answer that question, since they contain a detailed examination of the 'positivist' era in economic methodology viewed from the perspective of twentieth century philosophy of science. Almost all of the economic methodologists writing in this period made some reference to the philosophical literature; Friedman is the notable exception. It thus seems reasonable that a knowledge of the philosophy of science might be of use in coming to terms with the writings of economic methodologists.

In assessing the methodological literature, we discovered many ambiguities. Some economic methodologists had a firm grasp on the philosophical issues, and others did not. The meanings of terms employed by methodologists often differed, both from one another and from the meanings attached to them by philosophers; as a result, economists engaged in hot debates over methodological issues sometimes seemed to talk beyond each other, or to be involved in arguments about purely semantic issues. Perhaps most crucially, many of the economic methodologists discussed in the last few chapters would consider themselves positivists (though by now, that word seems to be losing some of its appeal), yet none of them seemed able to agree as to what it *means* to be a positivist. This broad assessment of the positivist period can be substantiated by briefly reviewing some of our findings regarding the positivist economic methodologists.

Terence Hutchison introduced falsificationism into economics over forty years ago, and has been one of its most consistent supporters. His most recent works are far more sophisticated than his earliest, in which he made a number of errors. He was mistaken in his assertion that the 'propositions of pure theory' are analytic. And he did not realize that his demand that the 'fundamental assumption' of maximizing, rational behavior be testable could not be achieved, that the indirect testability hypothesis is as applicable in economics (at least in this case) as it is in physics. Paradoxically, the specifics of Hutchison's analysis are incidental compared to his larger contribution: he brought to economics a methodological rhetoric which nicely fit the direction of substantive work by economists in the postwar era, that is, the construction of theories which must ultimately be tested by comparing their implications against data.

Since he was destined to make so many contributions in economic theory, Paul Samuelson's espousal of certain 'positivist' ideas probably had even more of an impact on the profession. He embraced operationalism, but it had little in common with Bridgman's position, resembling instead Hutchison's invocations that hypotheses be conceivably falsifiable and that theories make reference to observable data. Again, Samuelson's failure to accurately interpret a well-known position in the philosophy of science made little difference in economics.

Both Hutchison and Samuelson wrote in the late 1930s; if some of their methodological pronouncements seem naive, it should be remembered that a fully articulated logical empiricist position did not exist at that time. By the late 1940s and 1950s, however, the same cannot be said: logical empiricism was in its heyday. However, many economic methodologists did not seem cognizant of it, even though they referred to 'positivist' ideas in their writings.

His disclaimers notwithstanding, Hutchison certainly sounded like an ultra-empiricist in his debate with Machlup over whether the fundamental assumption of rational, maximizing behavior requires direct testing. Machlup, for his part, added some confusion by dubbing that issue 'the verification problem', though even a cursory reading of his article indicates that he was not using the term in the same way that philosophers use it. I have argued that Machlup was right, not simply because his position agreed with a similar one in the philosophy of science (the indirect testability hypothesis), but because in the absence of independently testable initial conditions, the rationality assumption as presently stated seems untestable. This underscores my belief that a knowledge of relevant issues in philosophy in no way guarantees the truth of a position, but is useful for purposes of clarifying debate.

Friedman's emphasis on predictive adequacy, his insistence that the 'realism' of assumptions is immaterial, and perhaps even his choice of the title 'The Methodology of Positive Economics' for his seminal methodological article, led many to interpret him as a positivist. His article was both sufficiently rich in detail and sufficiently ambiguous to generate a massive secondary literature. According to Boland's recent reinterpretation, and one with which I am in agreement, Friedman is not a positivist but an instrumentalist. Most of Friedman's critics writing in the 1950s and 1960s did not recognize this (nor, it seems, did Friedman himself), and as such, the force of their criticisms was vitiated by Boland's reinterpretation. I have argued that instrumentalism has been soundly criticized within the philosophy of science, so that Boland's defense need not be considered the final word. Such discussions might not have taken twenty-five years to emerge had the issues in philosophy been recognized more quickly.

Samuelson's advocacy of the descriptivist thesis in his critique of Friedman is a final example of methodological writing by a 'positivist' economist that fails to take into account well-established positions within logical empiricist philosophy of science. The covering-law models, which emphasize the importance of explanation in science, had been on the scene for almost two decades (longer if we take into account Popper's work on explanation in the 1930s) when Samuelson defended the descriptivist approach. His defense of descriptivism rests primarily on outdated arguments from philosophy (he would be hard-pressed to defend it on the grounds that it reflects actual scientific practice); as such, his arguments appear to be uniquely unconvincing.

In assessing the usefulness of a knowledge of the philosophy of science for an understanding of economic methodology, we find that the old saw about a little knowledge being dangerous seems entirely appropriate: the philosophy of science, taken in small doses, helped muddy the thinking of many of the 'positivist' methodologists. Yet our study has also demonstrated that a fuller understanding of the philosophical issues enables one to disentangle twisted arguments, to separate semantic debates from those which are more substantive, to clarify ambiguous positions and to systematize a literature which, on first examination, may appear to lack any coherence.

This analysis of the positivist era in economic methodology has shown that the philosophy of science can be a useful tool for the study of methodology. In Chapters 4 and 5 it was shown that all forms of positivism, including logical empiricism, have been subject to extensive criticism within contemporary philosophy of science. Karl Popper (whose work is vehemently anti-inductivist, and embraces the notions of fallibilism, critical rationalism, and the growth of scientific knowledge) may be considered the pivotal figure in the revolutionary transition from logical empiricism to the growth of knowledge tradition which is now so fashionable. In light of these developments, it makes sense to ask: Have economic methodologists kept up with the changing landscape in the philosophy of science?

Happily, it can be reported that they have. There is a growing number of articles on methodology in which the decline of positivist influence in philosophy is noted. At the same time, the growth of knowledge tradition has gained the attention of economists, though at this point it has had more influence on the history of economic thought than on methodology.[1]

While it is easy to criticize the mistakes of the past, it is more difficult to learn by them and thereby avoid committing similar errors in the future. Nonetheless, attempts to learn from the past should be made. We saw that a little knowledge was dangerous for the positivist economic methodologists; the same rule applies for the methodologists of today. Indeed, errors can already be found in the contemporary methodological literature, in the writings of both anti-positivists and those who draw on the growth of knowledge tradition.

Some of the critics of 'positivism' have caricatured the position. This occurs to some extent in Wilber and Harrison's article in which they claim Friedman is a positivist and that positivism may be equated with the covering-law models. Similarly, in books by Blaug and Katouzian in which positivist analysis is found wanting, the straw man of verificationism, an idea formulated by logical positivists but rejected by logical empiricists, is posited as an important 'positivist' doctrine.[2] Stanley Wong does the same in his critique of Samuelson's revealed preference theory, but the scope of his critique is far broader and indicates a thorough understanding of the philosophical literature.

Turning to the growth of knowledge tradition and the analysis of Popper, we find fewer mistakes in interpretation: most analysts have gotten their Kuhn and Lakatos down correctly. One possible problem area is in failing to distinguish between Popper and Lakatos: the former's prescriptions are really quite strict, while the latter's can be strict (if one emphasizes that problem shifts must be theoretically and empirically progressive) or lax (if one emphasizes the untestable hard core, the absence of instant rationality, and the like) depending on which aspect of his thought is invoked. Mark Blaug, who advocates falsificationism, sometimes sounds much more like a Lakatosian than a Popperian.[3] Another problem for those who make reference to the growth of knowledge literature is to use it productively. As was mentioned earlier, with the exception of a few of the papers in the Latsis volume, most articles on the growth of knowledge tradition have emphasized the historical models of change found in Kuhn and Lakatos, applying them to particular periods in doctrinal history. The vital methodological question of theory choice, though obviously implicit in such studies, is seldom explicitly addressed.

The point has been made: when used properly, the philosophy of science can be a valuable tool for studying economic methodology. The trick is to use it properly; the best safeguard is a thorough understanding of the field.

Can Philosophy of Science Make Economic Methodology Better?

In the last section it was claimed that a knowledge of philosophical issues would help the reader who is trying to understand methodology. It was also claimed that the practicing methodologist would benefit from some exposure to philosophy: his analyses would be clearer, and more comprehensible to others; debates with antagonists would be on firmer ground, since a common terminology would be employed; the wheel would not be repeatedly rediscovered; and, conversely, mistakes of the past could also be avoided.

Though these benefits are not trivial, some might wish more. While acknowledging the advantages just cited, some might hope that a knowledge of the philosophy of science could make economic methodology better in ways far grander than those mentioned above. Specifically, some might hope that the philosophy of science could serve as some sort of final arbiter in methodological debates. Not only would inconsistent and erroneous positions be exposed and weeded out, but ultimately, an 'optimal' methodology would emerge.

It is my belief that though error can be eliminated, it is a will-o'-the-wisp to hope for the emergence of a single methodology. Indeed, the emergence of a single methodology would be most unfortunate, for it would herald the dogmatic straightjacketing of the scientific process in economics. This point is treated in detail in the next two chapters; for now it must remain an assertion that one should not expect (and certainly not welcome) a single, ultimate methodology to be forthcoming when philosophical tools are applied to economic methodology – indeed, contemporary philosophy of science if anything points in exactly the opposite direction.

Can Other Approaches Be Taken?

Though the importance of a knowledge of the philosophy of science for the study of economic methodology has been emphasized in this chapter, my position should not be construed to imply that this is the only, or the penultimate, approach to the subject. There are other approaches, and in the best of all worlds, the economic methodologist should be able to make use of all of them.

One approach which to my knowledge has been completely ignored is the integration of economic methodology and philosophy with econometrics. Methodologists have generally skirted the issue of the methodological foundations of econometric theory, and the few econometricians who have addressed philosophical issues have seldom gone beyond gratuitous references to such figures as Feigl or Carnap.[4] This unexplored area could yield some extremely significant results.

Another approach (whose exclusion in this book must rankle more than a few readers) would make use of the growing field of philosophy of social science. It must indeed seem perverse to spend so many pages discussing the relationship between philosophy and the methodology of a social science while fastidiously avoiding a literature whose subject matter is obviously relevant.

The reason for ignoring this literature is straightforward: my primary task was to analyze the writings of economic methodologists in the positivist era, and for that task, a knowledge of the philosophy of social science is irrelevant.[5] (Positivists, we remember, adhere to the unity-of-science thesis, and as such, there is no distinction between philosophy of natural and philosophy of social science; there is only philosophy of science.) Surprisingly, few of the critics of the 'orthodoxy' have explored the philosophy of social science, either. An exception (though really, this has occurred only recently) is the Institutionalists, some of whom have been drawn to the pattern models of Kaplan and Deising. Some Austrian economists are currently examining the relationship between phenomenology and the science of human action. But by and large, the philosophy of social science remains a potentially fruitful but as yet untapped resource for the study of economic methodology.

A third approach that has made some headway in the last decade is the methodological analysis of particular research programs in economics. This began with the application of the Kuhnian and Lakatosian models of scientific change to selected epochs in the history of economic thought. Spiro Latsis took the significant step of applying Lakatos's framework in the evaluation of a contemporary research program, the theory of monopolistic competition. The suggestive vignettes in the latter third of Blaug's recent survey continue this approach, and several recent dissertations examine specific programs in great detail. Stanley Wong's appraisal of Samuelson's revealed preference theory using the internal criticism–external criticism dichotomy is perhaps the most sophisticated published example to date of this technique. And finally, Lawrence Boland's totally novel and predictably outspoken *The Foundations of Economic Method* (1982) should soon takes its place as another fine example of this type of analysis.[6]

The best of the studies cited above attempt a subtle blending and synthesis of many fields: the philosophy of science, the history of a particular research program in economics, economic methodology (both current and as it appeared to the theorist facing a given problem situation he was trying to solve), and the philosophy of history. (This last is included because one's interpretation of a particular historical incident is colored by one's methodology, as Lakatos so forcefully reminded us in his last major paper. If one does not explicitly take this into account in attempting such a study, the results are open to charges of bias. Whether such bias can ever be eliminated is, of course, one of the much-debated questions of the philosophy of history.)

The three approaches to the study of economic methodology mentioned above are only the most obvious ones and certainly do not exhaust the possibilities. One could, for example, study the sociology of the discipline, inspecting the various institutions, artifacts, and rituals which comprise the environment in which economists work.[7] Even more wide-ranging approaches are possible – I have occasionally wondered what a comparative study of, say, the rules of evidence in law, the canons of literary criticism, and various prescriptions in economic methodology might turn up. (I have never gotten beyond posing the question, and happily leave the task to a more ambitious scholar.) In methodology, as in other fields, there is plenty of room for novelty. And as in other fields, any successful alternative will have had to prove itself by surviving the critical scrutiny of antagonists bent on its destruction.

Notes

1 A listing of articles by economists who criticize various aspects of positivism would include Charles Wilber and Robert Harrison, 'The Methodological Basis of Institutional Economics: Pattern Model, Storytelling, and Holism,' *Journal of Economic Issues*, vol. 12 (March 1978), pp. 61–8; R. W. Pfouts, 'Some Proposals for a New Methodology for Economics,' *Atlantic Economic Journal*, vol. 1 (November 1973), pp. 13–22; S. Rosefielde, 'Post-Positivist Scientific Method and the Appraisal of Non-Market Economic Behavior, *Quarterly Journal of Ideology*, vol. 3 (Spring 1980), pp. 23–33; Homa Katouzian, 'Scientific Method and Positive Economics,' *Scottish Journal of Political Economy*, vol. 21 (November 1974), pp. 279–86; Alan Coddington, 'Positive Economics,' *Canadian Journal of Economics*, vol. 5 (1972), pp. 1–15; and Evan Jones, 'Positive Economics or What?' *Economic Record*, vol. 53 (September 1977), pp. 350–63. Cf. also the two books cited in note 2. See Chapter 9, note 24, for a list of articles by economists who use the Kuhnian and Lakatosian frameworks to analyze the history of thought.

2 In his *Ideology and Method in Economics* (New York: New York University Press, 1980), Homa Katouzian treats only logical positivism (and, when discussing Friedman, instrumentalism) in his search for the philosophical foundations of 'positive economics'. In Mark Blaug's first chapter on the philosophy of science, in *The Methodology of Economics*, there are ten pages devoted to 'the received view', (he discusses the 'hypothetico-deductive model of explanation' which we call the covering-law model, the symmetry thesis, and the verifiability principle of meaning), while Popper's views get twenty pages of text. They each have rather comprehensive later treatments of the growth of knowledge tradition, with emphasis on the works of Kuhn and Lakatos. For a fuller explication of my criticisms, see my two book reviews in the April and July 1981 issues of the *Southern Economic Journal*.

3 Cf. Chapter 6, note 64. Blaug's espousal of falsificationism is critiqued in Chapter 12.

4 An example of this approach is Arnold Zellner, 'Causality and Econometrics,' in K. Brunner and A. Meltzer (eds), *Three Aspects of Policy and Policymaking: Knowledge, Data and Institutions*, supplement to *Journal of Monetary Economics*, vol. 10 (1979), pp. 9–54.

5 *Unless* one is constructing a critique of positivism from a philosophy of social science perspective. Such a task could be attempted; for our purposes, it made more sense to get a firm understanding of positivism and to see how well positivist economic methodologists fared, given our understanding of the philosophical issues. In addition, if one agrees with methodological pluralism, the approach taken in the text is more robust, since it is internal criticism. A defense of methodological pluralism is contained in Chapter 13.

6 Four dissertations which examine the methodological and epistemological foundations of contemporary research programs are Arjo Klamer (Duke University) and James Wible (Penn State) on rational expectations, and Elba Brown (Duke) and William Guthrie (UNC) on the work of J. M. Keynes.

7 The development of a professional literature in economics is analyzed using a
   Kuhnian framework in Vincent J. Tarascio and Bruce Caldwell, 'Theory Choice
   in Economics: Philosophy and Practice,' *Journal of Economic Issues*, vol. 12
   (December 1979), pp. 983–1006. In Jerome Ravetz, *Scientific Knowledge and Its
   Social Problems* (Oxford: Clarendon Press, 1971), a 'common sense' approach to
   the sociology of science as a whole is taken; similar studies in economics could be
   revealing. On the lighter side, one should not neglect Axel Leijonhufvud, 'Life
   Among the Econ,' *Western Economic Journal*, vol. 11 (September, 1973), pp.
   327–37.

11

Prescription, Description, and Theory Appraisal

One of the most attractive features of logical empiricism was that it seemed to provide rigorous and objective formulas for identifying legitimate scientific procedure. The H-D model prescribed the structure and logical status of theories and theoretical terms; the covering-law models dictated which explanations were to qualify as scientific; and confirmationism provided criteria for the appraisal of theories. In a phrase, the logical empiricist program had prescriptive force.

As was shown in Chapter 4, the entirety of logical empiricism fell prey to extensive and severe criticism within the philosophy of science in the 1950s and 1960s. If the current climate of opinion continues, logical empiricism can no longer be considered a viable framework for explicating and assessing scientific activity. The question arises: Is there an equally prescriptively robust program to take the place of logical empiricism? If so, what is it; and if not, should other alternatives be considered?

Economists have generally neglected the topics of theory form and structure and the nature of scientific explanation in their methodological writings. (The exceptions are those analyses of explanation reviewed in Chapter 9.) The same cannot be said regarding the problem of theory appraisal. Indeed, much of the literature in economic methodology involves, either explicitly or implicitly, the defense or critique of various methods of theory assessment. As such, the question of whether prescriptive methodology is possible in economics turns on the question: Do objective canons of theory appraisal exist in economics?

In this chapter the philosophical issues are reviewed. The general conclusions can be stated in advance: no algorithm of choice exists;

because of this, any prescriptions that can be justified must be stated fairly broadly; a comprehensive approach to the theory appraisal question will involve both prescriptive and descriptive elements; the tension between prescription and description can be fruitful.

Before beginning, some definitional matters deserve attention. Throughout this chapter, the terms 'theory appraisal' and 'theory choice' are used interchangeably. Some may object to this, since the appraisal of a theory need not always imply that a choice must be made. It is clearly true that there are occasions when appraisal takes place but choice is absent, as when only a single theory is evaluated, or when the theories to be appraised are in different domains. Conversely, there are occasions when appraisal takes place and choice occurs without any problems: Kuhnian normal science is the classic example.

Neither of these scenarios creates problems, thus neither is very interesting. The *problem* of theory choice occurs when two (or more) theories in the same domain are appraised and each has some support. The question then is: Does some universally applicable prescriptive procedure exist for appraising such theories so that the 'best' (however defined) can be chosen? This is the interesting question, and in such cases the terms 'theory appraisal' and 'theory choice' can be used interchangeably.

Confirmationism and Falsificationism

In discussing the problem of theory appraisal, it may be useful to begin by looking at a related problem, the search for a criterion of cognitive significance, which was first formulated by the logical positivists of the Vienna Circle. In their attempts to discover a criterion that could be used to distinguish between meaningful and meaningless nonanalytic sentences, the logical positivists discovered that neither strict verifiability nor strict falsifiability was adequate: the former rules out sentences expressing laws of universal form, and the latter does not permit sentences expressing affirmative existential propositions into the domain of science. Though other alternatives were also proposed (e.g. Ayer's notion of weak verifiability, Carnap's suggestion that an empiricist language be developed), strength of confirmation was ultimately chosen as the logical empiricist criterion for judging the acceptability of theories. Confirmationism has a number of interesting features that deserve our attention.

1. First, a theory as a whole, rather than the individual sentences

contained within it, becomes the locus of testing. A theory is tested by comparing its predictions with the data. Since all the individual terms within a given theory are not generally given empirical counterparts, uninterpreted terms gain meaning indirectly when the theories in which they are embedded are confirmed. Operationalism is thus rejected by confirmationists.

2. Theories may be compared, and hopefully ranked, according to their relative strengths of confirmation. For this to occur, the predictions of competing theories first must be roughly comparable in terms of quantitative, qualitative, and temporal ranges of acceptability. The canons of inductive logic may then be applied to assess the relative strengths of confirmation of the theories in question. The following criteria of confirmation are employed to evaluate theories: quantity of favorable test outcomes, precision of procedures of observation and measurement, variety of supporting evidence, and confirmation by new test implications.

3. Confirmationists realize that the most highly confirmed theory need not be the true one. They also recognize that strength of confirmation alone may not be sufficient for unambiguous theory choice. They therefore recommend that additional criteria of acceptability, many of which refer to the structure and form of theories, be used to supplement strength of confirmation. These criteria include, among others, logical consistency, simplicity, elegance, generality, extensibility, and agreement with other well-established theories.

Confirmationists were hopeful that their prescriptive formulas would provide grounds for unambiguous theory choice in science. Disconfirmed, illogical, and cumbersome theories are rejected or reworked; highly confirmed, mutually consistent, logically complete and fruitful structures are retained. By this process, the frontiers of scientific knowledge are carefully, but inexorably, expanded; the growth of scientific knowledge is both rational and cumulative.

Karl Popper challenged all of this. Popper's starting points are the problem of induction and his belief that neither confirmationism nor any other form of inductivism offers successful responses to it. He emphasizes a fundamental asymmetry in the testing of hypotheses: propositions that make use of universal laws can never be proven true, but they can be falsified. The proper method of science is to advance bold conjectures – those that forbid much, thereby having high empirical content – which can be subjected to critical tests. Those that survive are considered corroborated, but significantly, they are not the most *probable* – empirical content and high probability vary inversely. As such the confirmationist quest for theories with high inductive probabilities is misguided.

Other problems with confirmationism exist. A universally-accepted, well-justified inductive logic has yet to be constructed. And various 'paradoxes of confirmation' pose additional difficulties. It would seem that it might be reasonable to reject confirmationism, and turn instead to Popper's methodological falsificationism.

But we find that Popper's approach has some weak points, too. There are elements of conventionalism in his approach that may be disturbing to some: the empirical basis, against which hypotheses are tested, is presumably based on facts from the protocol domain, but in the final analysis Popper admits that the empirical basis is a convention. The notion of verisimilitude may also be viewed with some skepticism; though it offers a formal solution to the problem that the theories with the highest empirical content are false, it can barely be considered an operational concept. Nor does Popper's refusal to critically assess the major prescription of critical rationalism ('Subject every belief to critical scrutiny.') sit well with many Popperian critics.

The Theory Choice Problem and the Growth of Knowledge Tradition

Though the names of such growth of knowledge theorists as Kuhn and Lakatos have become well known to economists, few in our profession seem to realize that their analyses, in many important ways, are direct responses to the perceived failure of both confirmationism and Popper's methodological falsificationism to provide viable frameworks for understanding the problem of theory choice in science. Though Popper may be considered one of the founders of the growth of knowledge approach, Feyerabend, Kuhn, and Lakatos have all criticized his particular formulation of the theory choice problem.

Feyerabend argues that any rules-oriented methodology (including Popper's) if ever followed, would be disastrous for science. In addition, he claims that the history of science offers no support for the view that scientists have ever followed a single, definable method; rather, the best of them have been 'unscrupulous opportunists' who bend the rules to fit the situation. Though not a lineal descendant of the Popperian growth of knowledge tradition (his work was influenced by Polyani, Koyré, and Conant), Thomas Kuhn's *Structure of Scientific Revolutions* was a pivotal work in the transition from the logical empiricist era to the present post-positivist period. He, too, has criticized Popper. Kuhn maintains that Popper's vision of science is fundamentally flawed: instead of being representable by the aphorism, 'Revolution in permanence', the true mark of a scientific discipline is normal science, in which scientists labor under a single paradigm and the results of tests are anticipated in advance. Furthermore, during periods of revolutionary science, there is no single method; rather, methodological debate proliferates. Finally, methods are paradigm-dependent, not universal. And Lakatos, who views his *MSRP* as a natural extension of Popper's work, questions Popper's insistence that falsifying tests should cause scientists to reject theories. Theory testing is a far more complex affair: series of theories are tested over long periods of time; few tests are crucial except in retrospect; tests are best viewed as 'three-sided affairs' in which competing programs are compared against data; even degenerating research programs may be retained for a time, especially if no replacement exists – an idea that is also central to Kuhn's program.

The problem of theory choice – whether objective and universally applicable criteria exist by which theories may be unambiguously compared, critically evaluated, and hopefully ranked – is thus viewed as an essential theme by the growth of knowledge analysts whose work was reviewed in Chapter 5. In the remainder of this section, I briefly document the response of each of these theorists to that question. Though all three agree that it is a problem of great significance, their responses to it vary widely, and each response leads to a different vision of the appropriate goal of methodological analysis. In particular, each analyst offers a unique answer to the question: What is the proper balance between prescription and description in formulating the theory choice problem?

Paul Feyerabend's greatest contribution may be that he, more than anyone else, shows that the theory choice problem is, indeed, a problem. In both *Against Method* and *Science in a Free Society*, Feyerabend repeatedly argues that scientists should not search for a rules-oriented methodology that would permit *choice* among theories; that the attempt to evaluate theories according to 'objective' rules is not only chimerical, but dangerous. It is chimerical because the definitions of all methodological criteria depend on the theories to which they are applied; as such, 'objective' criteria of choice are not independently definable or applicable. Methodological positions, like theories themselves, are not directly comparable due to the theory-dependence thesis. (This indicates the importance of that thesis even in Feyerabend's later work.) The attempt to apply canons of choice is dangerous because it leads to the elimination of theories, which by definition reduces empirical content: every theory has its own independent empirical content because facts are theory-dependent. Theory *proliferation* is Feyerabend's prescription for science, at least for the present; theoretical *pluralism* is the best way forward, since it increases empirical content; theory *choice* is inimical to the progress of science. Feyerabend claims further that his methodological dadaism is more accurate than is any artificial, rules-oriented approach for describing the true, erratic nature of scientific development. Thus he believes that the motto 'Anything goes' is not only sound prescriptive methodological advice, it also captures and illuminates the actual history of scientific development.

Feyerabend's insistence that scientists and philosophers stop taking themselves (and him!) so seriously is wonderful advice; nonetheless, his suggestion that scientists accept the nihilism of a nonmethodology has aroused considerable debate. Many critics question whether the pursuit of unrestrained theoretical pluralism promises any progress (however defined) in science; others wonder whether a dadaist nonmethodology accurately reflects the actual history of science. I will not try to resolve such debates here. But we can thank Feyerabend for his message to laugh at ourselves (and him) on occasion, and for highlighting that the theory choice problem is a real one. His *response* to it, however, is only one of many; there are alternatives to the complacent acceptance of the standard criteria and the anarchy of a dadaist nonmethodology.

Thomas Kuhn provides one such alternative. Kuhn argues that traditional criteria of choice (accuracy, scope, fruitfulness, simplicity, and the like) are easily applied during period of normal science because the goals, the methods, and indeed, even the results of research are widely known and accepted as unproblematical within the scientific community. During periods of revolutionary change, however, previously unquestioned scientific procedures come under scrutiny. If competing paradigms emerge, they may be incommensurable, so the usual tools of theory appraisal may not be sufficient for objective choice among them. Though debates over paradigms are usually couched in terms of evaluation via objective methodological standards, such standards are not generally logically compelling – they are incapable of providing conclusive grounds for choice. Kuhn's response is to interpret the standard criteria as *norms* and *values* for scientific research, rather than as strict *rules* of choice. He also suggests that while these norms and values form the shared objective basis for theory choice, their concrete application by scientists involves additional subjective factors which vary across individuals, and which may include such things as personality types, prior work experience in a field, and even such extra-scientific influences as dominant social and political theories. Finally, sociological studies of specific scientific communities may be useful for discovering which particular norms and values predominate.

Kuhn's analysis shares at least one thing in common with that of Feyerabend: both deny that any objective 'algorithm of choice' exists in science. In a recently published paper Kuhn emphasizes that, even though *when viewed as norms and values* the standard criteria provide the shared objective basis for theory appraisal, in their application by individual scientists, 'two men fully committed to the same list of criteria may nevertheless reach different conclusions'.[1] This is true for three reasons: many of the criteria are imprecisely defined; competing theories may meet different criteria; and if several criteria are employed together, individual scientists may differ on the weight to be accorded each criterion. Further, Kuhn (like Feyerabend) contends that it is *fortunate* that no such algorithmic procedures have been accepted by scientists, since few new theories could satisfy the criteria, and therefore scientific progress would be hindered if such procedures were applied to them.[2] Finally, Kuhn maintains that his model of scientific change is adequate for describing the history of science.

Kuhn's efforts are a bold attempt to go beyond Feyerabend's skepticism without being driven back into the camp that believes an algorithm of choice is discoverable. His proposals that the usual criteria provide a shared objective basis for theory choice, but are criteria which can nonetheless be interpreted differently by individual scientists, blend together both subjective and objective elements in choice. By positing the scientific community as the primary source of norms and individual scientists as interpreters of those norms, differences between communities and individuals can be rationalized. But the denial of the existence of unambiguously definable and applicable rules does not force us to accept Feyerabend's methodological anarchism; though admitting subjectivity, we need not embrace the concept that anything goes. Kuhn's approach also pinpoints where values enter science, and why they are important. Indeed, his contribution is more instructive than the by now rather tired debates over the normative–positive distinction or the endless arguments about whether science is, or can be, or should be either value-free or value-laden.[3] The descriptive advantages of Kuhn's approach are bought at a high price: norms and values need not provide grounds for choice; the prescriptive content of scientific methodology is reduced to the rather weak dictum, 'Scientific communities should instill in their members some workable and productive constellation of norms and values.' Before committing ourselves to the Kuhnian vision, the contribution of Imre Lakatos must be reviewed.

Lakatos believes that his methodology of scientific research programs (MSRP) provides a program for the critical evaluation of competing scientific theories, a program which, though fully cognizant that there is no instant rationality and that therefore both justificationists and probabilists are wrong, nevertheless retains a prescriptive role for methodology and avoids the subjective quagmire of Kuhn's 'social psychology' or Feyerabend's anarchism. Lakatos also argues that his model is an adequate descriptive vehicle for the 'rational reconstruction' of science.[4] Thus, at least in his own eyes, Lakatos's MSRP can claim both prescriptive and descriptive strengths. A closer look at his program allows us to judge whether that claim is justified.

His criterion for the long run evaluation of research programs, 'Choose the research program which over time has progressive problemshifts, that is, which continues over time to predict novel facts, some of which are corroborated', is easily stated, defined, and applied. It would seem that by following such a procedure, scientists could straightforwardly choose among theories, as well. Unfortunately, this is not necessarily the case.

The essential methodological message in Lakatos's works is that though 'instant rationality' does not exist, long run objectivity in theory appraisal is possible: one can, with the benefit of time, decide which research traditions are progressing and which are degenerating. But if one takes his principles of proliferation and tenacity seriously, it is clear that Lakatos never answers the fundamental question of when one should make the final decision to accept a program over its competitors. Without some decision rule or time specification appended to Lakatos's MSRP, a scientist could 'rationally' cling indefinitely to a degenerating research program by invoking the principle of tenacity. (The same situation exists if no replacement of the degenerating program has surfaced.) But if that is the case, the MSRP does not permit unambiguous choice. The situation is all the more intractable since its remedy (to add a decision rule or time horizon for choice) would be arbitrary; though it would allow choice and thereby make the Lakatosian program falsifiable, it would also falsify it descriptively.

The larger question here involves the entire notion of the long run, a concept whose power and limitations should be familiar to economists. We all learn as students that perfect competition ensures long run product exhaustion, and that changes in the supply of money affect only the price level in the long run, and that all expectations are realized and that all markets clear in the long run. Yet in our history of thought classes we are also taught either to disregard as 'unscientific', 'irrefutable', and 'unfalsifiable' the analyses of Marx and the Classicals because no time constraints were placed on their predictions, or to consider their long run predictions regarding capitalism as 'falsified' by (what may be a short span of) history. But surely there is a contradiction here: why should economists be so comfortable with the concept of the long run in some instances, and so disdainful of it in others? Though other differences between the historicism of Marx and the Classicals and the uses of the long run in more modern economic formulations may help resolve this particular dilemma, it seems that economists in general have paid too little attention to the slippery notion of the long run.

The same limitation plagues Lakatos. Though his MSRP successfully avoids the predicament of instant rationality, it loses prescriptive force by asserting that choice is unproblematical in some distant and nebulous future. This aspect of Lakatos's work leads Feyerabend to the conclusion that, for all its seeming emphasis on prescription, the MSRP is nothing more than 'anarchism in disguise'.[5] Indeed, his *Against Method* is dedicated, 'to Imre Lakatos, friend and fellow anarchist'.

And what of Lakatos's claim that his MSRP permits the rational reconstruction of the history of science? Lakatos's historical model is better than Kuhn's for describing both gradual change within a single research tradition and the existence over time of a number of competing traditions. Kuhn's model is superior for describing cataclysmic change and theoretical monism. The decision concerning which model is more appropriate for presenting the intellectual history of any given science will depend on how one views change within it. The obvious point that they may be best used as complements rather than as substitutes should not be overlooked, nor should the point that other models are possible, and perhaps more suitable for economics.

The Integration of Prescription and Description

In their attempts to solve the theory choice problem, no robust prescriptive algorithm of choice has been discovered by the growth of knowledge philosophers. Significantly, the problem is *not* that of finding criteria of choice that are easily definable, straightforwardly applicable, and which have weights attached to them to indicate relative order of importance. (The satisfaction of these conditions ensures that unambiguous choice is possible.) The problem is finding criteria that direct scientists to choose *correctly*. An example from economics will make this point quickly; a criterion of choice which is both unambiguously definable and remarkably easy to apply reads, 'Accept only those theories whose originator's surname is Friedman.' (Further criteria might restrict us to certain first names.) Though such invocations allow unambiguous theory choice, and may even seem to have been followed by members of the economics profession in the past, presumably most economists would reject such criteria as inadequate for a general method of theory appraisal.

The heart of the problem in attempting to formulate an algorithm of choice, then, is that we can never know prior to the fact which methods are most likely to lead us to true knowledge. If one accepts fallibilism, the problem can be stated even more strongly: since we can never know that we have found the truth (even if we have found it), we certainly can never know if we have found a method that invariably allows us to choose the true theory. Popper's great contribution was to recognize the problems of fallibilism yet still attempt to enunciate a prescriptive methodology. His falsification-ism does not solve the choice problem, but it does permit us to *eliminate error.* Yet even with this more modest goal, falsificationism runs into problems of its own, both logically (by refusing to apply its critical apparatus to itself) and descriptively (many of the criticisms of Popper by the growth of knowledge theorists involve pointing out instances in which falsificationism had not been applied and, further, should not have been applied).

In their unsuccessful attempts to solve the theory choice problem contemporary philosophers of science have discovered two extremely important insights concerning the relative importance of prescription and description in scientific methodology. The first is that only broadly stated prescriptions are reasonable if one wishes to truly understand the scientific process. The second is that there exists a significant role for descriptive studies in coming to terms with the process. It is of crucial importance that both prescription and description are necessary in any comprehensive treatment of methodology. A purely prescriptive methodology which has no link to actual scientific practice will never be followed. On the other hand, if methodological canons merely describe behavior, their prescriptive role is reduced to the Panglossian dictum: Whatever is, is correct.

Of the growth of knowledge theorists we have studied, Lakatos is the most ambitious: he claims to have discovered a descriptively accurate and prescriptively robust program for methodology. Kuhn's approach may be the most innovative (in looking at the usual choice criteria as norms and values), though his originality may simply be attributable to his coming from a non-Popperian tradition. And, as always, Feyerabend is the most playful: just as his approach to methodology is to embrace nonmethodology, his prescription of 'Anything goes' is perhaps best considered a nonprescription.

Those who would prefer that methodology offer a rigorous, objective, prescriptive framework will be disappointed by the results stated here. That methodology must always contain some blend of broad prescription with historical description should not be viewed as a counsel of despair. Only by the judicious application of these tools can we gain an accurate understanding of the true nature of scientific activity and change. These tools, in the hands of the growth of knowledge philosophers, have revealed some valuable insights about the scientific process, insights that were overlooked by positivist predecessors who thought they had discovered objective, immutable laws for distinguishing science from nonscience.

Notes

1   Thomas Kuhn, 'Objectivity, Value Judgement, and Theory Choice,' in *The Essential Tension: Selected Studies in Scientific Tradition and Change* (Chicago: University of Chicago Press, 1977), p. 324.
2   Ibid., pp. 322–5, 329–33.
3   We have nowhere discussed the perennial problem of the role of values in economics, but it is a methodological topic that has been hotly debated since the Methodenstreit. Some recent treatments of the subject include Mark Blaug, *The Methodology of Economics* (Cambridge, England: Cambridge University Press, 1980), Chapter 5; Homa Katouzian, *Ideology and Method in Economics* (New York: New York University Press, 1980), Chapter 6; Fritz Machlup, 'Positive and Normative Economics,' in *Methodology of Economics and Other Social Sciences* (New York: Academic Press, 1978), pp. 425–50; Terence Hutchison, *Positive Economics and Policy Judgements* (London: Allen and Unwin, 1964).
4   For Lakatos's views on the potential of his MSRP to provide a framework for the rational reconstruction of science, and some critical responses to his claims, see the articles cited in Chapter 5, note 63.
5   Paul K. Feyerabend, *Against Method, Outline of an Anarchistic Theory of Knowledge* (London: NLB, 1975), pp. 181–222.

12

Confirmationism and Falsificationism in Economics

That the theory choice problem seems insolvable was a major conclusion of the last chapter. The implications of that finding may not seem readily apparent to economists untrained in philosophy. The purpose of this chapter is to relate the philosophical analysis just completed to economics. It is argued that the methodological stance assumed by most practicing economists (some variant of confirmationism or instrumentalism) does not solve the choice problem, and that the methodological approach which dominates the rhetoric of economic methodologists (falsificationism) cannot be applied successfully in economics.

Confirmationism and the Practice of Economists

In the construction and evaluation of their theories, most economists adhere to some variant of confirmationism or instrumentalism.[1] Both of these approaches emphasize the testing of theories by their predictions. They differ in that instrumentalists consider the most highly confirmed theory the most useful instrument, whereas confirmationists consider the most highly confirmed theory the most probable: that is, confirmationists do and instrumentalists do not associate strength of confirmation with some notion of truth value.

Both confirmationists and instrumentalists recognize that empirical criteria are often insufficient for unambiguous choice among competing theories. Their solution is to supplement the empirical criteria with other criteria. Such criteria can be placed into four categories. The first category includes criteria that are used to evaluate the structure and form of theories. Among many that could be considered, perhaps six are most important. The first is logical consistency, which requires that no axioms or relationships postulated within a theoretical structure may contradict other relations or axioms in the structure, and that no mutually incompatible theorems may be deducible from the postulated axioms and relations. Logical consistency is probably the oldest and most generally accepted of the structural criteria of acceptability. The second is elegance, perhaps the most subjective standard. It focuses on the beauty and aesthetic appeal of a theoretical structure. In Henry Margenau's elegant prose, 'this regulative maxim separates what is ugly and cumbersome from sweeping ideas that carry élan and give pleasure on comprehension'.[2] The third is extensibility: A theory is preferred if it allows extension through deductions into other areas of investigation. The fourth, generality, maintains that a theory that incorporates an existing and well-established body of knowledge into a single unified framework is to be judged superior. The fifth criterion involves theoretical support, or multiple connectedness. If a new hypothesis fits in well with an established theoretical structure, it gains in acceptability. The last criterion, simplicity, is another ancient standard. It simply states that the simpler and more economical of two theories is preferred.

The second category involves criteria which are used to evaluate the intuitive plausibility of theories. These are twofold: realism and explanatory power. Realism, unless it is taken to mean truth value, or something similar, is notoriously difficult to define. Neither do its synonyms (e.g. understandability, reasonableness, intuitive plausibility) get us very far. And unless the covering laws are invoked, so that explanation is rigorously defined as the deduction of an explanandum from an explanans, explanatory power is a similarly troublesome term to pin down. Yet greater explanatory power and greater realism are often invoked by advocates engaged in arguing the merits of particular theories, so must be included among our criteria.[3]

A third criterion involves the pedagogic value of theories. Heuristic value, or the ability to illuminate a crucial point or to simplify a complex problem situation, is viewed as an advantageous characteristic of a theory.

The final category assesses the research potential of theories: fruitfulness and fertility are the terms used most often here. Theories which suggest new areas or methods of investigation, or new approaches to old problems, are judged favorably.

Of course, not all analysts would agree with the specifics of our choice of categories. As one example, Popper argues that simplicity is an empirical criterion: the simpler theory has more empirical content because it forbids more events. It is evident that many other organizational schemes are possible. My only intent is to offer one that includes those criteria which are most often mentioned by participants in debates over the merits of theories.

Can the addition of some or all of these criteria to the empirical ones help solve the problem of theory choice? An affirmative answer requires that the criteria outlined above be both justifiable and capable of straightforward application. Problems exist on both counts.

Most of the criteria are justifiable only on an intuitive basis. We generally like our theories to cohere well, or exhibit properties of simplicity or elegance, and that predilection is offered as justification. But clearly this will not do. A closer examination of our criteria indicates that many are based on metaphysical assumptions. The principle of simplicity, for example, has been justified on the grounds that nature is orderly, which clearly presupposes a metaphysics.[4] Other methodological justifications (such as Karl Popper's, which states that simpler theories are more 'falsifiable') depend on the results of individual tests and are thus themselves subject to practical 'falsification'. Similar criticisms could be advanced about theoretical criteria of theory choice, simply because criteria which impose constraints on the form and structure of theories implicitly presume a certain form and structure of the phenomenal world. The criteria are then justified because they guarantee the use of theories which are somehow optimal for the study of phenomenal reality. Any such justification assumes that one knows how reality is structured, and in making that assumption, one has entered the realm of metaphysics.

A likely response is, so what? After all, what matters to the working scientist is not justification, but workability. Even if the choice of various criteria is arbitrary (i.e. no ultimate foundation for that choice exists), could not their applicability be justification enough? If all economists agreed, for example, that economic theories should be logically consistent, and elegant, and so forth, would not such agreement be sufficient justification for retaining those criteria? Such an approach requires only that the criteria be easily applied in judging theories (i.e. that one know whether or not a given theory does meet a given criterion) and, further, that most economists agree about the value of the various criteria. This approach circumvents the problem of justification and attacks the issue of workability in a 'truth-by-consensus' manner. But it seems that even this defensive strategem encounters difficulties in economic science.

It is not always easy to determine whether a given hypothesis or theory meets a particular criterion. Some are so loosely defined that subjective interpretation is inevitable. Whether or not a theory is elegant is clearly a matter of opinion; heuristic value, too, depends greatly on whether an observer feels a theory is illuminating.

Some criteria cannot be employed for short run theory choice because they are often only distinguishable in retrospect. This seems to be the case for extensibility and generality; for example, a generation passed before economists realized that the tools of marginal utility analysis were general ones that could fruitfully be extended into such areas as production and distribution theory. The claim of greater generality is further hindered by the fact that future research may invalidate it. J. M. Keynes's *General Theory*, an obvious advance (in his eyes) over the work of 'classical' predecessors, was dubbed a 'special case' in the 1950s, by Don Patinkin and other founders of the neoclassical synthesis. Then, in the 1960s, revisionist Keynesians reinterpreted Keynes's work as more general again, since it isolated as explanatory principles the facts that expectations may not be realized and that information is costly. Theories that assume costless information and perfect expectation are limiting, special cases.

Even such ancient criteria as logical consistency and simplicity are not sacrosanct. A case may be made that it is logically inconsistent to assume that one knows the interest rate when one determines the value of capital, and then state with utter equanimity that the interest rate is determined by the marginal productivity of capital, which, of course, can only be determined if one knows the value of capital. And even simplicity, which has held the veneration of scientists since the time of William of Ockham, may encounter problems. As Hemple points out, simplicity is relative to a certain (often mathematical) background, and choice of the background is arbitrary. For example, let us posit three hypotheses:

$$H.1 \quad v = u^4 - 6u^3 + 11u^2 - 5u + 2$$
$$H.2 \quad v = u^5 - 4u^4 - u^3 + 16u^2 - 11u + 2$$
$$H.3 \quad v = u + 2$$

where $u = 0, 1, 2, 3$, and $v = 2, 3, 4, 5$, respectively. One would usually think of H.3 as being the simplest, but only if we define simplicity in terms of the order of a polynomial. If our background is in polar coordinates, H.3 would be more complex (since it describes a spiral) than, say, $v \cos (u - a) = p$, the polar equation for a straight line. It thus seems that identifying which theories meet which criteria can be annoyingly difficult.[5]

An even more important barrier to the application of these criteria is that no theory exhibits all of the criteria listed above. Some hypotheses are fruitful and suggestive but are insufficiently formalized; thus they do not meet the criteria of, say, logical consistency or elegance. Others may advance our understanding of a particular problem but may do little to satisfy generality or extensibility. That no theories meet all of the criteria makes theory choice on nonempirical grounds problematical, for competing theories may be incommensurable in terms of those criteria. This opens the door to a selective application of the nonempirical criteria of acceptability. Proponents of well-established theories, for example, might stress logical consistency, elegance, and multiple connectedness; proponents of alternatives might stress the fruitfulness or greater realism of their theories. Both camps, one assumes, would claim greater generality on the grounds that their theories cover areas which are not included in the domain of investigation of alternative formulations.

The implications of this discussion are disheartening for those seeking an algorithm of choice. Though empirical criteria can and are often supplemented with additional ones, it seems that their combined use permits the *rationalization* of theories, but not choice among theories. The only exception would occur when two theories share a number of the same attributes, and one is shown to be superior in terms of some of these attributes. For other cases, evaluation usually entails debates over which criteria should be employed, and agreement over which attributes a theory might possess usually occurs only in retrospect. Arguments have even been offered that certain criteria should not be employed; Milton Friedman's attack against 'realism of assumptions' is perhaps the most well-known example in economics. Indeed, even certain entrenched criteria have been subject to similar broadsides. (We remember Paul Feyerabend's argument that logical consistency and theoretical connectedness are arbitrarily strict and, therefore, inappropriate criteria for judging new, alternative theories; two defining characteristics of such theories are that they challenge existing approaches and that they are first expressed in rough form.)

To conclude, confirmationism even when supplemented with additional choice criteria cannot solve the choice problem.

Falsification and the Rhetoric of Methodologists

Though it is probably true that most practicing economists believe theirs to be a 'positivist' discipline, many recent writers in economic methodology have begun to reject positivism (or at least their interpretations of positivism, which is variously labeled the unity of science thesis, the covering-law models, verificationism, and the like). Significantly, certain recent analysts believe falsificationism to be a viable alternative to positivism. The most recent, sophisticated, and comprehensive plea for Popper's methodological falsificationism in economics is contained in Mark Blaug's 1980 study, *The Methodology of Economics*. As was argued earlier, Blaug's belief that there is no algorithm of choice is consistent with Popper's fallibilism, but also with Kuhn and Feyerabend's views on theory choice.

In any case, I will argue here that falsificationism should not be considered the only possible response to the failures of positivist doctrine in its many forms. I attempt to show that falsificationism has not been practiced in economics, and, more important, that it seems to be unpracticable. This is *not* an argument against the use of empirical tests in economics. Rather, it is an argument against the notion (which I feel is dogmatic) that falsificationism is the only responsible and legitimate methodology available to economists.

Arguments concerning the viability of Popper's methodological falsificationism in economics can be advanced on a number of levels. First, we should note that, given the criticisms of the growth of knowledge theorists, serious doubts have been raised about the viability of falsificationism as a methodology for *any* scientific discipline.

Next, there is little reason to expect that falsificationism can work in a social science like economics. Depending on where one stands regarding the unity of science thesis, one may view the differences between the natural and social sciences as dramatic, a matter of degree, or somewhere in between. No matter where one stands, however, no one has ever argued that it is easier to apply the scientific method in the social sciences than it is in physics. On the contrary, physics is called the queen of the sciences. Since Newton's time, celestial mechanics and later other branches of physics have provided the exemplars of sound scientific practice; if the scientific method works anywhere, it works in physics.

Significantly, the growth of knowledge critics chose many of their examples from the history of physics in arguing that there is no single best method that scientists have always followed. If serious questions have been raised about the applicability of confirmationism and falsificationism in physics, it requires a great leap of faith to imagine that they can succeed in a social science like economics.

Finally, the historical evidence suggests that falsificationism has never been practiced to any significant extent in economics, despite forty years of advocacy by proponents, and despite the entrance of falsificationist precepts into the methodological rhetoric of the discipline. Blaug points out that falsificationist ideas were non-existent in economics prior to the twentieth century. In 1938 Hutchison indirectly urged that Popper's methodology be adopted in the dismal science; in 1980 Blaug was more direct but no less insistent that falsificationism, which by that date so many economists had learned to mouth, be put into practice in economics. Had it been solely the opponents of falsificationism who argued that the method had yet to be successfully practiced in economics, one might question whether their perceptions could be trusted. When vocal advocates of falsificationism also agree that it has not yet been tried, one feels safer in believing that falsificationism has entered the rhetoric but not the practice of economists.

The three arguments advanced above – that falsificationism may be unpracticable in any science, that it may be especially unpracticable in a social science like economics, and that it has yet to be practiced to any significant extent in economics – should not deter an advocate of falsificationism. The true devotee would first remind us that Popper has responded to his growth of knowledge critics, and would argue that his responses are adequate. He would next argue that the absence of falsificationism in economics is no grounds for arguing that it should not be tried: the point of a prescriptivist methodology like falsificationism is to change the behavior of scientists, after all. Finally, a proponent would point out that the general claim that falsificationism may not work in the social sciences is unimpressive unless it is supported with specific reasons *why* we should expect it to be unsuccessful. Though the arguments above provide strong a priori grounds for suspecting that falsificationism may be unworkable in economics, it must be admitted that the case against it is not yet entirely persuasive. To strengthen the case, I now offer additional arguments which attempt to establish that there exist a number of specific and possibly irremovable obstacles to the practice of falsificationism in economics.

A necessary condition for the successful application of falsificationist methodology in any science is that straightforward tests of hypotheses, or theories, be possible. A test of a hypothesis is always conditional. Every conditional hyothesis is composed of two parts: an explanandum and an explanans. The explanandum is a sentence describing the phenomenon to be explained. The explanans contains sentences comprising a list of initial conditions which must obtain (these can include both the variables impounded in ceteris paribus and those in which a change is assumed to occur), and sentences presenting general laws. For a straightforward test of a hypothesis to occur, the initial conditions and general laws must be clearly specifiable and specified. In addition, any empirical proxies which are chosen to represent theoretical concepts must permit a true test of a theory. Finally, the data themselves must be clean.[6]

If all of these conditions are met, the results of tests of hypotheses are relatively easy to interpret. Confirming instances, as always, cannot prove that a hypothesis is true. But disconfirming test instances will direct us to reinspect the initial conditions, general laws, data, and test situation to see what went wrong. If each of those is clearly defined, we will find our mistake and correct it, and by this slow, critical, trial and error process, science may hopefully advance. My argument against the workability of falsificationism in economics is based on the contention that rarely will confirming and disconfirming test results be unambiguously interpretable in economics. This should come as no surprise: the growth of knowledge theorists offered similar objections regarding falsificationism in the natural sciences.[7] The arguments are even more persuasive in a social science like economics.

1. *Initial conditions are numerous*: Logically, it is impossible to specify all of the necessary initial conditions in any test situation, even in the laboratory sciences. As a practical matter, however, one can begin to have confidence about the results of a test if the important determining variables are finite in number and specifiable. A true test of a theory would occur if all the exogenous variables were known, one was varied while the others were held constant, and the effects noted. Obviously, such carefully controlled experimentation cannot occur in economics. In general, not all exogenous variables are known, and a number of them vary simultaneously. This does not preclude the possibility of testing in economics, however: multivariate analysis is expressly designed for handling these problems. Why then have certain economists claimed that a large number of exogenous variables somehow damages the credibility of tests of hypotheses in economics? There are, I think, two distinct complaints lying behind such a claim.

Some critics charge that the models of economists give a distorted, incorrect representation of reality. This argument is often made by Institutionalists, who prefer a more holistic approach to social phenomena. Thus Wilber and Harrison assert that the use of a ceteris paribus clause in a closed, causal model lends a 'degree of determinedness' to the model which does not exist in the subject matter. Sidney Schoeffler makes a similar point when he argues that economic systems, because they are 'essentially open', cannot be adequately captured by a closed model.[8]

A second concern of critics is that, while theories are stated causally, econometric specifications of theories are only capable of indicating correlations among variables. This has a number of implications. Few economists expect the estimates of coefficients to be the same when different observations of the same variables are used. It is often true that the addition or deletion of particular variables may profoundly affect the estimated values and significance of the coefficients of the remaining variables. The relationships among variables which emerge from an econometric model thus have little in common with the well-specified, causal relationships that exist in economic theories. And finally, there seems little hope that such a situation may be remedied someday, either when all the exogenous variables are discovered or when all of the relevant ones are 'endogenized'. The first solution is impossible, because the types of variables that may impinge on the results of any economic experiment are subject to change through time. And the second holds little promise because, as Emile Grunberg points out, 'endogenizing' exogenous variables leads to an infinite regress, since every variable now considered exogenous is itself determined by a number of exogenous variables.[9]

The first of these two complaints reflects a particular preference in theorizing: critics of the abstract, deductive method prefer a more holistic, broad-based approach to social reality. These are matters over which reasonable men can disagree. The second, however, involves certain limitations of econometric techniques that are well known within the profession. Less widely recognized are the implications of these limitations for falsificationism. Economists should rightly question a falsifying test instance if the number of exogenous variables is large, subject to change through time, and never completely specified: there simply are too many things that can affect the outcome of a test. Test results, either confirming or disconfirming, must be interpreted cautiously.

2. *Some initial conditions are uncheckable*: Certain initial conditions, though themselves exogenously determined and subject to change, cannot be independently checked. Two that figure prominently in many economic theories are the state of information (and, if it is not perfect, the role of expectations) and tastes and preferences. We saw in Chapter 7 that the uncheckable nature of these initial conditions vitiated any test of the rationality assumption – neither confirming nor disconfirming instances are unambiguously interpretable if these initial conditions cannot be independently checked.

3. *Absence of falsifiable general laws*: Though economists often use the term 'economic law', it is used to refer to a wide variety of propositions. Compared to the many debates (over how the term general law should be defined) within the philosophy of science, economists have virtually ignored the question in their method-ological debates.

Some consider the rationality postulate to be the fundamental behavioral law in economics: Hutchison and Machlup took this approach in their debate in the 1950s, for example. If that is the case, then economists must admit that their most basic general law is not directly testable. This poses no problem for confirmationists, who only require that theories be evaluated by how well their predictions conform to reality. But a falsificationist, who requires that disconfirming test instances be treated seriously, would be alarmed to find out that disconfirming test instances cannot be unambiguously interpreted, that we can never know whether the assumed initial conditions or the behavioral law has been falsified. Though the theoretical definition of rationality has been resolved by economists (transitivity in choice over a well-ordered preference function), its empirical interpretation has always remained problematical. Can rationality be defined in the absence of full information? Is there a difference between short run and long run rationality? Does Simon's distinction between substantive and procedural rationality hold any promise for resolving this dilemma?[10] The questions go on and on.

There are other candidates for general laws in economics. The 'law' of diminishing marginal returns is certainly one. But, as is often noted, this hypothesis when correctly stated only implies that returns will *eventually* diminish. This necessary caveat renders the 'law' unfalsifiable, however: one can always respond to a disconfirming instance that 'we simply have not reached the point of diminishing returns yet'. And indeed, perhaps the major difference between Classical and modern treatments of the 'law of diminishing returns' is that, whereas they believed the law was operative and observable in history, modern economists view it as an analytic device.

The 'law' of demand is another example. In a recent work, Terence Hutchison points out that, in the absence of checkable initial conditions, especially regarding tastes, prices of other goods, and price expectations, the law is effectively untestable.[11] Hutchison also comments on so-called empirical laws in economics, and compares them with laws in the natural sciences.

> Since very few or no fully adequate scientific laws, in the physico-chemical or natural scientific sense, have been established in economics, on which economists can base predictions, what are used, *and have to be used*, for predictive purposes are *trends, tendencies, or patterns*, expressed in empirical or historical generalizations of less than universal validity, restricted by local and temporal limits.[12]

Hutchison cites as an example that, even if the elasticity of demand for herrings over a period of years lay between 1.2 and 1.45, 'it surely cannot be claimed to be a universal law, that in all markets, in all countries, at all times, the elasticity of demand for herrings is, and has always been, between 1.2 and 1.45'. Hutchison concludes that the primary contribution of economists 'must inevitably come from *trend-spotting*, not by deduction from laws'.[13]

As he did some forty years ago, Hutchison argues in his book against the idea that economics proceeds by deduction from universal laws. As he admits, his is a somewhat skeptical position: even well-tested generalizations that have performed perfectly in the past need not be applicable in the future, especially if the structural relationships within an economy change.[14] Empiricism is then still quite important to Hutchison. But it must also be recognized that, in the absence of checkable initial conditions and general laws, the hope for the success of falsificationism in economics grows dimmer.

4. *Tests of models are not tests of theories*: Though this idea can be found in Papandreau's *Economics as a Science* (1958), it has been forcefully and eloquently restated in a recent piece by Boland. He notes that the concept of testability has been variously interpreted by economists, but settles on the definition, 'empirically refutable'. He then argues that, for three reasons, 'it is impossible to test any economic theory convincingly even when it is not tautological'.[15] Two of these reasons concern the natures of testing and of logic, and are similar to arguments that have already been made. The third, however, is unique. Boland shows that, to test a theory, a model must be constructed. However, a wide variety of models may be constructed to represent any theory. As a result, the empirical falsification of any single model does not imply the falsification of the theory. Falsification of *theories*, as opposed to models, is thus impossible in economics.[16]

5. *Empirical data may not accurately represent theoretical constructs*: A final obstacle to falsificationism in economics concerns the interpretation of data. Many economists have commented on the 'aggregation problem' in economics, which refers to the difficulties that may be encountered in aggregating data in macroeconomics, and in providing meaningful interpretations of what those data are meant to represent.[17] But even when microeconomic data are used, problems may arise. We have already mentioned Machlup's discussion of the many alternatives available if one wishes to empirically define 'the price of steel'. Wilber and Harrison offer a more general, and even more skeptical, assessment of empirical testing in economics.

Both the methods of collection and construction of economic data are unreliable. Typically, economic data are statistically constructed and are not conceptually the same as the corresponding variables in the theory.

Therefore, econometricians and statisticians engage in data massaging. If a test disconfirms a hypothesis, the investigator can always blame the data: they have been massaged, either too much or not enough.[18]

Falsificationism does not guarantee that its use will lead scientists always to choose the 'true' theory. It is a more modest methodology of theory appraisal – its aim is only the avoidance of error; its method is to eliminate theories that have been falsified by strict empirical tests. But for falsificationism to be viable, straightforward empirical tests must be possible. This requires that general laws be present; that initial conditions be relatively few in number, known, not subject to change, and easily checkable; that a test be a test of a theory, not a model; that data be trustworthy, complete, and accurately representative of analogous constructs in the theory. It is now perhaps understandable why falsificationism, though dominant in the methodological literature, seems to have been little practiced by working economists.

The invocation to *try* to put falsificationism into practice in economics need not be dropped, though it seems that there is little chance for its successful application. What must be avoided is the wholesale rejection of research programs that do not meet the falsificationist criteria of acceptability, for that would lead to an elimination, not only of alternative research programs like those proposed by Austrians and Institutionalists, but much of standard economic theory as well.

Notes

Parts of this chapter are drawn from my paper with Vincent J. Tarascio, 'Theory Choice in Economics: Philosophy and Practice,' *Journal of Economic Issues*, vol. 13 (December 1979), pp. 983–1006.

1 The exceptions are those purely theoretical exercises in which theorems or lemmas are proven and no attempt is made to relate the results to empirical work.

2 Henry Margenau, 'What Is a Theory?' in Sherman R. Krupp (ed.), *Structure of Economic Science: Essays on Methodology* (Englewood Cliffs, N.J: Prentice-Hall, 1966), p. 33.

3 In the introductory chapter of his dissertation, Arjo Klamer mentions four types of arguments which economists use in discussing the merits and weaknesses of theories: empirical, theoretical, commonsensical, and philosophical. The third of these corresponds closely to my category, intuitive plausibility. See Arjo Klamer, 'The So-Called Rational Expectations Approach from a Methodological Perspective,' unpublished dissertation, Duke University, Durham, N.C.

In my article with Tarascio cited above, criteria of choice were divided into only two categories, empirical and nonempirical. Soon after its publication, I began to suspect that the second category was too broad and should be broken down further. The discussion in the text attempts to do this. I found a reading of Klamer's first chapter and a subsequent discussion with him to be extremely helpful in clarifying my thought on these matters.

4 A more detailed discussion of the simplicity criterion as well as further citations of relevant works can be found in Carl G. Hempel, *Philosophy of Natural Science* (Englewood Cliffs, N.J.: Prentice-Hall, 1966), pp. 40–5.

5 Ibid., pp. 40–2.

6 This discussion follows Hempel and Oppenheim's presentation of explanation under covering laws, but is completely compatible with Popper's view of deductive explanation as developed in his *Logic of Scientific Discovery*. For both confirmationists and falsificationists, hypothesis testing and scientific explanation are two sides of the same coin.

7 As Lakatos argues in his 'Falsificationism and the Methodology of Scientific Research Programmes,' there are few crucial tests in science because one can seldom be sure just what is falsified by a disconfirming instance. In his words, 'The main difference from Popper's original version is, I think, that in my conception criticism does not – and must not – kill as fast as Popper imagined,' (p. 179).

8 Charles Wilber and Robert Harrison, 'The Methodological Basis of Institutional Economics: Pattern Model, Storytelling, and Holism,' *Journal of Economic Issues*, vol. 12 (March, 1978), pp. 67–8; Sidney Schoeffler, *The Failure of Economics: A Diagnostic Study* (Cambridge, Mass: Harvard University Press, 1955).

9 Emile Grunberg, ' "Complexity" and "Open Systems" in Economic Discourse,' *Journal of Economic Issues*, vol. 12 (September 1978), pp. 541–60.

10 The reference is to Herbert Simon, 'From Substantive to Procedural Rationality,' in Spiro Latsis (ed.), *Method and Appraisal in Economics* (Cambridge, England: Cambridge University Press, 1976), pp. 129–48.

11 Terence W. Hutchison, *Knowledge and Ignorance in Economics* (Chicago: University of Chicago Press, 1977), p. 15.

12 Ibid., pp. 19–20.

13 Ibid., pp. 21, 22. Though Hutchison notes that the herring example is from Lipsey's introductory text, its choice is significant: Lionel Robbins used the same example in his tract, *An Essay on the Nature and Significance of Economic Science*, 2nd edn (London: Macmillan, 1935), pp. 107–8, to denigrate 'empirical economics'. Hutchison no doubt perceives his own position as lying between the two extremes; in any case, he seems to be having fun here.

14 This position finds further support from Wassily Leontief in his 'Theoretical Assumptions and Nonobserved Facts,' *American Economic Review*, vol. 61 (March 1971), pp. 1–7.

15 Lawrence Boland, 'Testability in Economic Science,' *South African Journal of Economics*, vol. 45 (1977), p. 93.

16 Ibid., 93–103.

17 For some discussions of the many forms of aggregation problems confronting economists see Mark Blaug, *The Cambridge Revolution: Success or Failure?* (first published, 1974) (London: The Institute of Economic Affairs, 1975), Chapter 2; Kelvin Lancaster, 'Economic Aggregation and Additivity,' in Sherman Krupp, (ed.), *Structure of Economic Science*, op. cit., pp. 201–15; Oskar Morgenstern, *National Income Statistics: A Critique of Macroeconomic Aggregation* (first published, 1950) (San Francisco: Cato Institute, 1979). For an eclectic and highly readable approach to the aggregation problem generally, suitable for classroom use, see Thomas C. Schelling, *Micromotives and Macro-behavior* (New York: Norton, 1978).

18 Wilber and Harrison, 'Methodological Basis. . .,' loc. cit., p. 69.

13

A Program for Economic Methodologists – Methodological Pluralism

The most significant contribution of the growth of knowledge philosophers was the demonstration that the quest for a single, universal, prescriptive scientific methodology is quixotic. Confirmationism provides no logically compelling algorithm of choice. Instrumentalism is viable only in those situations in which predictive adequacy is the sole goal. And Popper's falsificationism, though it recognizes the problem of induction and seeks only to eliminate error, runs into problems in application when interpreted strictly, and loses prescriptive force when interpreted loosely. That these philosophical matters have direct application in economics was demonstrated in the last chapter.

Such findings challenge the long-held views that scientific activity is best distinguishable by the rigor and objectivity of its methods, and that science progresses by the gradual accumulation of true knowledge, either in the form of brute, atomic facts or in the form of theories whose structural characteristics mimic an objectively discernable phenomenal reality. The growth of knowledge tradition emphasizes that science is a dynamic, growing enterprise, that its growth cannot be described by a straight line, that its impressive successes are not due to its having followed immutable and objective procedures. The story of science involves both constancy and flux, both bold conjectures and rigorous criticism, both normal science and revolutionary crisis. The positivist fixation on the objective side of science missed half of a beautiful and complex tale.

What is the role of the methodologist in this new environment? Clearly, it is not to discover some universal method. Yet other significant tasks can be attempted. A partial listing of these would include: to foster an understanding of the scientific process among members of his profession; to systematize jargon; to rationally reconstruct the methodological content of various research programs; to promote an environment in which both novelty and criticism can operate freely. Few, I think, would disagree with the desirability of attempting to reach such goals. The problem lies in showing, concretely, how one might go about these tasks. In the next section, some specific recommendations for putting such a program into operation within economics are offered.

Methodological Pluralism

The approach to economic methodology advocated here is labeled 'methodological pluralism' because it takes as a starting assumption that no universally applicable, logically compelling method of theory appraisal exists. (Or, more correctly, even if it exists, we can never be sure that we have found it, even if we have.) The goals of methodological analysis stated above are also accepted as general desiderata. The specific tasks of the economic methodologist under methodological pluralism are as follows.

1. The starting point of methodological analysis is the rational reconstruction of the methodological content both of the writings of economic methodologists and of the various research programs within the discipline.

This is the descriptive side of economic methodology. The rational reconstruction of the methodological content of a particular research program in economics is no casual endeavor: if done well, it requires that the methodologist be knowledgeable in many fields, including economic theory, economic methodology, doctrinal history (if the research program has existed for any length of time), philosophy of science, and the philosophy of history. Stanley Wong's treatment of Samuelson's revealed preference theory, and Lawrence Boland's ambitious attempt to lay bare the foundations of both standard and avant-garde neoclassical theory, provide superlative examples of how such work can be done. In Chapters 5 through 9 of the present volume, a rational reconstruction of the writings of positivist economic methodologists was attempted; similar treatments of other methodological traditions (Austrian, Marxian, Institutionalist, and post-Keynesian are the broad contemporary categories; one might also look at other time periods or at the writings of individuals like Mises, Shackle, Leibenstein, Simon, Lowe, or Hayek) would be useful. Every such reconstruction should be from a particular point of view that should be explicitly stated. This has been the case in the three studies mentioned: Wong begins with the problem-situation that Samuelson the theorist tries to solve; Boland investigates the 'hidden agenda' of neoclassical theory; I attempted to reconcile the positivist tradition in economics with that same tradition within philosophy. The explicit statement of the goals of any rational reconstruction allows critics to see if the goals were reached, and to see what other approaches to the subject are possible. Such criticism is useful and should be encouraged.

2. The next step is the critical assessment of the methodological content revealed in the rational reconstruction. Such criticism should highlight the strengths (if any) and limitations of the particular approach under examination. In undertaking such an exercise, it is crucial that the methodologist be aware that its purpose is not the discovery of the optimal method. Indeed, one of the fundamental critical tasks of the methodologist is to repeatedly point out the futility of such a search, while at the same time emphasizing that a place for criticism still exists. A brief digression serves to illustrate this point.

In a paper written in the early 1970s, Lawrence Boland tersely comments, 'methodology, in attempting to solve the choice problem, is pursuing an uninteresting (because unsolvable) problem'.[1] The rationale behind this remark is Boland's fallibilism: as a fallibilist, he recognizes that the search for a methodology that will yield true theories is futile, since we can never know when we have reached the truth, even if we do reach it. Boland is correct in asserting that the problem is unsolvable, but he errs in thinking that it is therefore uninteresting. On the contrary, understanding that the problem is unsolvable is a key to understanding the true nature of scientific inquiry, with all of its complexities and ambiguities. Simply put, most economists either think that the problem is solvable and solved, or think that it is not and that methodological debate is a waste of time. Both attitudes are wrong, and must be exposed as such.

It is usually the practitioner of normal science who holds such views. Paradoxically, the two views, though mutually exclusive, are often held by the same scientist!

A practitioner of normal science working in a well-established research tradition can safely assert that the choice problem is solved. Using the techniques he learned in graduate school, he busies himself doing substantive work in economics, applying those methods to various problems, solving puzzles in good Kuhnian style. For such a scientist, explicit discussions of methodology seem utterly inane. When pushed to discuss methodological matters, however, the same scientist often responds that methodological debate is useless because the questions asked are unanswerable. 'No one ever agrees on methodological questions, so why waste time studying them?' he is apt to counter, 'And besides, only people working in fringe areas, like Institutionalists or Marxists, ever talk about methodology, and those people shouldn't even be considered scientists!'

When the research tradition in which this normal scientist works breaks down in a revolutionary period, he may briefly turn to methodology or to history to see what went wrong. What he wants to find is some definitive answer about the 'correct' method. What he discovers instead is a plurality of answers, each with its own weaknesses and strengths. This reinforces his prior antagonistic attitude toward methodological discussion, but luckily for him, it is not necessary to ruminate over the idiocy of methodology for too long. A new paradigm emerges, with its own accepted methods and procedures, and he can happily busy himself with substantive work once more.

This caricature of the normal scientist with anti-methodological biases is harshly drawn, but sadly enough, the general attitude attributed to him is not all that hard to find. (As an aside, it has been my experience that such biases are more likely to be encountered in academics from 'high-powered' research institutions. A study of this would be interesting.) In any case, the point has been made; it is grossly inconsistent to simultaneously hold the views that methodology is useless because the correct methods are given and that methodology is useless because there are no answers to methodological debates. Similarly, it is inconsistent to view methodological discussion as useless while dismissing alternative approaches to economics on methodological grounds. The role of the methodologist is first to show that there is no single 'given' method, and then to demonstrate that reasonable and fruitful criticism and debate is still possible.

3. This latter task is achieved by the critical discussion of the strengths (if any) and limitations of the rationally reconstructed methodological positions under examination.

Again, the books by Wong and Boland, and Chapters 5 through 9 of this volume, provide examples of this procedure. Wong shows that Samuelson's revealed preference program attempted to resolve three mutually inconsistent problem situations, and further, that the program was unable to successfully resolve any of them. Boland demonstrates that the 'hidden agenda' of neoclassical theory contains two tenets that determine the direction of research within the program, then criticizes those tenets on a variety of grounds. And in the chapters above, the writings of positivist economic methodologists are rationally reconstructed in philosophical terms, then subjected to critical scrutiny of various sorts. At times the criticisms were designed to show that a position was inconsistent with positions in philosophy of science (e.g. Hutchison's proofs of the analyticity of the postulates of pure theory). At other times, the potential usefulness of positions was demonstrated. (Machlup's ideal-type approach applies when economists seek heuristic, explanatory theories; Friedman's instrumentalism can be invoked when truth value is unimportant but predictive adequacy is.) Sometimes positions were rejected as inapplicable to or unworkable in economics (e.g. descriptivism, operationalism, and falsificationism were rejected on these grounds). The point of all of this was not to resolve these issues once and for all, but to demonstrate that there are, indeed, many roads to criticism and that critical discussion can obtain results even if there is no solution to the theory choice problem.

4. There are a number of research programs within economics whose epistemological and methodological foundations differ radically from those of mainstream theory, broadly defined. One of these, the Austrian program, was mentioned in Chapter 6. How are such alternative programs to be handled?

It is in this area, the methodological evaluation of alternative research programs, that methodological pluralism has the most to offer. Such programs should be criticized either on their own terms, or for failing to show how they can be compared to other programs. This approach ensures that novelty is promoted, that criticism is not dogmatic, and that a dialogue takes place among members of alternative research programs. Since this prescription is the most controversial aspect of methodological pluralism, it is worth our time to examine it carefully. Though the example we use is Austrian economics, the same principles apply to any alternative research program.

In many debates in methodology, adversaries seem perpetually to talk beyond each other. This occurs most dramatically when the methodologies of opposing camps are founded on rival epistemological systems. We examined the Austrian revival with this point in mind, and found that though the Austrians have a fairly well-established research tradition (they can claim both historical antecedents and a vocal group of contemporary advocates), their objections to the standard analysis and their substantive contributions to economic theory often seem unintelligible to non-Austrians, with the results that their contributions are either ignored or dismissed as inconsequential.

When opponents of Austrian economics claim that the Austrian position is unintelligible, they are engaging in external criticism – more specifically, they are (usually) challenging the epistemological situational constraints advanced by their adversaries. That criticism is based on an alternative epistemological theory, one that rejects an a priorist approach to the foundations of scientific knowledge. Since each camp holds a rival epistemological theory, external criticism which simply *posits* one theory as correct, then finds all antagonistic viewpoints to be wanting, can hardly be considered convincing. At the minimum, a comparison can properly be made only after the relative strengths and weaknesses of the competing epistemological theories are carefully investigated. In this particular case (since a priorism has a rather extensive history itself), that task would be an ambitious one even for professional philosophers. It is not false modesty to suggest that economists are unqualified to attempt it.

As an alternative, economists might try internal criticism, and criticize the Austrians from within the Austrian framework. This route has a number of distinct advantages. Opponents would first of all have to immerse themselves in the Austrian worldview. If they did so, many semantic debates could be avoided: if non-Austrians still found the Austrian position unintelligible, at least it would not be because the Austrian 'language' had never been translated. Divisive issues would be clarified, even if they might not be resolved; in the best of worlds, the two groups might start talking to each other rather than beyond each other. Finally, if one is convinced that the Austrian position must be discredited, internal criticism as a strategic weapon is more powerful when successful than external criticism, since it takes the theoretical aims and situational constraints of an adversary as given.

For their part, the Austrians and other such groups must show their opponents how their theories may be compared with their competitors. Instead of attempting to insulate their views from criticism, they must show that their systems are capable of withstanding criticism. If it seems simplistic to expect proponents of minority views to open themselves to criticism, one need only recall that there is an incentive mechanism at work: without such exposure, few new members will be persuaded to join the ranks. Minority groups must recognize that though self-imposed isolation ensures doctrinal purity, it also endangers the prospects for the successful recruitment of novitiates. Finally, and this perhaps reflects accurately on the ultimate impact of methodological debate, substantive contributions to economic analysis in the end outweigh even the most persuasive methodological criticism for gaining the attention of other members of the profession: that insight is implicit in the Kuhnian view that methodological attacks seldom accomplish the goal of unseating a dominant paradigm until a suitable replacement has also been articulated.

These, then, are the broad prescriptions of methodological pluralism, a program for economic methodologists to follow. Methodological pluralism begins with the assumption that no single optimal methodology is discoverable. Rational reconstruction, either of research programs in economic theory or of the writings of economic methodologists, is the first step of analysis. Since such reconstructions can be attempted from a variety of viewpoints, the methodologist must be explicit about the framework of analysis employed. Criticism of the reconstruction follows according to the stated framework. Criticism can take place on a number of levels, but internal criticism is the most powerful (since it takes a program on its own terms) and is often the most fruitful (since critics must fully understand the program being criticized). As such, internal criticism is the preferred form of criticism, especially for those programs that do not share the epistemological foundations and methodological approach of the dominant body of theory.

Answers To Some Possible Objections

Methodological pluralism can itself be criticized on a number of grounds. Any methodological pluralist worth his salt welcomes such criticism, and hopes that methodological pluralism is either improved by the ensuing debate, or, if a superior alternative emerges, that it is superceded. Some possible objections are raised here, and answers to them attempted.

1. The initial assumption is wrong; methodologists should search for a universally applicable method of choice. A variation of this objection reads, 'Thus-and-so methodology (falsificationism, a priorism, instrumentalism, and so on) is the best methodology for economic science to follow.'

The response of the methodological pluralist must be – convince me.

2. Methodological pluralism, if taken seriously, undermines all substantive work in economic science. How can a working economist try to make a contribution in his chosen field if he is always aware that the methodology he uses is open to criticism?

The response of the methodological pluralist is that substantive work in economics need not halt; neither angst nor inaction are necessary byproducts of methodological pluralism.

Dropping the existentialist metaphor, the point of methodological pluralism is not the impossibility of science, but the knowledge that results obtained within specific research programs which of necessity follow particular methodological precepts are program-specific. Indeed, a major concern is to show that criticism is an essential aspect of any scientific endeavor, even though the search for a logically compelling, universally applicable critical apparatus is chimerical.

It can also be added that methodological pluralism is a program for *methodologists*. Though its insights should be useful to any economist, the working economist of necessity chooses a given framework when making a contribution to a field. If acquaintance with pluralism encourages the working economist to be conscious in his choice of a framework, all the better. But he need not, for example, state the framework at the outset of each article. Methodology fixation is not a goal of pluralism; it would be lethal for the prospects of the field.

3. Methodological pluralism, if taken seriously, leads to methodological anarchism, under which any particular methodological view could claim legitimacy.

There are safeguards against this outcome. Simply put, methodological discussion is as much a form of persuasion as it is a means of ensuring that problems are viewed from different perspectives. Unless a particular methodological view is persuasive, its existence is usually inconsequential. And again, the advocacy of a particular methodological position will rarely convince outsiders until substantive examples of the benefits of holding such a view also exist: only after substantive contributions to economic *theory* are made will opponents be ready to listen to discussions of methodology proper.

4. Due to its relativism, methodological pluralism will lead to a backlash of dogmatism, and ultimately to the abrogation of scientific freedom.

It should first be noted that dogmatism exists today. It does not derive from methodological pluralism, but from its opposite: alternative programs which do not meet the standards of scientific practice alleged to be followed by the mainstream are often summarily (hence dogmatically) rejected. Given this environment, it makes more sense to attempt to overcome the present problem than to fail to act due to fear of future ones.

But more important, it is far from clear that such problems can be avoided by following a particular methodological framework. Though methodological pluralism may contain the seeds of dogmatism, methodological monism can also be dogmatic, if alternative visions of economic reality are dismissed without a fair hearing. Methodological pluralism does presume the existence of a free science. The protection of scientific freedom should be of concern to all scientists. But it is a value that is meta-methodological: no particular methodological approach can ensure its continued existence; like most freedoms, its perpetuation cannot be guaranteed by following some simple formula.

Some closing words: methodological pluralism is not meant to be taken as an attempt at systematic philosophy of science. There is no discussion of the status of the initial assumption, or of its relationship to the other prescriptions. Methodological pluralism is an attempt by an economic methodologist to come up with some common-sense procedural norms for his field. The exercise derives its impetus from certain findings in contemporary philosophy of science, and from my perception that methodological debate in economics has too often degenerated into dogmatic, sterile exchanges whose primary result is to call into question the usefulness of methodology itself.

This study ends with the same thought with which it began – that methodology is a frustrating and rewarding area in which to work. Just as there is no best way to listen to a Tchaikovsky symphony, or to write a book, or to raise a child, there is no best way to investigate social reality. Yet methodology has a role to play in all of this. By showing that science is not the objective, rigorous intellectual endeavor it was once thought to be, and by demonstrating that this need not lead to anarchy, that critical discourse still has a place, the hope is held out that a true picture of the strengths and limitations of scientific practice will emerge. And with luck, this insight may lead to a better, and certainly a more honest, science.

Notes

1 Lawrence Boland, 'Conventionalism and Economic Theory,' *Philosophy of Science,* vol. 37 (June 1970), p. 116. Actually, the quote begins, 'Conventionalist methodology, in attempting to solve the choice problem. . .'. As I read Boland, however, he defines a conventionalist as anyone who attempts to solve the choice problem: since any attempted solution involves positing specific criteria, or conventions, of choice, anyone trying to solve the problem must be a conventionalist.

This reading of Boland is supported by his responses to critics (including myself) of his article on Friedman – we are all conventionalists, and thus we miss the point of instrumentalism, which does not seek true, explanatory theories. See Lawrence Boland, 'Friedman's Methodology vs. Conventional Empiricism: A Reply to Rotwein,' *Journal of Economic Literature*, vol. 18 (December 1980), pp. 1555–7.

Boland and I, then, both agree that the choice problem (his Problem of Conventions) is unsolvable. Our *responses* to that differ: whereas he seeks out logically compelling arguments (since they are 'interesting'), I maintain that rational debate in the absence of logically compelling arguments is still possible.

Notes for Further Reading – Philosophy of Science

I   Logical Positivism

Taken together two books provide a brief but adequate introduction to the philosophy of the Vienna Circle. Joergen Joergensen's *The Development of Logical Empiricism* (1951) is a solid, succinct account of the development of the Vienna Circle. The monograph is part of the International Encyclopedia of Unified Science, begun in the 1930s to advance the ideas of the group. A. J. Ayer's 'Editor's Introduction' to his *Logical Positivism* (1959) is also beneficial. More important, that volume contains a number of translations of articles by Schlick, Carnap, and others, articles that were originally published in the journal *Erkenntnis* in the 1930s. The unquestioned conviction on the part of members of the movement that they had discovered the true task of philosophy is perhaps nowhere better expressed than in these pages.

Though most of the members of the Circle (and many of their immediate predecessors) wrote in German, much of their work has by now been translated. Mach's theory of elements and his views on perceptions are contained in his *The Analysis of Sensations* (1959); his fictionalist stance on theories is best exemplified in the chapter entitled 'On the Economical Nature of Physical Inquiry' in his *Popular Scientific Lectures* (1895). A sympathetic evaluation of Mach's philosophy of science is J. Bradley's *Mach's Philosophy of Science* (1971).

Carnap's *Aufbau der Welt* was translated as *The Logical Structure of the World: Pseudoproblems in Philosophy* (1967). An autobiograhical sketch with some fascinating comments on the personalities of Wittgenstein and Einstein, as well as a summary of his work is found in *The Philosophy of Rudolf Carnap*, edited by Paul Schilpp (1963). Conversations between Wittgenstein and Friedrich Waismann (who are occasionally joined by other members of the Circle) which occurred between 1929 and 1932 were transcribed in notebooks by Waismann. These are collected, edited, and translated by Brian McGuiness with Joachim Schulte in *Wittgenstein and the Vienna Circle* (1979).

The D. Reidel Publishing Company, which handles the superlative *Boston Studies in the Philosophy of Sciences* series, began publishing in the early 1970s the Vienna Circle collection, which is a series of translations of previously untranslated works of members of the group, as well as certain predecessors. Economists who associate 'positivism' with Chicago and laissez-faire economics will be surprised at the socialist leanings of some of these thinkers; see, in particular, Neurath's 'Empirical Sociology' in the collection of articles published under *Empiricism and Sociology* (1973). This collection of his essays also contains a translation of the pamphlet, 'Der Wiener Kreis'.

Evaluations of the impact of logical positivism on modern philosophy of science by those both sympathetic to (e.g. Feigl, Hempel) and critical of (e.g. Scriven, Hanson) its development are found in Peter Achinstein and Stephen Barker (eds), *The Legacy of Logical Positivism* (1969).

II Logical Empiricism

The best concise introductory statement of modern positivist thought is C. Hempel's *Philosophy of Natural Science* (1966). For a collection of Hempel's work, see *Aspects of Scientific Explanation* (1965). E. Nagel's *Structure of Science* (1961) is still probably the most complete and judicious statement of the principles of logical empiricism.

Various collections of articles that have been published through the years serve as excellent sourcebooks on the philosophical debates of the forties and fifties. Some of these appeared periodically, for example, *Philosophy of Science: The Delaware Seminar*, Vols I, II (1963); *Minnesota Studies in Philosophy of Science*, Vols I–VIII (1956, 1958, 1962, 1970, 1975, 1976, 1977). Others appeared as single volumes, for example, H. Feigl and M. Brodbeck (eds), *Readings in the Philosophy of Science* (1953); H. Feigl and G. Maxwell (eds), *Current Issues in the Philosophy of Science* (1961); and, more recently, B. Brody, *Readings in the Philosophy of Science* (1970).

Volume XI of the *Library of Living Philosophers* series, edited by P. Schilpp, is entitled *The Philosophy of Rudolf Carnap* (1963), and is an invaluable guide to the work of that great analyst. Each volume in this remarkable series begins with an autobiographical sketch by the philosopher, followed by critical essays by equally distinguished colleagues, the philosopher then replies, and the book closes with a comprehensive bibliography. For articles dealing with the subsequent development of some of Carnap's pathbreaking ideas, see Jaakko Hintikka (ed.), *Rudolf Carnap, Logical Empiricist* (1975).

III Post-Positivist Thought

The best secondary source on Popper is R. Ackermann's *The Philosophy of Karl Popper* (1976). To study Popper, begin with either the 'Autobiography of Karl Popper' in P. Schilpp (ed.), *The Philosophy of Karl Popper* (1976), or, for a shorter version, Chapter One of *Conjectures and Refutations* (1963; 2nd edn. 1965). Next, see his *Logic of Scientific Discovery* (1934; Eng. Trans. 1959), *Conjectures and Refutations* (1965), and finally, *Objective Knowledge* (1972).

Post-positivist contributions in book form include P. Achinstein,

Concepts of Science (1968), J. Agassi, *Science in Flux* (1975), J. Feibelman, *Scientific Method* (1972), R. Harré, *Philosophies of Science* (1972), and S. Toulmin, *Human Understanding* (1972). Consultations with journals and collections of articles should also be fruitful; for example, P. Achinstein and S. Barker, *The Legacy of Logical Positivism* (1969), contains an excellent collection of critical articles on the impact of positivism. The preeminent journals are *Philosophy of Science, British Journal for the Philosophy of Science,* and *Synthese.* Volumes published by major universities (especially Johns Hopkins, the University of Minnesota, and the University of Delaware) as well as the superlative *Boston Studies in the Philosophy of Science* are often the best sources for first rate work by practitioners on the frontiers.

The introduction and afterward of Frederick Suppe's *The Structure of Scientific Theories* (2nd ed., 1977) is still probably the best single critical survey of twentieth century thought in the philosophy of science.

The best sourcebook on the growth of knowledge tradition is the Lakatos and Musgrave volume, *Criticism and the Growth of Knowledge* (1970), with our three protagonists all making contributions. Some of Kuhn's early work, as well as some recent pieces, can be found in his *The Essential Tension: Selected Studies in Scientific Tradition and Change* (1977). Lakatos' work is collected in J. Worrall and G. Currie (eds), *Imre Lakatos – Philosphical Papers* (1977, 1978), the first volume entitled *The Methodology of Scientific Research Programmes,* and the second entitled *Mathematics, Science, and Epistemology.*

Notes for Further Reading – Methodology of Economics

The best general introduction to economic methodology is M. Blaug's *The Methodology of Economics* (1980). In addition to treating twentieth century philosophy of science and economic methodology, which I have done, Blaug examines nineteenth century methodologists and nine contemporary 'research programs' in economics. His bibliography is comprehensive.

Collections of articles on methodology are rare. *The Structure of Economic Science: Essays on Methodology* (1966), edited by S. R. Krupp, contains some excellent pieces, though others seem a bit dated. The source book for articles dealing with the importance of the work of Kuhn and Lakatos for economics is S. Latsis (ed.), *Method and Appraisal in Economics* (1976). Two journals, *Journal of Economic Issues* and *History of Political Economy*, frequently publish articles which relate the work of growth of knowledge theorists to economics. Finally, F. Machlup's *Methodology of Economics and Other Social Sciences* (1978) is a valuable collection of that economist's methodological output.

Terence Hutchison's contributions to the literature have continued throughout his academic career, and in my opinion, each successive volume is better than the last, which is no small feat. In addition to his original classic, Hutchison has produced *'Positive' Economics and Policy Judgements* (1964), *Knowledge and Ignorance in Economics* (1977), and *On Revolutions and Progress in Economic Knowledge* (1978). The final chapter of the latest book carefully addresses what should count as a revolution and as progress in economics, and he goes far beyond the growth of knowledge philosophers (and integrates the history of the discipline, as well) in coming up with an answer. It is a masterful piece.

Frank Knight's forays into methodology, including his scathing review of Hutchison's book, are collected in his *On the History and Method of Economics* (1956). The exchange between Knight and Hutchison in the October 1941 *Journal of Political Economy* should not be neglected.

In addition to the growing number of books produced by advocates of each view, both the Institutionalists and the Post-Keynesians have their own journals – the *Journal of Economic Issues* and *Journal of Post-Keynesian Economics*. The Institutionalists have been the more self-conscious methodologically – a number of articles comparing Institutionalist and neoclassical methodologies can be found in the pages of the *JEI*. For the post-Keynesians, methodology is often mentioned but rarely directly addressed; the exception is M. Hollis and E. J. Nell's *Rational Economic Man* (1976). Two general expositions of Cambridge theorizing, with full bibliographies and conflicting assessments of contributions, are M. Blaug, *The Cambridge Revolution: Success or Failure?* (1975); and J. A. Kregel, *The Reconstruction of Political Economy: An Introduction to Post-Keynesian Economics* (1973).

A brief overview of the methodological positions of Austrian economists from Menger to Rothbard is L. White, 'Methodology of the Austrian School,' (1977). Mises wrote two tracts on methodology, *Epistemological Problems of Economics* (1933, 1960) and *The Ultimate Foundation of Economic Science* (1962), but the first seven chapters of *Human Action: A Treatise on Economics* (1949, 1966) is probably the best introduction to praxeological reasoning. Hayek's major methodological contribution is 'Scientism and the Study of Society,' reprinted in *The Counter-Revolution of Science* (1952, 1979); other books containing articles on methodology are his *Studies in Philosophy, Politics and Economics* (1967) and *New Studies in Philosophy, Politics, Economics and the History of Ideas* (1978). The last includes his Nobel Lecture, 'The Pretence of Knowledge.'

Modern Austrians are also interested in methodology: articles by J. Egger, I. Kirzner, M. Rizzo, and M. Rothbard in the introductory collections, *The Foundations of Modern Austrian Economics* (1976), edited by E. Dolan; and *New Directions in Austrian Economics* (1978), edited by L. Spadaro, concern methodology. O'Driscoll and Rizzo will soon publish a book offering a modern statement of the Austrian position, with a research agenda for future work.

A great number of economists have offered alternative conceptions to the rationality postulate; we will mention here only some of the more important studies. William Baumol and Albert Ando offer their assessments of Simon's work in 'On the Contributions of Herbert A. Simon to Economics,' *Scandanavian Journal of Economics* (1979). Simon's massive bibliography (twenty pages long, in very small print) is also included. Two surveys of alternative theories of the firm are Oliver Williamson, 'Firms and Markets,' in Sidney Weintraub (ed.), *Modern Economic Thought* (1977); and F. M. Scherer, *Industrial Market Structure and Economic Performance* (1980), Chapter 2.

Those with an interest in experimental economics may wish to consult the annual, *Research in Experimental Economics: A Research Annual*, edited by Vernon Smith.

Bibliography – Philosophy of Science

Achinstein, P., *Concepts of Science: A Philosophical Analysis* (Baltimore: Johns Hopkins Press, 1968).
Achinstein, P., 'A Reply to Cohen,' in Suppe (ed.) (1977), pp. 350–60.
Achinstein, P. and Barker, S. (eds), *The Legacy of Logical Positivism* (Baltimore: John Hopkins Press, 1969).
Ackermann, R. J., *The Philosophy of Karl Popper* (Amherst, Mass.: The University of Massachusetts Press, 1976).
Agassi, J., *Towards an Historigraphy of Science* (The Hague: Mouton, 1963).
Agassi, J., *Science in Flux. Boston Studies in the Philosophy of Science*, Vol. XXVIII (Dordrecht, Holland: D. Reidel, 1975).
Ayer, A. J., *Language, Truth, and Logic*, 2nd edn (New York: Dover, 1946).
Ayer, A. J. (ed.), *Logical Positivism* (Glencoe, Ill.: The Free Press, 1959).
Ayer, A. J., 'Editor's Introduction,' in Ayer (ed.) (1959), pp. 3–28.
Ayer, A. J., 'What Is a Law of Nature?' in Brody (ed.) (1970), pp. 39–54.
Bartley, W. W., *The Retreat to Commitment* (New York: Knopf, 1962).
Bartley, W. W., 'Rationality versus the Theory of Rationality,' in Bunge (ed.) (1964), pp. 3–31.
Baumrin, B. (ed.), *Philosophy of Science: The Delware Seminar*, 2 Vols (New York: Wiley, 1962–63).
Beardsley, M. (ed.), *The European Philosophers from Descartes to Nietzsche* (New York: Modern Library, 1960).
Bradley, J., *Mach's Philosophy of Science* (London: Athlone Press of the University of London, 1971).
Braithwaite, R., *Scientific Explanation*, 2nd edn (Cambridge, England.: Cambridge University Press, 1959).
Bridgman, P. W., *The Logic of Modern Physics* (New York: Macmillan, 1927).
Brody, B. (ed.), *Readings in the Philosophy of Science* (Englewood Cliffs, N.J.: Prentice-Hall, 1970).
Bromberger, S., 'Why-Questions,' in Brody (ed.) (1970), pp. 66–87.
Buck, R. and Cohen, R. (eds), *PSA 1970: In Memory of Rudolf Carnap. Boston Studies in the Philosophy of Science*, Vol. VIII (Dordrecht, Holland: D. Reidel, 1971).
Bunge, M. (ed.), *The Critical Approach to Science and Philosophy* (London: The Free Press of Glencoe, 1964).
Campbell, N. R., *Physics: The Elements* (Cambridge, England: Cambridge University Press, 1920).
Carnap, R., *Der Logische Aufbau Der Welt* (1928), transl. by R. A. George as *The Logical Structure of the World: Pseudoproblems in Philosophy* (Berkeley and Los Angeles: University of California Press, 1967).
Carnap, R., *The Logical Syntax of Language* (1934), trans. by A. Smeaton (New York: Harcourt, Brace, 1937).

Carnap, R., 'Testability and Meaning,' *Philosophy of Science*, vol. 3 (1936), pp. 420–68; ibid., vol. 4 (1937), pp. 1–40.

Carnap, R., *Foundations of Logic and Mathematics. International Encyclopedia of Unified Science*, Vol. I, no. 3 (Chicago: University of Chicago Press, 1939).

Carnap, R., *Introduction to Semantics* (Cambridge, Mass.: Harvard University Press, 1942).

Carnap, R., *Formalization of Logic* (Cambridge, Mass.: Harvard University Press, 1942).

Carnap, R., *Meaning and Necessity. A Study in Semantics and Modal Logic* (Chicago: University of Chicago Press, 1947).

Carnap, R., *Logical Foundations of Probability* (Chicago: University of Chicago Press, 1950).

Carnap, R., *The Continuum of Inductive Methods* (Chicago: University of Chicago Press, 1952).

Carnap, R., 'The Elimination of Metaphysics through Logical Analysis of Language,' transl. by A. Pap, in Ayer (ed.) (1959), pp. 60–81.

Carnap, R., 'The Old and the New Logic,' transl. by I. Levi, in Ayer (ed.) (1959), pp. 133–46.

Carnap, R. and Jeffrey, R. C. (eds), *Studies in Inductive Logic and Probability*, Vol. I (Berkeley: University of California Press, 1971).

Cohen, I. B., 'History and the Philosopher of Science,' in Suppe (ed.) (1977), pp. 308–49.

Cohen, R. and Wartofsky, M. (eds), *Boston Studies in the Philosophy of Science*, Vol. II (New York: The Humanities Press, 1965).

Cohen, R, and Wartofsky, M. (eds), *Philosophical Foundations of Science. Boston Studies in the Philosophy of Science,* Vol. XI (Dordrecht, Holland: D. Reidel, 1974).

Cohen, R., Feyerabend, P. K. and Wartofsky, M. (eds), *Essays in Memory of Imre Lakatos. Boston Studies in the Philosophy of Science.* Vol. XXXIX (Dordrecht, Holland: D. Reidel, 1976).

Collingwood, R. G., *The Idea of History* (Oxford: Clarendon Press, 1946).

Colodny, R. (ed.), *Mind and Cosmos: Essays in Contemporary Science and Philosophy* (Pittsburgh: University of Pittsburgh Press, 1966).

Comte, A., *A General View of Positivism*, translated by J. H. Bridges, in Beardsley (ed.) (1960), pp. 730–64.

Conant, J. B., *On Understanding Science* (New Haven: Yale University Press, 1947).

Davidson, D., 'Actions, Reasons and Causes,' *Journal of Philosophy*, vol. 60 (1963), pp. 690–700.

Dray, W. H., 'Historical Understanding as Re-Thinking,' In Brody, (ed.) (1970), pp. 167–79.

Feibelman, J. K., *Scientific Method: The Hypothetico-Experimental Laboratory Procedure of the Physical Sciences* (The Hague: Martinus Nijhoff, 1972).

Feigl, H. and Brodbeck, M. (eds), *Readings in the Philosophy of Science* (New York: Meredith Corporation, 1953).

Feigl, H. and Scriven, M. (eds), *Minnesota Studies in the Philosophy of*

Science, Vol. I (Minneapolis: University of Minnesota Press, 1956).

Feigl, H., Maxwell, G. and Scriven, M. (eds), *Minnesota Studies in the Philosophy of Science*, Vol. II (Minneapolis: University of Minnesota Press, 1958).

Feigl, H., Maxwell, G. and Scriven, M. (eds), *Minnesota Studies in the Philosophy of Science,* Vol. III (Minneapolis: University of Minnesota Press, 1962).

Feyerabend, P. K., 'Explanation, Reduction and Empiricism,' in Feigl, Maxwell, and Scriven (eds), Vol. III (1962), pp. 28–97.

Feyerabend, P. K., 'Reply to Criticism,' In Cohen and Wartofsky (eds) (1965), pp. 223–61.

Feyerabend, P. K., 'On the "Meaning" of Scientific Terms,' *Journal of Philosophy*, vol. 62 (1965), pp. 267–9.

Feyerabend, P. K., 'Consolations for the Specialist,' In Lakatos and Musgrave (eds) (1970), pp. 197–230.

Feyerabend, P. K., 'How To Be A Good Empiricist – A Plea for Tolerance in Matters Epistemological', in Brody (ed.) (1970), pp. 319–42.

Feyerabend, P. K., *Against Method: Outline of an Anarchistic Theory of Knowledge* (London: NLB, 1975).

Feyerabend, P. K., *Science in a Free Society* (London: NLB, 1978).

Gallie, W. B., 'Explanations in History and the Genetic Sciences,' in Brody (ed.) (1970), pp. 150–66.

Giedymin, J., 'Instrumentalism and Its Critique: A Reappraisal,' in Cohen, Feyerabend, and Wartofsky (eds) (1976), pp. 179–207.

Goodman, N., *Fact, Fiction and Forecast*, 2nd edn (New York: Bobbs-Merrill, 1965).

Grandy, R. (ed.), *Theories and Observation in Science* (Englewood Cliffs, N.J.: Prentice Hall, 1973).

Grunbaum, A., 'Temporally Asymmetric Principles, Parity between Explanation and Prediction and Mechanism versus Teleology,' in Baumrin (ed.) (1963), Vol. I, pp. 57–96.

Hahn, H., Carnap, R. and Neurath, O., 'Wissenschaftliche Weltauffasung: Der Wiener Kreis,' transl. by P. Foulkes and M. Neurath in Neurath (1973), pp. 299–318.

Hanson, N., *Patterns of Discovery* (Cambridge, England: Cambridge University Press, 1958).

Harré, R., *An Introduction to the Logic of the Sciences* (New York: St. Martin Press, 1967).

Harré, R., *The Principles of Scientific Thinking* (Chicago: University of Chicago Press, 1970).

Harré, R., *The Philosophies of Science: An Introductory Survey* (London: Oxford University Press, 1972).

Hempel, C., 'A Logical Appraisal of Operationalism,' *Scientific Monthly*, vol. 79 (1954), pp. 215–20.

Hempel, C., 'The Theoretician's Dilemma,' in Feigl, Maxwell, and Scriven (eds) (1958), pp. 37–98.

Hempel, C., 'The Empiricist Criterion of Meaning,' in Ayer (ed.) (1959), pp. 108–29.

Hempel, C., 'Explanation and Prediction by Covering Laws,' in Baumrin (ed.) (1963), Vol. I, pp. 107–33.

Hempel, C., *Philosophy of Natural Science* (Englewood Cliffs, N.J.: Prentice-Hall, 1966).

Hempel, C., 'Studies in the Logic of Confirmation,' in Brody (ed.) (1970), pp. 384–409.

Hempel, C., 'On the "Standard Conception" of Scientific Theories,' in Radner and Winokur (eds) (1970), pp. 142–63.

Hempel, C. and Oppenheim, P., 'Studies in the Logic of Explanation,' in Feigl and Brodbeck (eds) (1953), pp. 319–52.

Hesse, M., *Models and Analogies in Science* (Notre Dame, Ind.: University of Notre Dame Press, 1966).

Hintikka, J., *Rudolf Carnap, Logical Empiricist: Materials and Perspectives* (Dordrecht, Holland: D. Reidel, 1975).

Hume, D., *An Inquiry Concerning Human Understanding* (1748) (Indianapolis: Bobbs-Merrill, 1955).

Jeffrey, R. C., 'Review of Putnam,' in Grandy (ed.) (1973), pp. 124–8.

Joergensen, J., *The Development of Logical Empiricism. International Encyclopedia of Unified Science*, Vol. III, no. 9 (Chicago: University of Chicago Press, 1951).

Koertge, N., 'Bartley's Theory of Rationality,' *Philosophy of Social Science*, vol. 4 (1974), pp. 75–81.

Koertge, N., 'Rational Reconstructions,' in Cohen, Feyerabend, and Wartofsky (eds) (1976), Vol. XXXIX, pp. 359–70.

Kuhn, T., *The Structure of Scientific Revolutions. International Encyclopedia of Unified Science*, Vol. II, no. 2, 2nd enlarged edn (Chicago: University of Chicago Press, 1970).

Kuhn, T., 'Logic of Discovery or Psychology of Research?' in Lakatos and Musgrave (eds) (1970), pp. 1–23.

Kuhn, T., 'Reflections on My Critics,' in Lakatos and Musgrave (eds) (1970), pp. 231–78.

Kuhn, T., *The Essential Tension: Selected Studies in Scientific Tradition and Change* (Chicago: University of Chicago Press, 1977).

Kuhn, T., 'Objectivity, Value Judgement, and Theory Choice,' in Kuhn (1977), pp. 320–39.

Lakatos, I., 'Falsification and the Methodology of Scientific Research Programmes,' in Lakatos and Musgrave (eds) (1970), pp. 91–196.

Lakatos, I., 'History of Science and Its Rational Reconstructions,' in Buck and Cohen (eds) (1971), pp. 91–139.

Lakatos, I. and Musgrave, A. (eds) *Criticism and the Growth of Knowledge* (Cambridge, England: Cambridge University Press, 1970).

Lenzer, G. (ed.), *Auguste Comte and Positivism: The Essential Writings* (New York: Harper Torchbooks, 1975).

Mach, E., *Popular Scientific Lectures*, transl. by T. J. McCormack (Chicago: Open Court, 1898).

Mach, E., *The Analysis of Sensations,* transl. by C. M. Williams supplemented by S. Waterlaw (New York: Dover, 1959).

Masterman, M., 'The Nature of a Paradigm,' in Lakatos and Musgrave (eds) (1970), pp. 59–89.

McGuiness, B. (ed.), *Wittgenstein and the Vienna Circle*, transl. by J. Schutte and B. McGuiness (New York: Barnes and Noble, 1978).

McMullin, E., 'Logicality and Rationality,' in Cohen and Wartofsky (eds) (1974), pp. 415–30.

Michalos, A. C., *The Popper-Carnap Controversy* (The Hague: Martinus Nijhoff, 1971).

Nagel, E., *The Structure of Science: Problems in the Logic of Scientific Explanation* (New York: Harcourt, Brace and World, 1961).

Natanson, M. (ed.), *Philosophy of the Social Sciences: A Reader* (New York: Random House, 1963).

Neurath, O., 'Protocol Sentences,' transl. by G. Schick in Ayer (ed.) (1959) pp. 199–208.

Neurath, O., *Empiricism and Sociology*, transl. by P. Foulkes and M. Neurath, edited by M. Neurath and R. S. Cohen (Dordrecht, Holland: D. Reidel, 1973).

Popper, K., *Logik der Forschung* (1934) transl. as *The Logic of Scientific Discovery* (New York: Basic Books, 1959; Harper Torchbooks, 1968).

Popper, K., *The Open Society and Its Enemies* (Princeton, N.J.: Princeton University Press, 1950).

Popper, K., *The Poverty of Historicism* (London: Routledge and Kegan Paul, 1957).

Popper, K., *Conjectures and Refutations: The Growth of Scientific Knowledge*, 2nd edn (New York: Basic Books, 1965).

Popper, K., 'On the Sources of Knowledge and Ignorance,' in Popper (1965), pp. 3–30.

Popper, K., 'Science: Conjectures and Refutations,' in Popper (1965), pp. 33–65.

Popper, K., 'Three Views Concerning Human Knowledge,' in Popper (1965), pp. 97–119.

Popper, K., 'Truth, Rationality, and the Growth of Scientific Knowledge,' in Popper (1965), pp. 215–50.

Popper, K., 'The Demarcation between Science and Metaphysics,' in Popper (1965), pp. 253–92.

Popper, K., 'Normal Science and Its Dangers,' in Lakatos and Musgrave (eds) (1970), pp. 51–8.

Popper, K., *Objective Knowledge: An Evolutionary Approach* (Oxford: Clarendon Press, 1972).

Popper, K., 'Conjectural Knowledge: My Solution to the Problem of Induction,' in Popper (1972), pp. 1–31.

Popper, K., 'Intellectual Autobiography,' in Schilpp (ed.) (1974), pp. 3–181.

Putnam, H., 'What Theories Are Not,' in Grandy (ed.) (1973), pp. 111–23.

Quine, W. V. O., *From a Logical Point of View* (Cambridge, Mass.: Harvard University Press, 1953).

Quine, W. V. O., 'Two Dogmas of Empiricism,' in Quine (1953), pp. 20–46.

Radner, M. and Winokur, S., *Minnesota Studies in the Philosophy of Science*, Vol. IV (Minneapolis: University of Minnesota Press, 1970).

Rapoport, A., 'Various Meanings of "Theory",' *American Political Science Review*, vol. 52 (1958), pp. 927–88.

Reichenbach, H., *Experience and Prediction: An Analysis of the Foundations and Structure of Knowledge* (Chicago: University of Chicago Press, 1938).

Reichenbach, H., *Philosophical Foundations of Quantum Mechanics* (Berkeley and Los Angeles: University of California Press, 1944).

Russell, B. and Whitehead, A. N., *Principia Mathematica*, 3 Vols (Cambridge, England: Cambridge University Press, 1910–13).

Salmon, W. (ed.), *The Foundations of Scientific Inference* (Pittsburgh: University of Pittsburgh Press, 1966).

Scheffler, I., *Science and Subjectivity* (New York: Bobbs Merrill, 1967).

Scheffler, I., 'The Fictionalist View of Scientific Theories,' in Brody (ed.) (1970), pp. 211–22.

Schilpp, P. A. (ed.), *The Philosophy of Rudolf Carnap*. Vol. XI, *The Library of Living Philosophers* (LaSalle, Ill.: Open Court, 1963).

Schilpp, P. A. (ed.), *The Philosophy of Karl Popper*. Books I and II, *The Library of Living Philosophers*, Vol. XIV (LaSalle, Ill.: Open Court, 1974).

Schlick, M., 'The Turning Point in Philosophy,' transl. by D. Rynin, in Ayer (ed.) 1959), pp. 53–9.

Schlick, M., 'Positivism and Realism,' transl. by D. Rynin, in Ayer (ed.) (1959), pp. 82–107.

Scriven, M., 'The Temporal Asymmetry of Explanations and Predictions', in Baumrin (ed.) (1963) Vol. I, pp. 97–105.

Scriven, M., 'The Philosophy of Science,' *International Encyclopedia of the Social Sciences*, vol. 14 (1968).

Shapere, D., 'Meaning and Scientific Change,' in Colodny (ed.) (1966), pp. 41–85.

Shapere, D., 'The Paradigm Concept,' *Science*, vol. 172 (1972), pp. 706–9.

Shapere, D., 'Scientific Theories and Their Domains,' in Suppe (ed.) (1977), pp. 518–65.

Skyrms, B., *Choice and Change: An Introduction to Inductive Logic*, 2nd edn (Encino, Calif.: Dickenson, 1975).

Stuewer, R., *Minnesota Studies in the Philosophy of Science*, Vol. V (Minneapolis: University of Minnesota Press, 1970).

Suppe, F. (ed.), *The Structure of Scientific Theories*, 2nd edn (Urbana, Ill.: University of Illinois Press, 1977).

Suppe, F., 'Critical Introduction – The Search for Philosophic Understanding of Scientific Theories,' in Suppe (ed.) (1977), pp. 3–241.

Tarski, A., *Logic, Semantics, Metamathematics* (Oxford: Clarendon Press, 1956).

Toulmin, S., 'Does the Distinction between Normal and Revolutionary Science Hold Water?' in Lakatos and Musgrave (eds) (1970), pp. 39–47.

Toulmin, S., *Human Understanding*, Vol. I (Princeton, N.J.: Princeton University Press, 1972).

Toulmin, S., 'Scientific Strategies and Historical Change,' in Cohen and Wartofsky (eds) (1974), pp. 401–14.

Wartofsky, M., 'The Relation between Philosophy of Science and History of Science,' in Cohen, Feyerabend, and Wartofsky (eds) (1976), pp. 717–38.

Watkins, J. W. N., 'Comprehensively Critical Rationalism,' *Philosophy*, vol. 44 (1969), pp. 57–62.

Watkins, J. W. N., 'Against "Normal Science",' in Lakatos and Musgrave (eds) (1970), pp. 25–37.

Watkins, J. W. N., 'C.C.R.: A Refutation,' *Philosophy*, vol. 46 (1971), pp. 56–71.

Whitehead, A. N., *Science and the Modern World* (New York: Macmillan, 1925; Free Press, 1967).

Wittgenstein, L., *Tractus Logico-philosophicus*, transl. by D. F. Pears and B. F. McGuinness, Introduction by Bertrand Russell (New York: Humanities Press, 1961).

Worral, J. and Currie, G. (eds), *Imre Lakatos–Philosophical Papers*, 2 Vols (New York: Cambridge University Press, 1977–78).

Bibliography – Methodology of Economics

Agassi, J., 'Tautology and Testability in Economics,' *Philosophy of Social Sciences*, vol. 1 (1971), pp. 49–63.

Alchian, A., *Economic Forces at Work* (Indianapolis, Ind.: Liberty Press, 1977).

Alchian, A., 'Uncertainty, Evolution and Economic Theory,' in Alchian (1977), pp. 15–35.

Ando, A., 'On the Contributions of Herbert A. Simon to Economics,' *Scandanavian Journal of Economics*, vol. 81 (1979), pp. 83–93.

Battalio, R., Kagel, J., et al., 'A Test of Consumer Demand Theory Using Observations of Individual Consumer Purchases,' *Western Economic Journal*, vol. 11 (December 1973), pp. 411–28.

Baumol, W., 'On the Contribution of Herbert A. Simon to Economics,' *Scandanavian Journal of Economics*, vol. 81 (1979), pp. 74–82.

Bear, D. V. T. and Orr, D., 'Logic and Expediency in Economic Theorizing,' *Journal of Political Economy*, vol. 75 (April 1967), pp. 188–96.

Becker, G., 'Irrational Behavior and Economic Theory,' *Journal of Political Economy*, vol. 70 (February 1962), pp. 1–13.

Becker, G., *The Economic Approach to Human Behavior* (Chicago: University of Chicago Press, 1976).

Blaug, M., *The Cambridge Revolution: Success or Failure?*, revised edn (London: Institute of Economic Affairs, 1975).

Blaug, M., *The Methodology of Economics: Or How Economists Explain* (Cambridge, England: Cambridge University Press, 1980).

Boland, L., 'Economic Understanding and Understanding Economics,' *South African Journal of Economics*, vol. 37 (1969), pp. 144–60.

Boland, L., 'Conventionalism and Economic Theory,' *Philosophy of Science*, vol. 37 (June 1970), pp. 239–48.

Boland, L., 'Discussion: Methodology as an Exercise in Economic Analysis,' *Philosophy of Science*, vol. 38 (March 1971), pp. 105–17.

Boland, L., 'Testability in Economic Science,' *South African Journal of Economics*, vol. 45 (1977), pp. 93–105.

Boland, L., 'Model Specification and Stochasticism in Economic Methodology,' *South African Journal of Economics*, vol. 45 (1977), pp. 182–9.

Boland, L., 'A Critique of Friedman's Critics,' *Journal of Economic Literature*, vol. 17 (June 1979), pp. 503–22.

Boland, L., 'Friedman's Methodology vs. Conventional Empiricism: A Reply to Rotwein,' *Journal of Economic Literature*, vol. 18 (December 1980), pp. 1555–7.

Boland, L., *The Foundations of Economic Method* (London: Allen and Unwin, 1982).

Brunner, K. and Meltzer, A. (eds), *Three Aspects of Policy and Policy-*

Making: Knowledge, Data and Institutions. Supplement to *Journal of Monetary Economics*, vol. 10 (1979).

Buchanan, J., *Cost and Choice: An Inquiry in Economic Theory* (Chicago: University of Chicago Press, 1969; Midway Reprint, Chicago: University of Chicago Press, 1978).

Buchanan, J., *What Should Economists Do?* (Indianapolis, Ind.: Liberty Press, 1979).

Buchanan, J., 'Is Economics the Science of Choice?' in Buchanan (1979), pp. 39–63.

Caldwell, B., 'Positivist Philosophy of Science and the Methodology of Economics,' *Journal of Economic Issues*, vol. 14 (March 1980), pp. 53–76.

Caldwell, B., 'A Critique of Friedman's Methodological Instrumentalism,' *Southern Economic Journal*, vol. 47 (October 1980), pp. 366–74.

Caldwell, B., 'Book Review: Homa Katouzian's *Ideology and Method in Economics*,' *Southern Economic Journal*, vol. 47 (April 1981), pp. 1167–68.

Caldwell, B., 'Book Review: Mark Blaug's *The Methodology of Economics: Or How Economists Explain*,' *Southern Economic Journal*, vol. 48 (July, 1981), pp. 242–45.

Coats, A. W., 'Is There a "Structure of Scientific Revolutions" in Economics?' *Kyklos*, vol. 22 (1969), pp. 289–96.

Coddington, A., 'Positive Economics,' *Canadian Journal of Economics*, vol. 5 (1972), pp. 1–15.

Commission on Money and Credit, *Stabilization Policies* (Englewood Cliffs, N.J.: Prentice-Hall, 1963).

Crews, J. M., 'Econometric Models: The Monetarist and Non-Monetarist Views Compared,' in Havrilesky and Boorman (eds) (1976), pp. 179–90.

Cyert, R. and March, J., *A Behavioral Theory of the Firm* (Englewood Cliffs, N.J.: Prentice-Hall, 1963).

Deane, P., *The Evolution of Economic Ideas* (Cambridge, England: Cambridge University Press, 1978).

Devroey, M., 'The Transition from Classical to Neoclassical Economics: A Scientific Revolution, *Journal of Economic Issues*, vol. 9 (September 1975), pp. 415–39.

Dillard, D., 'Revolutions in Economic Theory,' *Southern Economic Journal*, vol. 44 (April 1978), pp. 705–24.

Dolan, E. (ed.), *The Foundations of Modern Austrian Economics* (Kansas City: Sheed and Ward, 1976).

Dugger, W., 'Methodological Differences between Institutional and Neo-classical Economics,' *Journal of Economic Issues*, vol. 13 (December 1979), pp. 899–909.

Friedman, M., *Essays in Positive Economics* (Chicago: University of Chicago Press, 1953).

Friedman, M., 'The Methodology of Positive Economics,' in Friedman (1953), pp. 3–43.

Friedman, M., 'Nobel Lecture: Inflation and Unemployment,' *Journal of Political Economy*, vol. 85 (June 1977), pp. 451–72.

Friedman, M. and Meiselman, D., 'The Relative Stability of Monetary

Velocity and the Investment Multiplier in the United States 1897–1958,' in Commission on Money and Credit (1963), pp. 165–268.

Garrison, R., 'Austrian Macroeconomics: A Diagrammatical Exposition,' in Spadaro (ed.) (1978), pp. 167–204.

Gordon, D. F., 'Operational Propositions in Economic Theory,' *Journal of Political Economy*, vol. 63 (April 1955), pp. 150–62.

Gordon, D. F., 'The Role of History of Thought in the Understanding of Modern Economic Theory,' *American Economic Review*, vol. 55 (May 1965), pp. 119–27.

Grossack, I. M. and Loescher, S. M., 'Institutional and Mainstream Economics: Choice and Power as a Basis for a Synthesis,' *Journal of Economic Issues*, vol. 14 (December 1980), pp. 925–36.

Grunberg, E., ' "Complexity" and "Open Systems" in Economic Discourse,' *Journal of Economic Issues,* vol. 12 (September 1978), pp. 541–60.

Havrilesky, T. and Boorman, J. (eds), *Current Issues in Monetary Theory and Policy* (Arlington Heights, Ill.: AHM Publishing Corporation, 1976).

Hayek, F. A., *Studies in Philosophy, Politics and Economics* (Chicago: University of Chicago Press, 1967).

Hayek, F. A., *Law, Legislation, and Liberty*, 3 Vols (Chicago: University of Chicago Press, 1973–79).

Hayek, F. A., *New Studies in Philosophy, Politics, Economics and the History of Ideas* (Chicago: University of Chicago Press, 1978).

Hayek, F. A., 'The Pretence of Knowledge,' in Hayek (1978), pp. 23–34.

Hayek, F. A., *The Counter-Revolution of Science: Studies on the Abuse of Reason*, 2nd edn (Indianapolis, Ind.: Liberty Press, 1979).

Hicks, J., *Value and Capital*, 2nd edn (Oxford: Clarendon Press, 1946).

Hirshleifer, J. and Riley, J., 'The Analytics of Uncertainty and Information: An Expository Survey,' *Journal of Economic Literature*, vol. 17 (December 1979), pp. 1375–421.

Hirshleifer, J., *Price Theory and Applications*, 2nd edn (Englewood Cliffs, N.J.: Prentice-Hall, 1980).

Hollis, M. and Nell, E. J., *Rational Economic Man: A Philosophical Critique of Neo-Classical Economics* (Cambridge, England: Cambridge University Press, 1975).

Houthakker, H., 'Revealed Preference and the Utility Function,' *Economica*, vol. 17 (May 1950), pp. 159–74.

Hutchison, T. W., *The Significance and Basic Postulates of Economic Theory* (London: Macmillan, 1938: reprint edn, New York: Augustus M. Kelley, 1960).

Hutchison, T. W., 'Reply,' *Journal of Political Economy*, vol. 49 (October 1941), pp. 732–50.

Hutchison, T. W., 'Professor Machlup on Verification in Economics,' *Southern Economic Journal*, vol. 22 (April 1956), pp. 476–83.

Hutchison, T. W., *Positive Economics and Policy Judgements* (London: Allen and Unwin, 1964).

Hutchison, T. W., *Knowledge and Ignorance in Economics* (Chicago: University of Chicago Press, 1977).

Hutchison, T. W., *On Revolutions and Progress in Economic Knowledge* (Cambridge: Cambridge University Press, 1978).

Jones, E., 'Positive Economics or What?' *Economic Record*, vol. 53 (September 1977), pp. 350–63.

Kagel, J., Battalio, R., et al., 'Experimental Studies of Consumer Demand Behavior Using Laboratory Animals,' *Economic Inquiry*, vol. 13 (March 1975), pp. 22–38.

Katouzian, H., 'Scientific Method and Positive Economics,' *Scottish Journal of Political Economy*, vol. 31 (November 1974), pp. 279–86.

Katouzian, H., *Ideology and Method in Economics* (New York: New York University Press, 1980).

Keynes, J. N., *The Scope and Method of Political Economy* (New York: Kelley and Millman, 1891).

Kirzner, I., 'Rational Action and Economic Theory,' *Journal of Political Economy*, vol. 70 (August 1962), pp. 380–85.

Kirzner, I., *Competition and Entrepreneurship* (Chicago: University of Chicago Press, 1973).

Kirzner, I., 'On the Method of Austrian Economics,' in Dolan (ed.) (1976), pp. 40–51.

Kirzner, I., 'Philosophical and Ethical Implications of Austrian Economics,' in Dolan (ed.) (1976), pp. 75–88.

Kirzner, I., 'Economics and Error,' in Spadaro (ed.) (1978), pp. 57–76.

Kirzner, I., *Perception, Opportunity and Profit: Studies in the Theory of Entrepreneurship* (Chicago: University of Chicago Press, 1979).

Klamer, A., 'The So-Called Rational Expectations Approach from a Methodological Perspective,' unpublished dissertation, Duke University, Durham, N.C.

Knight, F., ' "What Is Truth" in Economics?' *Journal of Political Economy*, vol. 48 (Feb.–Dec. 1940), pp. 1–32.

Knight, F., 'A Rejoinder,' *Journal of Political Economy*, vol. 49 (October 1941), pp. 750–3.

Knight, F., *On The History and Method of Economics* (Chicago: University of Chicago Press, 1956).

Koo, A. Y. C., 'An Empirical Test of Revealed Preference Theory,' *Econometrica*, vol. 30 (October 1963), pp. 646–64.

Koo, A. Y. C. and Hasenkamp, G., 'Structure of Revealed Preference: Some Preliminary Evidence,' *Journal of Political Economy*, vol. 80 (July–August 1972), pp. 724–44.

Koopmanns, T., 'Measurement without Theory,' *Review of Economic Statistics*, vol. 29 (August 1947), pp. 161–72.

Kregel, J. A., *The Reconstruction of Political Economy: An Introduction to Post-Keynesian Economics* (London: Macmillan, 1973).

Krupp, S. R. (ed.), *The Structure of Economic Science: Essays on Methodology* (Englewood Cliffs, N. J.: Prentice-Hall, 1966).

Lancaster, K., 'Economic Aggregation and Additivity,' in Krupp (ed.) (1966), pp. 201–15.

Latsis, S. (ed.), *Method and Appraisal in Economics* (Cambridge, England: Cambridge University Press, 1976).

Leibenstein, H., *Beyond Economic Man: A New Foundation for Micro-economics*, 2nd edn (Cambridge, Mass.: Harvard University Press, 1980).

Leijonhufvud, A., 'Schools, "Revolutions," and Research Programmes in Economics,' in Latsis (ed.) (1976), pp. 65-108.

Leijonhufvud, A., 'Life Among the Econ,' *Western Economic Journal*, vol. 11 (September 1973), pp. 327-37.

Leontieff, W., 'Theoretical Assumptions and Nonobserved Facts,' *American Economic Review*, vol. 61 (March 1971), pp. 1-7.

Lerner, M. (ed.), *The Portable Veblen* (New York: The Viking Press, 1948).

Loasby, B. J., *Choice, Complexity and Ignorance: An Enquiry into Economic Theory and the Practice of Decision Making* (Cambridge, England: Cambridge University Press, 1976).

Machlup, F., *Essays on Economic Semantics* (Englewood Cliffs, N. J.: Prentice-Hall, 1963).

Machlup, F. (ed.), *Essays on Hayek* (New York: New York University Press, 1976).

Machlup, F., 'Hayek's Contributions to Economics,' in Machlup (ed.) (1976), pp. 13-59.

Machlup, F., *Methodology of Economics and Other Social Sciences* (New York: Academic Press, 1978).

Machlup, F., 'The Problem of Verification in Economics,' in Machlup (1978), pp. 137-57.

Machlup, F., 'Operational Concepts and Mental Constructs in Model and Theory Formation,' in Machlup (1978), pp. 159-88.

Machlup, F., 'Operationalism and Pure Theory in Economics,' in Machlup (1978), pp. 189-203.

Machlup, F., 'The Ideal Type: A Bad Name for a Good Construct,' in Machlup (1978), pp. 211-21.

Machlup, F., 'Ideal Types, Reality, and Construction,' in Machlup (1978), pp. 223-65.

Machlup, F., 'Homo Oeconomicus and his Class Mates,' in Machlup (1978), pp. 267-81.

Machlup, F., 'The Universal Bogey: Economic Man,' in Machlup (1978), pp. 283-301.

Machlup, F., 'Theories of the Firm: Marginalist, Behavioral, Managerial,' in Machlup (1978), pp. 391-423.

Machlup, F., 'Rejoinder to a Reluctant Ultra-Empiricist,' in Machlup (1978), pp. 493-503.

Margenau, H., 'What Is a Theory?' in Krupp (ed.) (1966), pp. 25-38.

McKensie, R. and Tullock, G., *Modern Political Economy: An Introduction to Economics* (New York: McGraw-Hill, 1978).

Melitz, J., 'Friedman and Machlup on the Significance of Testing Economic Assumptions,' *Journal of Political Economy*, vol. 73 (February 1965), pp. 37-60.

von Mises, L. *Epistemological Problems of Economics*, translated by George Reisman (Princeton, N.J.: van Nostrand, 1960).

von Mises, L., *Human Action: A Treatise on Economics*, 3rd revised edn (Chicago: Henry Regnery, 1963).

von Mises, L., *The Ultimate Foundation of Economic Science*, 2nd edn (Kansas City: Sheed, Andrews, and McMeel, 1978).

Morgenstern, O., *National Income Statistics: A Critique of Macroeconomic Aggregation*, 2nd edn (San Francisco: Cato Institute, 1979).

Nagel, E., 'Assumptions in Economic Theory,' *American Economic Review Papers and Proceedings*, vol. 53 (May 1963), pp. 211–19.

Nelson, C. R., 'The Predictive Performance of the FRB–MIT–PENN Model of the U.S. Economy,' *American Economic Review*, vol. 62 (December 1972), pp. 902–17.

Nozick, R., 'On Austrian Methodology,' *Synthese*, vol. 36 (1977), pp. 353–92.

O'Driscoll, G. and Rizzo, M., 'What Is Austrian Economics: A Survey,' N.Y.U. Department of Economics, Discussion Paper no. 80–15.

Papandreou, A., *Economics as a Science* (Chicago: J.B. Lippencott, 1958).

Pfouts, R. W., 'Some Proposals for a New Methodology in Economics,' *Atlantic Economic Journal*, vol. 1 (November 1973), pp. 13–22.

Ravetz, J., *Scientific Knowledge and Its Social Problems* (Oxford: Clarendon Press, 1971).

Redman, B., 'On Economic Theory and Explanation,' *Journal of Behavioral Economics*, vol. 5 (Summer 1976), pp. 161–76.

Rizzo, M., *Time, Uncertainty and Disequilibrium: Exploration of Austrian Themes* (Massachusetts: Lexington Books, 1979).

Robbins, L., *An Essay on the Nature and Significance of Economic Science*, 2nd edn (London: Macmillan, 1935).

Rosefielde, S., 'Post-Positivist Scientific Method and the Appraisal of Non-Market Economic Behavior,' *Quarterly Journal of Ideology*, vol. 3 (Spring 1980), pp. 23–33.

Rosenberg, A., *Microeconomic Laws: A Philosophical Analysis* (Pittsburgh, Pa.: University of Pittsburgh Press, 1976).

Rosenberg, A., 'Can Economic Theory Explain Everything?' *Philosophy of Social Science*, vol. 9 (1979), pp. 509–29.

Rothbard, M., 'Praxeology: The Methodology of Austrian Economics,' in Dolan (ed.) (1976), pp. 19–39.

Rotwein, E., 'Reply,' *Quarterly Journal of Economics*, vol. 76 (November 1972), pp. 666–8.

Samuelson, P., 'A Note on the Pure Theory of Consumer's Behavior,' *Economica*, vol. 5 (February 1938), pp. 51–61.

Samuelson, P., 'The Empirical Implications of Utility Analysis,' *Econometrica*, vol. 6 (October 1938), pp. 344–56.

Samuelson, P., 'International Trade and the Equalization of Factor Prices,' *Economic Journal*, vol. 57 (June 1948), pp. 163–84.

Samuelson, P., 'Consumption Theory in Terms of Revealed Preference,' *Economica*, vol. 15 (November 1948), pp. 243–53.

Samuelson, P., 'The Problem of Integrability in Utility Theory,' *Economica*, vol. 17 (November 1950), pp. 355–85.

Samuelson, P., 'Economic Theory and Mathematics: An Appraisal,' *American Economic Review*, vol. 42 (May 1952), pp. 56–66.

Samuelson, P., 'Discussion,' *American Economic Review Papers and Proceedings*, vol. 53 (May 1963), pp. 231–36.

Samuelson, P., 'Theory and Realism: A Reply,' *American Economic Review*, vol. 54 (September 1964), pp. 736–9.

Samuelson, P., 'Economic Forecasting and Science,' *Michigan Quarterly Review*, vol. 4 (October 1965), pp. 274–80.

Samuelson, P. 'Professor Samuelson on Theory and Realism: Reply,' *American Economic Review*, vol. 55 (December 1965), pp. 1164–72.

Samuelson, P., 'Lessons from the Current Economic Expansion,' *American Economic Review Papers and Proceedings*, vol. 64 (May 1974), pp. 75–7.

Samuelson, P., *Foundations of Economic Analysis*, 2nd edn (New York: Atheneum, 1965).

Schelling, T. C., *Micromotives and Macrobehavior* (New York: Norton, 1978).

Scherer, F. M., *Industrial Market Structure and Economic Performance*, 2nd edn (Chicago: Rand McNally, 1980).

Schoeck, H. and Wiggins, J., *Scientism and Values* (Princeton, N. J.: van Nostrand, 1960).

Schoeffler, S., *The Failure of Economics: A Diagnostic Study* (Cambridge, Mass.: Harvard University Press, 1955).

Shackle, G. L. S., *The Years of High Theory: Invention and Tradition in Economic Thought 1926–1939* (Cambridge, England: Cambridge University Press, 1967).

Shackle, G. L. S., *Decision, Order and Time in Human Affairs*, 2nd edn (Cambridge, England: Cambridge University Press, 1969).

Shackle, G. L. S., *Epistemics and Economics: A Critique of Economic Doctrines* (Cambridge, England: Cambridge University Press, 1972).

Simon, H., 'From Substantive to Procedural Rationality,' in Latsis (ed.) (1976), pp. 129–48.

Simon, H. A., 'Bibliography,' *Scandanavian Journal of Economics*, vol. 81 (1979), pp. 94–114.

Smith, V. (ed.), *Research in Experimental Economics: A Research Annual* (Greenwich, Conn.: Jai Press, 1979).

Sowell, T., *Classical Economics Reconsidered* (Princeton, N.J.: Princeton University Press, 1974).

Spadaro, L. M. (ed.), *New Directions in Austrian Economics* (Kansas City: Sheed, Andrews and McMeel, 1978).

Stanfield, R., 'Kuhnian Scientific Revolutions and the Keynesian Revolution,' *Journal of Economic Issues*, vol. 8 (March 1974), pp. 97–109.

Stigler, G. and Becker, G., 'De Gustibus Non Est Disputandum,' *American Economic Review*, vol. 67 (March 1977), pp. 76–90.

Stiglitz, J. (ed.), *The Collected Scientific Papers of Paul A. Samuelson*, 2 Vols (Cambridge, Mass.: MIT Press, 1966).

Sweezy, A., 'The Interpretation of Subjective Value Theory in the Writings of Austrian Economists,' *Review of Economic Studies*, vol. 1 (June 1934), pp. 176–85.

Tarascio, V. J., *Pareto's Methodological Approach to Economics: A Study in the History of Some Scientific Aspects of Economic Thought* (Chapel Hill, N.C.: University of North Carolina Press, 1966).

Tarascio, V. and Caldwell, B., 'Theory-Choice in Economics: Philosophy and Practice,' *Journal of Economic Issues*, vol. 13 (December 1979), pp. 983–1006.

Tisdale, C., 'Concepts of Rationality in Economics,' *Philosophy of Social Science*, vol. 5 (1975), pp. 259–72.

Veblen, T., 'Why Is Economics Not an Evolutionary Science?' in Lerner (ed.) (1948), pp. 215–40.

Weinstein, A., 'Transitivity of Preference: A Comparison Among Age Groups,' *Journal of Political Economy*, vol. 76 (March–April 1968), pp. 307–11.

Weintraub, S. (ed.), *Modern Economic Thought* (Philadelphia: University of Pennsylvania Press, 1977).

White, L., 'Methodology of the Austrian School,' *Center For Libertarian Studies, Occasional Paper Series*, No. 1, New York, 1977.

Wilber, C., 'Empirical Verification and Theory Selection: The Monetarist–Keynesian Debate,' *Journal of Economic Issues*, vol. 13 (December 1979), pp. 973–82.

Wilber, C. and Harrison, R., 'The Methodological Basis of Institutional Economics: Pattern Model, Storytelling, and Holism,' *Journal of Economic Issues*, vol. 12 (March 1978), pp. 61–89.

Williamson, O., 'Firms and Markets,' in Weintraub (ed.) (1977), pp. 185–202.

Winter, S., 'Economic "Natural Selection" and the Theory of the Firm,' *Yale Economic Essays*, vol. 4 (Spring 1964), pp. 224–72.

Wong, S., 'The F-Twist and the Methodology of Paul Samuelson,' *American Economic Review*, vol. 62 (June 1973), pp. 312–25.

Wong, S., *The Foundations of Paul Samuelson's Revealed Preference Theory: A Study by the Method of Rational Reconstruction* (London: Routledge and Kegan Paul, 1978).

Woodbury, S. A., 'Methodological Controversy in Labor Economics,' *Journal of Economic Issues*, vol. 13 (December 1979), pp. 933–55.

Zellner, A., 'Causality and Econometrics,' in Brunner and Meltzer (eds) (1979), pp. 9–54.

Index